Guardians of the Digital Age

The internet wasn't built for time travelers. But when ethical hacker and mother Elsa and her 14-year-old son, Aiden, uncover a hidden code buried deep within cyberspace, they are pulled into a high-stakes journey through cybersecurity history – from the birth of ARPANET in 1969 to the artificial intelligence (AI)-driven cyberwars of 2040.

Their mission? Trace the origins of digital security before an unknown force alters history and reshapes the future of technology forever. As they jump across decades, they encounter internet pioneers, legendary hackers, and cyber-rebels who changed the digital world. But not everything in the past wants to stay in the past.

Real dangers lurk in the timeline. Elsa and Aiden must navigate malware, mass surveillance, cyberwarfare, and a growing mystery that threatens the foundation of the internet itself. As they race against time, they also face their own fears and shifting trust in each other.

A thrilling bridge between past and future, this book introduces parents and teens to the evolution of the internet and the most essential skill of our time – digital security.

The future is written in code – but cybersecurity is about trust and humanity. Will they protect it, or rewrite it?

Elçin Biren is a seasoned, award-winning cybersecurity leader with 20 years of experience. With a background in industrial engineering, ethical hacking, and executive leadership, she brings a unique, multidimensional perspective to the evolving threat landscape. As CEO of SwissCyberSmart and Global AI Ambassador, Elçin has led major cyber risk initiatives and advised global organizations on security strategy, compliance, and ethical AI adoption. She has served as a CISO advisor, cyber risk manager, and strategist, and currently sits on various international advisory boards and councils shaping the future of digital safety. A frequent keynote speaker and guest lecturer across academic platforms and global conferences, Elçin is also a mentor and advocate for women in tech, passionately working to make cybersecurity more diverse, inclusive, and accessible. As a mother of two, she has seen firsthand the digital threats facing children in today's AI-driven world. Her personal experience fuels her mission to educate and empower not just professionals, but also parents, educators, and other individuals at large.

Security, Audit and Leadership Series

Series Editor: Dan Swanson, Dan Swanson and Associates, Ltd., Winnipeg, Manitoba, Canada.

The scope and mandate for internal audit continues to evolve each year, as does the complexity of the business environment and speed of the changing risk landscape in which it must operate. The fundamental goal of this exciting series is to produce leading-edge books on critical subjects facing security and audit executives and practitioners. Key topics addressed include Leadership, Cybersecurity, Security Leadership, Privacy, Strategic Risk Management, Auditing IT, Audit Management and Leadership, and Operational Auditing.

Securing Talent: Building and Retaining High-Performance Cybersecurity Teams
By Kevin Lynn McLaughlin

Digitalization and Women's Rights: Volume 1
By Muharrem Kılıç and Sezer Bozkus Kahyaoglu

Analysis of Threat Perceptions: NATO and Türkiye's Cyber Terrorism Policies
By Mehmet Emin Erendor

Members, Methods, and Measures: Unlocking the Secrets of IT Leadership
By Thomas E. Armstrong

Philosophy.exe: The Techno-Philosophical Toolkit for Modern Minds
By Matthias Muhlert

Guardians of the Digital Age: Securing the Future
By Elçin Biren

For more information about this series please visit: www.routledge.com/Security-Audit-and-Leadership-Series/book-series/CRCINTAUDITA?

Guardians of the Digital Age

Securing the Future

Elçin Biren

CRC Press
Taylor & Francis Group
Boca Raton London New York

CRC Press is an imprint of the
Taylor & Francis Group, **an informa** business

Designed cover image: Elçin Biren

First edition published 2026
by CRC Press
2385 NW Executive Center Drive, Suite 320, Boca Raton FL 33431

and by CRC Press
4 Park Square, Milton Park, Abingdon, Oxon, OX14 4RN

CRC Press is an imprint of Taylor & Francis Group, LLC

© 2026 Elçin Biren

ISBN: 978-1-032-80224-4 (hbk)
ISBN: 978-1-032-81839-9 (pbk)
ISBN: 978-1-003-50162-6 (ebk)

DOI: 10.1201/9781003501626

Typeset in Sabon
by Newgen Publishing UK

To Arel and Bartu, my endless sources of inspiration,
and to Sinan, my greatest love.

Contents

Preface

I've always known that one day I would write a book. There are so many stories, experiences, and lessons stored in my mind – like dozens of open tabs on a browser, each waiting to be addressed. But, like those tabs, I often found myself overwhelmed, jumping from one thought to another, never quite getting the chance to close them or bring them to life. Until now.

Cybersecurity has been one of the greatest passions of my life, a field that continues to challenge and inspire me. Alongside it, my role as a mother has shaped who I am in ways I could never have imagined. These two worlds – cybersecurity and motherhood – may seem distant, but for me, they are deeply connected. Both require vigilance, nurturing, and, above all, a profound sense of responsibility.

In today's fast-paced world, many nonfiction books on cybersecurity awareness sit untouched on shelves, gradually becoming outdated while technology and cyber risks evolve rapidly. Most of these books speak directly to professionals, businesses, and IT experts, leaving out the most vulnerable and essential audience: families. Parents, teenagers, and everyday individuals are often left to navigate this vast, complex digital landscape without guidance. I wanted to create a book that I, as both a parent and a professional, would want to read – a book that bridges the gap between the technical and the deeply personal, between the past and the future.

Initially, I thought this would be just another cybersecurity awareness book filled with tips and strategies. But I soon realized I wanted something more. I wanted this book to focus on connection – understanding the history of the internet, the evolution of cybersecurity, and how these forces shape our mental health, relationships, and daily lives. I wanted to move beyond facts and figures and tell a story that parents and teenagers alike could relate to and reflect on.

That's when I made the decision to lean into fiction, even science fiction, weaving a narrative through the journey of a character. This character journeys from the dawn of the internet, beginning with the ARPANET era, and explores the triumphs and mistakes that many in my field have long forgotten or overlooked. Through this story, I aim to bring the past, present, and future of cybersecurity to life in a way that is both relatable and meaningful.

This book is more than a passion project – it's a mission. It's an effort to connect families, bridge generational gaps, and provide a guide for navigating the digital world safely and meaningfully. I want parents and teenagers to not only understand the dangers but also to appreciate the incredible opportunities that come with living in a globally connected world.

Cybersecurity is not just about protecting devices; it's about protecting people – our loved ones, our communities, and ourselves. This book is my contribution to that goal. It's a story of connection, resilience, and the lessons we can learn from the past to safeguard our future.

Thank you for embarking on this journey with me.

Journal entry – Elçin – October 7, 2024

From *Elçin*: When I discovered how fragile I was beneath the polished armor of success, I felt as though I'd found a stranger within myself – a young girl I had long forgotten. She carried a quiet wisdom, a truth I had ignored. But somewhere along the way, a bug crept into her mind. Society's expectations, the relentless push to achieve, had planted it there. And as I climbed higher, the bug spread deeper, feeding on every moment I hid behind that shiny, unyielding facade of accomplishment.

The more I suppressed her wishes – to give, to create, to realize her true self – the heavier the weight of my burnout grew. Burdens on my soul, the vulnerabilities and pain I had tried so hard to hide, became unbearable. The shield I clung to, once my refuge, wasn't protecting me; it was suffocating me, reflecting only a hollow image of triumph. It wasn't until I let the shield fall, allowed myself to feel the pain and embrace the parts of myself I had been taught to suppress, that I began to heal.

I realized that true strength isn't about perfection or hiding pain – it's about standing unguarded in your own truth. It's about recognizing that vulnerability is not a weakness but a profound source of power. When I allowed myself to feel, to break, to rebuild, I discovered a strength I had never known. Being true to myself became my strongest shield.

And now, with that shield forged from honesty and hope, I am ready – not just to protect myself, but to help protect the world.

To Elsa: She is a dreamer. She was a dreamer. She will always be a dreamer.

She lives her life through her daydreams first, and in the time that remains, she becomes a witness to the world she creates in her boundless imagination. She has mastered the art of silencing her fears, anxieties, and negativity. When they creep into her mind, she acknowledges them with grace: "Yes, I see you," she says. Then, with unwavering resolve, she declares, "You are not serving me. Goodbye." And it works. Most of the time. The challenge? Remembering to do it consistently.

Life's complexity is shaped by our perceptions and imagination. If you let yourself spiral into a mental web – like a spider endlessly circling – you risk getting trapped in that web. It becomes suffocating instead of a sanctuary.

She is melancholic, fun, and endlessly curious. She is sharp yet hopelessly naïve, at times foolish in her trust. But once she decides on something, it's done. No turning back. In her mind, there is no such thing as a rewrite.

Her strengths are in her stubborn consistency, yet life constantly challenges her to embrace flexibility. The lessons come in waves – sometimes crashing, harsh and painful; other times lapping gently, teaching her with kindness.

It's hard, yes. But it's also so simple – if only you let yourself embrace life instead of resisting it. She is a magician, spinning a world of her own creation, resilient even when the threads unravel.

CYBERSECURITY, SIMPLIFIED FOR ALL GENERATIONS

From a hacker mom's heart to everyone – even newborn babies and the generations yet to come.

DISCLAIMER

This book draws inspiration from the history of the internet and cyber security. While certain individuals and events mentioned are real, various scenes, dialogues, and narratives have been fictionalized for storytelling purposes. The goal is to present these complex topics in an engaging and accessible manner. Readers are encouraged to consult verified sources for accurate historical and technical details.

Chapter 1

Lucid dreams and chasing digital ghosts

Journal entry – Aiden – January 10, 2028

I'll always remember this moment – this moment where I felt the first connection with my mom in forever. She is always all about work. It sometimes feels more important than anything. Even me. I feel like I'm not even on her radar sometimes. I can tell she's stressed 24/7. Why is it so important to her? There must be more to life than the grind? She doesn't have time for anything else. I don't know how to help. At least I have gaming to zone out.

The kitchen glowed faintly in the dim light of the early evening. Outside, rain streaked down the windows, tracing jagged paths that disappeared into the black void beyond. Inside, the only sound was the faint hum of a holographic screen hovering above the table. Elsa Winters sat at her kitchen table, the weight of burnout pressing down on her shoulders like a leaden blanket. Her fingers hovered above the keyboard, hesitant to engage with digital demands that seemed to multiply by the hour.

Notifications pulsed softly in the corner of the screen, their glow rhythmic, like a patient heartbeat. Each one carried a weight she couldn't bear to lift – another message unanswered, another demand unmet. Elsa stared at them as if they were living things, creatures clawing at her mind.

She knew she should care. Once, she had cared deeply. Once, this life – this world of endless connections, infinite possibilities – had been her dream. Now it felt like a trap. The freedom of the digital age had become her oppressor.

Her eyes drifted to the corner of the table where a coffee mug sat untouched. She didn't remember brewing it. She didn't remember much of anything these days. The days bled into each other, a blur of notifications, deadlines, and the faint ache behind her temples that no amount of sleep seemed to cure.

DOI: 10.1201/9781003501626-1

Her hand twitched toward the keyboard, but a sudden, sharp sound broke the silence, the door slamming. Elsa tossed her AR specs onto the cluttered table with a clatter. Lines of code still danced behind her eyes, taunting her with another long day of chasing down digital ghosts. She exhaled, her breath heavy with exhaustion and disillusionment.

"Mom?" Aiden's voice broke through her trance. "Can we talk about the new VR rig? I thought maybe we could – "

"Not now, Aiden," Elsa sighed. "I need to finish this penetration test report and tackle some of Grandma Janet's stuff today."

She caught the crestfallen look on her son's face in her peripheral vision before he slouched out of her office. A pang of guilt twisted in her gut, but she pushed it down. This was important work, even if the endless slog of identifying security flaws had long ago lost its shine.

The AI assistant in her glasses chirped, "Incoming message from Zephyr Media. Based on past interactions, I predict a high likelihood of unwanted algorithmic content suggestions."

"Mute notifications," Elsa growled, silencing the AI's too-chipper voice. She closed her eyes against the relentless onslaught of digital noise that pervaded every waking moment. Pop-up ads hovered at the edges of her vision, personalized based on her search history and biometric responses.

When had it all started to feel so hollow? Her younger self had been filled with such fierce idealism, determined to use her skills to build a better world. But now, two decades into her "white hat" hacker career, the noble intentions had been buried under an avalanche of data breaches, corporate malfeasance, and the creeping realization that every code she cracked only revealed three more vulnerabilities beneath.

Dully, Elsa reached to activate the coffee implant embedded in her wrist, wincing as the needle pierced her vein to deliver a precisely calibrated dose of caffeine. The momentary rush of energy did little to dispel her bone-deep weariness.

She glanced at the framed photo on her desk, her fingers tracing the smiling faces of her mother and a young Aiden. Janet had always made it seem so easy, spinning stories of ARPANET's early days and the thrill of discovery. But she'd been gone five years now, and the sense of purpose she'd instilled in Elsa felt like a distant memory.

As the caffeine ignited her bloodstream, Elsa turned back to her screen with grim determination. Lose yourself in the work, like always. The alternative – facing the disappointed looks from Aiden, the oppressive weight of her own disillusionment – didn't bear contemplating.

Her fingers danced across the keyboard once more, lines of Python filling the screen. She would finish this report, then the next one, each task blurring into an endless string of days defined by the glow of her monitor. Distantly, she heard Aiden's animated voice drifting from his room, excitement crackling through the walls as he undoubtedly regaled his friends with tales of his latest gaming exploits.

Elsa's heart clenched. When had the distance between them grown so vast? He was the one spark of warmth in her life, and yet she couldn't summon the energy to bridge the gap.

The notifications flickered at the edges of her vision once more – a colleague pinging her with a databurst, an automated calendar reminder flashing an upcoming security conference, each message dragging her from the promise of undisturbed focus.

With a deep breath, Elsa muted them all, sinking back into the cold comfort of the code. This was the world she knew, the domain she could control, even if the victories rang hollow. She would endure, like always, ignoring the small voice whispering that there had to be more to life than this endless digital twilight.

Elsa stood and stretched, her joints popping in protest. A leather-bound journal seemed to call to her from across the room, its worn cover an invitation to connect with the real world, to connect with her mother again. She'd been putting off sorting through her mother's things for months, each box a Pandora's enchantment of emotion she feared to unleash.

Aiden bounded into the room, his tablet clutched in his hands. "Mom, you've gotta check out this new augmented reality game! It's like the whole world becomes your battleground."

"Maybe later. Once I am done with Grandma's stuff, kiddo." Elsa managed a tired smile.

Aiden's eyes lit up. "Can I help? I bet there's all kinds of mad lit retro-tech in there!"

Elsa hesitated, but the eagerness in Aiden's face was impossible to resist. "Alright, but be careful. Some of this might be fragile."

Together, they began to sort through the boxes, Aiden's running commentary filling the air. "Whoa, check out these ancient floppy disks! And is this a first-gen VR headset?"

Elsa barely heard him, her attention captivated by the journal she hadn't had the courage to open. She lifted it reverently, running her fingers over the embossed initials: J.W. The pages crackled as she opened it, revealing Janet's precise handwriting interspersed with complex diagrams and cryptic equations. Something clattered to the floor.

"Mom, look at this!" Aiden held up a strange device, all-gleaming metal and pulsing lights. "It was hidden in the back of the journal."

Elsa took it gingerly, turning it over in her hands. "I've never seen anything like it. It almost looks like some kind of cipher machine."

As if in response, the device hummed to life, projecting a holographic interface into the air. The words "**ChronoCipher Activated. Decrypt the Timeline?**" glowed in pale blue light.

Elsa's heart raced. She had read about ARPANET before, but where? Flashes of fragmented notes scattered over her mother's desk took her back to her childhood as the memories fell into place. "**ARPANET** … " she murmured, the word echoing in her mind. ARPANET, the great-grandparent of today's internet, was designed to link scientists and researchers across distant locations, laying the groundwork for the connected world we now take for granted. Hardly anyone outside of academic or government circles even knew it existed.

Had her mother really been involved in its creation? And what was this ChronoCipher device … some kind of time capsule linking the present to those early days of networked communication? Elsa swallowed hard.

She flipped through the pages frantically, snippets of Janet's entries leaping out at her. " … *the potential for abuse is staggering, but so too is the opportunity for enlightenment … " " … must ensure the ethical foundations are laid now, before it's too late … "*

Aiden leaned over her shoulder, his eyes wide. "Sheesh, was Grandma Janet like a digital prophet or something?"

Elsa nodded slowly, a chill running down her spine. The weight of her mother's legacy settled upon her, a mantle she'd never asked to bear.

The ChronoCipher pulsed insistently, the invitation to decrypt the timeline hanging in the air. Elsa's finger hovered over the holographic "Yes," a lifetime of questions crystallizing into one breathless moment.

She glanced at Aiden, seeing her own wonder and trepidation mirrored in his eyes. This was their inheritance, the key to a puzzle spanning generations. Together, they would unravel its secrets, navigating the landscape of the past to chart a course for the future.

Elsa took a deep breath and pressed "Yes." The world dissolved in a cascade of light, time unspooling around them as the ChronoCipher whirred to life. And so, their journey into the tangled web of history and technology began, a mother and son united in their quest for understanding.

Elsa's hand trembled as she held the ChronoCipher. "This is crazy," she muttered, shaking her head. "We can't just … just jump into this like it's some kind of virtual reality game. We have no idea what this entails. What the implications could be."

Aiden's voice rose slightly, his expression intent. "But Mom, think about it! Grandma Janet left this for us. For you. She wanted you to see something, to understand what she was working on."

"I know, but … " Elsa's voice trailed off as she stared at the device, her reflection distorted in its metallic surface. The exhaustion of years spent battling digital threats, the endless cycle of patch and hack, patch and hack, seemed etched into her features. Did she have the strength to take on this new challenge, to confront the ghosts of her family's past?

Aiden's hand on her arm jolted her back to the present. "We can do this, Mom. Together. Like a co-op mission, right? You've got the skills, and I've got the fire!" His grin was infectious, a reminder of the joy and curiosity that had once driven her own passion for technology.

Elsa felt a smile tugging at the corners of her mouth. "Alright, kid. Let's see what this thing can do." She took a deep breath and tapped YES, watching as lines of code cascaded across the holographic display.

The ChronoCipher hummed to life, the air around them shimmering with energy. Elsa's fingers danced across the interface, muscle memory taking over as she navigated the complex encryption. It was like slipping into a familiar code library, the patterns and structures as comforting as they were challenging.

Aiden watched in awe, his eyes tracking the flow of data. "It's lit," he whispered. "Like a digital galaxy, all those connections and pathways."

Elsa nodded, her focus never wavering. This was her element, the world of logic and algorithms where she could lose herself for hours. But this time, there was something more at stake than just another security patch. This was about her family, about the legacy that had shaped her life in ways she had never fully understood.

With a final keystroke, the encryption fell away, and the ChronoCipher's full potential was revealed. The holographic display expanded, filling the room with a glowing web of timelines and data points. Elsa and Aiden stood at the center, unsure of what they had gotten themselves into.

"Decrypt the timeline," Elsa read aloud, her voice hushed with apprehension. "Well, here goes nothing."

A swirl of light and data engulfed Elsa and Aiden as the ChronoCipher hummed with energy, projecting a cryptic message in glowing text:

"KYZJB DRO MYWK. COXSFO DRO MYNO. QOXSFO DRO XSFSDR."

Elsa's eyes narrowed, the gears in her mind already turning as she analyzed the cipher. Aiden inched closer, drawn in by the mystery like a gamer tackling a final boss level.

"It's a substitution cipher," Elsa explained, her voice taking on the familiar cadence of a teacher. "Each letter is replaced by another letter, shifting the alphabet by a certain number of positions."

Aiden nodded, his eyes never leaving the hologram. "But how do we know the shift?"

A smile tugged at the corner of Elsa's mouth. "That's where the hint comes in." She gestured to a smaller, almost invisible, line of text beneath the cipher:

"Shift as ELIZA would."

Elsa's mind raced, connections forming like sparks in her neural pathways. ELIZA, the groundbreaking chatbot developed in 1966, had inspired her name. Her full name, Elizabeth, was a tribute to that pioneering creation, a fact her mother had often recounted with pride. ELIZA operated on basic patterns and keywords, an early attempt at mimicking human conversation.

Binary, the language of computers, a sequence of zeroes and ones, was the backbone of its design.

"Of course," she breathed, her fingers flying across the holographic keyboard. "ELIZA, the first chatbot, used a binary shift of 010, or 2 positions in the alphabet."

With a few swift keystrokes, the cipher unraveled, the letters rearranging themselves into a coherent message within the blinding light of the interface: "BREAK THE CODE. DECIPHER THE PAST. RECOVER THE FUTURE."

Aiden grinned, the thrill of the solve evident on his face.

"Break the code, decipher the past, recover the future," he read aloud, his voice filled with excitement. "We did it, Mom!"

Elsa smiled, a genuine warmth spreading through her chest. For a moment, the weight of her exhaustion lifted, replaced by the pure joy of sharing this moment with her son. But beneath the surface, her thoughts churned with the implications of the message.

Break the code. Decipher the past. Recover the future. The words echoed in her mind, a call to action that she couldn't ignore. Her mother's legacy, the secrets of her family's past, all tied to the very foundations of the digital world she had devoted her life to protecting.

She took a deep breath, steeling herself. There would be challenges, both technical and emotional, but with Aiden by her side, she felt a flicker of hope. Together, they would unravel the mysteries of the ChronoCipher and perhaps, in the process, find a way to mend the fractures in their own relationship.

Elsa blinked as the blinding light faded, her eyes adjusting to the now softer glow of the ChronoCipher's holographic display. The interface had transformed, presenting a detailed explanation of the cryptographic principles they had just employed.

"Whoa," Aiden breathed, leaning in closer. "It's like a built-in crypto textbook!"

Elsa nodded, her gaze scanning the text. "Substitution ciphers, like the one we just solved, were some of the earliest forms of encryption. Each letter in the plaintext is replaced by another letter, creating the ciphertext."

The display shifted, illustrating the concept with animated letters dancing across the screen. Aiden watched, enthralled, as the device walked them through the process step by step.

"So, that's how they kept messages secure back then?" he asked, glancing up at Elsa.

"It was a start," she replied, a hint of nostalgia in her voice. "But as technology advanced, so did the complexity of the ciphers. The key was to stay one step ahead of those trying to crack the codes."

Elsa's mind drifted to her own work in cybersecurity, the constant battle to protect data from prying eyes. The ChronoCipher seemed to sense her thoughts, the display shifting once more to highlight the role of cryptography in the early days of the internet.

"Look!" Aiden exclaimed, pointing at the screen. "It says here that encryption was crucial in securing communication between the first ARPANET nodes."

Elsa leaned in. The device was offering a glimpse into the very foundations of the digital world, the building blocks upon which everything she knew had been constructed.

As they delved deeper into the lessons of the crypto textbook, Elsa felt a spark of her old passion reigniting – the elegance of the algorithms, the ingenuity behind each new cipher. It was a reminder of why she had fallen in love with technology in the first place.

Aiden, too, seemed to be catching the excitement, his eyes alight with the thrill of discovery. "I never got how important cryptography was," he mused. "It's like the secret language of the internet."

Elsa couldn't help but smile at his enthusiasm. "And it's a language that's always evolving," she added. "Every new challenge, every new threat, pushes us to innovate, to find new ways to protect what matters."

The ChronoCipher pulsed, as if in agreement, and Elsa felt a sense of purpose creeping into her that she had thought long lost. This device, this legacy from her mother, was more than just a puzzle to be solved. It was a reminder of the greater mission, the responsibility they had to safeguard the digital frontier.

As the lesson came to a close, Elsa and Aiden shared a look of understanding. They were ready, armed with the knowledge of the past, to face whatever challenges lay ahead. The ChronoCipher had opened their eyes to the importance of their task, and together, they would see it through to the end.

Elsa ran her fingers over the ChronoCipher's surface, the cool metal thrumming with potential beneath her touch. The holographic interface shimmered, casting an ethereal glow across the room. Aiden leaned in closer, his eyes wide with anticipation.

"So, what now?" he asked, his voice barely above a whisper. "Where do we go from here?"

Elsa's eyes narrowed, her focus zeroing in on the device as she examined its details. The cryptographic puzzle had been just the beginning, a test of their understanding. But now, with the basics of encryption fresh in their minds, they were ready for the next challenge.

She tapped the interface, and a new message appeared, the text shimmering in the air before them. "Congratulations," it read. "You have unlocked the first destination."

Aiden's breath caught in his throat. "The first destination? You mean, like, in time?"

Elsa shrugged slowly, her heart pounding with a mixture of excitement and trepidation. Could it be possible? Could this device somehow transport them physically through time or space? Surely not. It had to be a digital destination.

She thought of her mother, of the cryptic notes and diagrams that filled her journal. Janet had been a visionary, a pioneer in the world of digital communication. But she had also been a mother, a wife, a woman torn between her passion for technology and her love for her family. Elsa's fingers trembled as she reached for the device, her resolve wavering for a moment. Was she ready to follow in her mother's footsteps? To take on the mantle of responsibility that came with the ChronoCipher?

"I don't know, Aiden. How do we possibly know unless we accept the invitation? And then how do we know that it is safe? Time travel surely is not truly possible."

She felt Aiden's hand on her shoulder, his touch unusually gentle and reassuring. "We can do this," he said with confidence. "Together."

Elsa took a deep breath, letting his words wash over her. He was right. They were a team, bound by blood and a shared purpose. And with the ChronoCipher as their guide, they would navigate the twists and turns of time – if that was indeed what would come.

She met Aiden's gaze, a smile tugging at the corners of her lips. "Together," she echoed, her voice strong and clear. "Alright, kid," Elsa said with a deep breath. "Let's see where this thing takes us."

She reached out, her finger a hair's breadth from the holographic interface. A final glance at Aiden, a silent acknowledgment of the adventure they were about to embark on, and then her hand passed through the hologram to select the unknown.

The device flared to life once more: Welcome to 1969 – The Birthplace of ARPANET.

Elsa and Aiden looked at each other with wide eyes. "Could we really be about to TIME TRAVEL? Skibidi!" Aiden breathed.

"It would seem so, kid. Hold on tight!" Elsa grabbed Aiden's hand, fear gripping her. The first destination awaited them, a portal to a world long gone but never forgotten. A world where the seeds of the digital revolution had first been planted, where visionaries like her mother had dared to dream of a future where technology and humanity could coexist in harmony.

Elsa felt a thrill of anticipation as the ChronoCipher began to hum, the air around them vibrating with energy. They were on the cusp of something extraordinary, a journey that would potentially test their wits and their resolve. But with each other to lean on, and the lessons of the past to guide them, they would face whatever challenges lay ahead.

The gloomy weather in Oregon faded away, replaced by the warm glow of the device. They were ready, poised on the brink of a new adventure. And as the ChronoCipher prepared to transport them across the boundaries of time and space, Elsa knew that they were exactly where they were meant to be.

The world shifted, realigning itself in a dizzying kaleidoscope of light and color. The room filled with a blinding light, the boundaries of space and time dissolving around them. And then, they were gone, pulled into the vortex of the past.

Elsa felt a sudden lurch in her stomach as the ground seemed to fall away beneath her feet. Beside her, Aiden let out a whoop of exhilaration, his hand gripping hers tightly.

The ChronoCipher was more than just a puzzle box – it was a key, a gateway to the past. And with each destination they unlocked, they would be one step closer to unraveling the mysteries of her family's legacy.

And then, as suddenly as it had begun, the sensation of falling ceased. Elsa blinked, her eyes adjusting to the sudden change in light. They were standing in a long, fluorescent-lit corridor, the walls lined with posters and flyers bearing the distinctive logo of the Stanford Research Institute.

"That was FIRE!" Aiden breathed in hushed awe. "We're here. The birth-place of ARPANET."

Chapter 2

Opening Pandora's box (1969)

Journal entry – Elsa – January 10, 2028

I loved coding with my mom – that was our thing. Outside of that, was there much of a relationship? Mom's work was so important to her, so I made it important to me. How does Aiden feel about this? Sometimes I lie awake at night wondering if I'm giving him enough of what he needs, or if he sees me as I saw Mom sometimes – distant, caught up in the world of code, too busy to spend time with me. Is it too late to form something real, something deep with my son? Will he ever understand why it is so important that I do what I do? How will I teach him? Is he even interested?

I see him hiding in video games like I hide in my world of coding – we have more in common than he realizes. We both hide in the digital world.

Elsa nodded, her heart racing. She recognized this place from the old photographs her mother had shown her, the grainy black-and-white images now brought to vivid life. The air hummed with a sense of barely contained energy, the thrill of discovery and innovation.

But beneath the excitement, Elsa felt a twinge of unease. What secrets lay hidden in these halls? What role had her family played in the creation of this groundbreaking technology, and what implications might that have for the future? And, more practically, how would they explain their presence in the building? Their clothing would surely raise some eyebrows if nothing else did!

Aiden tugged at her hand, his eyes shining with eagerness. Not an ounce of practicality in his young mind. "Come on, let's explore!" He'd forgotten his too-cool-for-school persona for the moment, totally caught up in the excitement. Elsa missed those days.

Elsa hesitated, wanting to hold Aiden back. But as she looked into her son's face and saw the pure, unbridled curiosity there, she felt her own reservations melt away.

DOI: 10.1201/9781003501626-2

"Alright," she said, squaring her shoulders. "But we need to be careful. We don't know what we might find here, or how it might affect the timeline. Let alone how people might react to us being here."

Aiden nodded solemnly, his expression sobering. "Got it, Mom. But we have to try. For Grandma's sake, and for the sake of everyone who came after her."

Elsa felt a surge of pride at her son's words, at the wisdom and compassion that belied his youth. Together, they set off down the corridor, their footsteps echoing in the stillness despite their efforts to move in silence.

Their breath caught in their throats as a door opened off to the side and a group of engineers turned into the corridor toward them. This was the moment of truth, come sooner than expected. They were caught. The group looked directly at the mother and son duo, standing frozen in corridor ahead, and walked right through them.

"Sheesh!" Aiden cried; his eyes gleaming. "That was mad weird! Did you feel that, Mom? My whole body is buzzing!"

"An interesting sensation, indeed," Elsa said with a giggle. "So, kid. Looks like we're invisible here. Let's go check things out!"

The hum of early computers filled the air, accompanied by the muted whispers of scientists as they prepared for a moment that would change history forever.

"Can you feel the vibe, Mom?" Aiden whispered, his voice tinged with awe.

Elsa nodded, her heart pounding in time with the steady rhythm of progress. She could sense it too – the excitement, the tension, and the weight of responsibility that rested on the shoulders of everyone present.

"Let's move closer," she suggested, her gaze locked on a group huddled around a massive computer console. As they edged forward, Elsa felt a surge of determination course through her veins, fueled by the knowledge that she was helping her son uncover a pivotal moment in history. And perhaps, in doing so, she was finding a new purpose for herself as well.

"Stay close," she murmured to Aiden, her hand reaching out to grasp him.

The cacophony of excited voices and the mechanical whir of computer reels surrounded Elsa and Aiden as they stood at the epicenter of technological innovation. Scientists hustled about, their eyes darting between monitors and printouts while fingers danced across keyboards.

Elsa's gaze shifted from the flurry of activity to the tense faces of the scientists, each a tapestry of hope and apprehension. The duality struck her – the birth of ARPANET was both a symbol of connection and control. She couldn't help but wonder what these pioneers envisioned, whether they knew they were on the cusp of creating something that would come to define humanity's relationship with technology.

"Mom, check it out!" Aiden's voice cut through her thoughts like a laser beam. His green eyes were wide as he pointed toward a group of researchers huddled around a teletype machine. "Is that ... ?"

"Yes," Elsa whispered. "This is it. The first message sent over ARPANET."

As the scientists prepared to transmit the groundbreaking message, an electrifying current of anticipation surged through the room. Elsa felt it intertwining with her own nerves, a tangible manifestation of the significance of this moment in time.

"LO" appeared on the distant screen, followed by a cheer erupting from the researchers. Elsa watched as they exchanged relieved smiles and hearty pats on the back. Aiden turned to her, his face lit with excitement.

"Did they know, Mom?" he asked breathlessly. "Did they have any idea how much this would change everything?"

Elsa hesitated for a moment, weighing her response. "I think they had some idea of the potential, but even they couldn't imagine just how far-reaching the impact would be," she said, her voice steady and contemplative.

What lay ahead wasn't simply a marvel of science; it was a doorway to something deeper, something unknown – like opening a digital Pandora's box.

Aiden's gaze flickered as he mused on her words. The ARPANET project, initiated by the Advanced Research Projects Agency (ARPA) within the US Department of Defense, had started with a clear and noble goal: to create a robust, resilient network that could connect American research institutions and keep information flowing, even under the threat of attack. Revolutionary packet-switching technology made this possible, breaking data into independent packets that could travel different paths and reassemble seamlessly at their destination.

But questions lingered: would this network remain a tool to share knowledge, or could it become a vessel for darker purposes?

The parallels to mythology were hard to ignore. Pandora's box came once again to Elsa's mind – the ancient Greek myth of the first woman, created by Zeus, who was given a sealed jar and told never to open it. Consumed by curiosity, Pandora eventually broke the seal, unleashing all the evils of the world: pain, disease, envy, and death. Only hope remained, trapped within the jar.

Just as Pandora had unleashed chaos, Elsa realized, the ARPANET's foundational principles of openness and freedom would also become its most dangerous vulnerabilities. Pandora's box had been opened, and closing it was no longer an option.

Elsa's green eyes sharpened, her gaze cutting through the hum of the lab. "ARPANET was groundbreaking, Aiden," she began. "It marked the birth of a new era, one where information could be shared across vast distances in mere seconds."

The importance of the moment settled on them both as they stood invisible amid the engineers and programmers, their excitement contagious. Elsa continued, "But with every great leap forward comes the potential for misuse and vulnerability."

Aiden's eyes flickered between his mother and the researchers. He shifted his weight from one foot to the other, absorbing the magnitude of what they were witnessing.

"Imagine," Elsa said, gesturing to the room around them, "the power that comes with connecting entire nations, expanding human knowledge at an unprecedented rate. But also consider the risks – the loss of privacy, the potential for manipulation and control."

Aiden's expression tightened as he processed her words. His focus remained fixed on his mother, her wisdom a beacon in this foreign environment. The lab buzzed with activity, but Aiden tuned it out, concentrating solely on Elsa's explanation.

"Mom," he said, "how did they balance it all? How'd they make sure the good stuff hit harder than the bad?"

Elsa smiled, her face softening as she met Aiden's intense gaze. "It would be a while before they'd have to consider that. But it's been a constant struggle throughout history, Aiden, and it still is today. There will always be those who push boundaries for progress and those who exploit vulnerabilities for their own gain."

Her fingers brushed against the edge of the ChronoCipher, a reminder of the technology tethering them to the past. "Our role, as individuals, is to educate ourselves and remain vigilant. To understand the tools we wield and use them responsibly."

Aiden's eyes widened, his perspective shifting as he saw the internet in a new light. Not just as a tool, but as a complex web of possibilities and challenges. He nodded, the seed of newfound understanding blossoming within him.

The hum of conversation and the whirring of machines filled Elsa's ears as they navigated through the lab. Aiden trailed behind her, his gaze darting from one side of the room to another, soaking in every detail.

"Look at that," Elsa said, nodding toward a group huddled around an early computer terminal. "Just think of how far we've come."

"From room-sized machines to smartphones," Aiden mused. "It's insane." He mentally cataloged each interaction, each piece of equipment, eager to share this information with his classmates.

Elsa's thoughts raced, drawing parallels between the past and present. The challenges faced by these pioneers mirrored her own experiences with cybersecurity – a constant battle between innovation and exploitation. She watched as the researchers exchanged ideas, their collaboration laying the foundation for a digital revolution.

A sudden hum broke through the clatter of the lab, faint at first but growing louder, until it was impossible to ignore. Elsa and Aiden froze, their gazes snapping to the ChronoCipher. It buzzed in her hand, the glow beneath its intricate surface intensifying until it cast long, dancing shadows across the room. The scientists worked on, oblivious to the time travelers and their strange device.

"What's it doing now?" Aiden whispered, his voice quivering with nervous excitement.

The device pulsed once, and then a soft beam of light projected upward, splitting the air with a hiss. Lines of glowing text materialized in the space above, flickering as though alive: **"Decrypt the Past to Understand the Future."**

"What does that even mean?" Aiden asked, stepping closer, his face illuminated by the holographic glow.

Elsa didn't answer immediately. Her gaze hardened as the text on the screen was replaced by a chaotic storm of symbols, fragmented code, and scattered diagrams. They hovered in midair like shattered pieces of a puzzle, rotating slowly, waiting.

"It's a puzzle," Elsa said finally. "It looks like ... the Network Control Protocol. The foundation of ARPANET."

Aiden tilted his head, his curiosity overtaking his nerves. "You mean the first rules of the internet?" He reached out, his hand wavering as it passed through the projection, disrupting the light. "This is bussin."

Cool wasn't the word Elsa would have used. There was something eerie about the way the fragments floated, as though they had been plucked straight from her mother's notes. The way the ChronoCipher vibrated in her hand made her skin crawl, as if it was alive – aware.

"Let's solve it!" Aiden said, his enthusiasm cutting through her hesitation.

Elsa's fingers hovered over the hologram, but she hesitated. "This isn't a game, Aiden. This ... This means something."

"Yeah, but we won't know what until we finish it," he countered, his face lit with the kind of excitement only a teenager could muster. "Come on, Mom. You said progress comes with risks, right?"

Her lips pressed into a thin line, but she couldn't argue with his logic. With a reluctant nod, she said, "Okay. Let's see what it wants."

Aiden reached out first, his fingers tracing one of the glowing fragments. As he pulled it into place, the piece snapped into alignment with a faint chime, locking into the pale outline of a larger diagram.

Elsa studied the emerging framework, her mind racing. It was familiar – too familiar. Her mother's handwriting appeared on several of the fragments, neat and precise, but slightly rushed, as though she had scribbled them down in a frenzy of ideas.

"Check this one," Aiden said, dragging a fragment into view. "What's this squiggly stuff?"

Elsa leaned closer, her eyes narrowing. "Packet switching," she said softly. "This is what made ARPANET possible. It broke data into packets, sent them independently, and reassembled them at the destination."

Aiden's fingers paused mid-motion. "Like … digital puzzle pieces?"

"Exactly," Elsa said, nodding. "But if even one packet gets lost or corrupted, the whole thing falls apart."

Aiden grinned, the comparison clearly sparking his interest. "So, the internet's basically a giant jigsaw puzzle?"

"More like a puzzle that constantly changes," Elsa said. "And in 1969, this puzzle was delicate. One wrong move, and the whole thing could crash." She glanced toward the group of scientists, who were still hunched over their terminal, unaware of their observers. "Which it did. A lot."

They continued working, each fragment clicking into place with a satisfying hum. Aiden's confidence grew as the diagram took shape, his movements quick and deliberate. But Elsa's unease deepened. Each piece revealed more of the protocol's structure – and its flaws.

"This part," she murmured, dragging a diagram of error correction into focus. "It's so basic. They didn't have redundancy yet. If a node failed, the whole network could collapse."

Aiden frowned. "Didn't they think about backups?"

"They were making it up as they went," Elsa replied. "Backups, firewalls, encryption – those came later, when it was too late to build them into the foundation."

As the last few fragments floated into alignment, Elsa's chest tightened. Her mother's notes contained annotations she hadn't noticed before – questions scribbled in the margins. *What happens if control is lost? Who decides who gets access?*

Her mother had known, even then, that the network's openness was a double-edged sword. She hadn't been able to fix it.

With a final click, the last fragment slid into place. The hologram flared brighter, and the swirling lines of code coalesced into a single sentence: **"The Box Is Open. What Lies Within?"**

Elsa's stomach turned. The words felt like an accusation, as if the ChronoCipher had pulled them from her own thoughts. Aiden stepped back, his wide eyes reflecting the hologram's glow.

"What's it mean?" he asked.

Elsa didn't answer immediately. Her mind raced with the implications. ARPANET's creators had opened the box, but they hadn't understood what lay inside – the vulnerabilities, the exploitation, the chaos.

"It means," Elsa said finally, her voice low, "that once something is unleashed, you can't take it back. You can only try to control what happens next."

The ChronoCipher buzzed again, louder this time. The hologram flickered, its light growing brighter until it bathed the lab in an otherworldly glow.

Aiden turned to Elsa, his face pale. "Is it ... doing that by itself?"

Elsa tightened her grip on the device, her knuckles whitening. "It's leading us somewhere."

Before they could react, the lab around them dissolved in a cascade of light and sound. The scientists, the machines, the faint hum of the terminal – they all vanished, replaced by the sensation of falling.

"Where are we going?" Aiden asked, his voice trembling with a mix of fear and excitement.

Elsa held his hand tightly, her own heart pounding. "My guess is to find out what's inside the box."

The light consumed them, and the world spun out of focus, pulling them forward into the unknown.

The rain was still falling outside, streaking down the glass in restless rivulets. Inside, the glow of the holographic screen had dimmed, but the faint hum of the ChronoCipher filled the silence. Elsa turned the device over in her lap, her fingers tracing the smooth contours absentmindedly.

They were back home, sitting in the living room, trying to process what they'd just experienced.

"I always thought of it like magic," Aiden said suddenly, breaking the quiet. His gaze was fixed on the raindrops, his voice softer now. "When I was little, I mean. You'd tell me stories about the internet, how it connected everything. It sounded like ... I don't know, like a fairy tale."

Elsa's lips curved into a faint smile. "That's how it felt, at first," she admitted. "Back then, we didn't call it magic, though. We called it progress. We believed it would make everything better. Easier. Fairer."

"And did it?" Aiden turned to her, his expression open, curious.

Elsa hesitated, the question hanging between them like the rain clouds outside. "Sometimes," she said finally. "But magic – real magic – isn't perfect. It has a price."

Aiden frowned. "What kind of price?"

"With every great leap forward comes the potential for misuse and vulnerability."

Elsa reflected on a timeless truth: humanity has always been granted the freedom to choose between light and dark. ARPANET, too, would embody this duality. It could be a vessel for knowledge and progress, yet also a refuge for shadows and exploitation. Users would ultimately have to decide – to walk in the light or embrace the shadows.

She watched her son, his excitement contagious and heartwarming.

"Hey, Mom," Aiden said, turning toward her. "Thanks for doing this with me. I know you've been stressed lately, but this ... .This was lit."

In that moment, something shifted within Elsa. She felt a warmth in her chest, a subtle rekindling of the passion that had once fueled her every waking moment. The weight of her burnout seemed to lift a little more, incrementally being replaced by a growing sense of purpose and connection.

"Thank you, Aiden," she replied with gratitude. "You reminded me why I fell in love with technology in the first place. It's not just about the innovation – it's about the people we connect with along the way."

Their eyes met, and in the depths of Aiden's green irises, Elsa saw a reflection of her younger self – the same curiosity, determination, and resilience that had carried her through countless challenges.

"Promise me something, Aiden," Elsa said, her voice soft but resolute. "Never lose sight of what truly matters in this digital world. Stay curious, stay cautious, and above all, stay connected to the people you love."

Aiden's lips curved into a determined smile. "I promise, Mom."

As they sat there, their hands clasped together, Elsa knew that this journey was not only about guiding her son – it was about rediscovering herself, her passion, and the boundless possibilities that lay ahead.

Chapter 3

The first glitches (1970s)

Journal entry – Aiden – January 11, 2028

What the Sigma?! Time travel is an actual thing? No cap ... it's kind of cool I get to do it with Mom though. She's actually pretty awesome.

The air around Elsa and Aiden shimmered as the ChronoCipher completed its transition. The duo hadn't had long to recuperate in the quiet comfort of their living room before the device had buzzed to life again. This time, they were sucked from reality without any warning at all. Their almost empty coffee cups clattering to the floor as they went.

The gentle drumming of rain on windows was replaced by a quieter, more methodical energy. They found themselves standing in a corridor lined with beige walls, dimly lit by fluorescent lights. A faint whiff of coffee and ink hung in the air, mingled with the subtle heat of electronics.

"Where are we?" Aiden asked, his voice breaking the stillness. He rubbed his arms as if shaking off the feeling of displacement.

Elsa scanned their surroundings as she fought off a wave of motion sickness. Her gaze fell on a cluster of terminals at the far end of the hallway, where men and women hunched over keyboards, their faces illuminated by green screens. "Judging by the technology, I would say this is the early 1970s," she said quietly. "ARPANET has grown. It's no longer just an experiment – it's becoming a network."

The word felt heavy as it left her mouth. Network. The precursor to the internet, the web that would unite humanity in ways once unimaginable – and divide it in ways no one could have foreseen. She motioned for Aiden to follow her, the sound of their steps muffled by the linoleum floor.

As they entered the main room, they were greeted by the rhythmic clatter of teletype machines and the low murmur of conversation. Stacks of printouts, coffee-stained and crumpled, cluttered every available surface. Elsa's sharp green eyes swept the room, noting the palpable excitement among the researchers.

DOI: 10.1201/9781003501626-3

"They're proud," she said, almost to herself. "They should be. They've built something extraordinary."

Aiden's gaze darted from one terminal to another, taking in the glowing monitors and rows of blinking lights. "So, this is ARPANET? It's kind of … cheugy."

Elsa smirked as she took a second to interpret his Gen Alpha slang. "It may look that way to you now, but this was revolutionary. Remote login, file sharing, electronic mail – these were concepts that didn't exist before. These people weren't just building machines; they were building possibilities."

A burst of laughter erupted from the far side of the room. Elsa and Aiden turned to see a cluster of researchers gathered around a teletype machine. One of them was typing furiously, the rhythmic click-clack punctuated by stifled giggles.

"What's going on?" Aiden asked, inching closer.

Elsa followed him. The text spilling from the machine caught her attention: **"This is the first spam message! Congratulations, ARPANET users!"**

Aiden squinted at the line of text. "Spam? So this is ground zero for it?"

Elsa gave a quick nod. "Spam, as in unsolicited messages. This is what some call the first instance of it – though it's more like a mass broadcast message. They thought it was harmless fun, but … " Her voice trailed off, and her smile faded.

"But what?" Aiden pressed, his brow furrowing.

She gestured toward the researchers, who were now exchanging bemused looks as the machine churned out more lines of text. "That 'harmless' message caused a system slowdown. ARPANET wasn't designed for this kind of unexpected load. Every node that received the message had to process it, and that clogged up the system."

Aiden's jaw dropped. "Seriously? Just one little message could do that?"

"It wasn't the message itself," Elsa explained. "It was the volume that was sent and how it interacted with the network. ARPANET was built on trust – users were expected to follow certain unwritten rules. No one thought to put limits on what could be sent because they assumed people wouldn't abuse it."

Aiden frowned. "That seems… naïve."

Elsa turned to him, her expression somber. "It was. But that naivety was also what made it beautiful. The system wasn't just built to connect machines – it was built to connect people. And that's where the cracks began to show."

"Like this spam message?" Aiden asked, piecing it together.

Elsa nodded. "Exactly. It's not just about coding and hacking, Aiden. It's about understanding the human impact of our actions. Every innovation has consequences, especially in the digital world."

Aiden absorbed her words, his expression sobering as he looked back at the terminal. "I want to understand, Mom. All of it."

Elsa reached out, her hand resting gently on his shoulder. "You will. That's why we're here – to learn from the past and protect the future."

They stood there for a moment, surrounded by the low thrum of mainframes and the distant chatter of researchers. The glow of the ARPANET terminal wavered, casting faint shadows on their faces as it signaled that it was nearing time to move on.

Aiden leaned closer to a humming terminal, his fingers hovering over the chunky keys. "Mom, when did all this stop being about just sharing research and become ... you know, spam and scams?"

Elsa let out a measured sigh, her gaze fixed on an oscilloscope's flickering green line. "The first recorded instance of what we'd call spam was in the late '70s," she began, her voice threading through the electronic symphony of the lab. "It was an unsolicited message sent to hundreds of ARPANET users, promoting a presentation. It wasn't malicious like today's phishing scams, but it crossed a boundary – using a shared network for personal gain without consent."

"Did people even know what to do with it?"

"Some were baffled, others were annoyed. A few even laughed it off," Elsa said, her words falling in rhythm with the blinking lights of a nearby mainframe. "But it was a wake-up call. It showed how trust in a system could be exploited."

The familiar blinding light engulfed them, and before they knew it, they opened their eyes to find themselves standing in the same lab. "Has it glitched?" Aiden asked with concern. They looked at each other with mild confusion, before they realized that the computers had been updated. They had left and returned a few years later – at the moment the first unsolicited spam message was sent out over ARPANET.

Aiden scribbled notes onto his tablet, his stylus moving swiftly across the screen, picking up where he'd left off. "So, that's why we're here – to see it firsthand?"

"Exactly." Elsa nodded, watching him work. "History isn't just about dates and facts. It's about understanding these moments, feeling their weight."

Their conversation melted into the background as they approached a cluster of researchers gathered around a printout. The group's voices rose and fell in a heated exchange. Elsa and Aiden hung back, invisible observers to a pivotal scene unfolding in real time.

"Unbelievable," one researcher muttered, shaking his head at the document in his hands.

"Is it a prank?" another asked, adjusting his glasses.

"Could be a demonstration," a third suggested, tapping the paper with his pen. "But it wasn't scheduled or approved."

Elsa's focus honed in, catching every subtle shift – the tightening of jaws, the flicker of hesitation in their eyes, and the faint sighs of indifference. Aiden, meanwhile, scribbled furiously, his youthful script barely keeping pace with the unfolding discussion.

"See their faces?" Elsa whispered, leaning down to Aiden's level. "Curiosity is there, but so is the seed of concern. They can't see the full picture yet, not like we can."

"Because we know where this leads … " Aiden's voice trailed off, connecting past to future.

"Right." Elsa straightened up, a shadow crossing her features. "We know the cost of curiosity without caution."

They stepped away from the researchers, leaving the heated debate behind as they continued to weave through the lab, the echoes of history resonating with lessons still relevant decades later.

Elsa drew Aiden to the fringes of the lab, where the staccato rhythm of keystrokes played a counterpoint to their hushed conversation. She motioned toward the ARPANET terminals that stood like monoliths to progress, and her gaze lingered on the amber glow of the screens.

"Think of it, Aiden," she began. "That message, sent without a thought for consent, is like the first crack in a dam." She locked eyes with him, ensuring each word resonated. "It's small, almost innocuous, but it's the beginning of a flood – digital trust exploitation."

Aiden absorbed her words. "So, this is where it starts to get a little messy? Like sharing info versus crossing the line and violating trust?"

"Exactly." Elsa nodded, her mouth set in a firm line. "And that's why the human element in cybersecurity can't be overstressed. Technology may evolve, but people … people are constant. Our desires, fears, vulnerabilities – they remain the same."

As they spoke, Elsa led Aiden to an empty workstation tucked away behind the main flurry of activity. On the table lay a series of printouts, lines of code interspersed with fragments of text. She gestured to them, a spark igniting in her weary eyes.

"Here's our ChronoPuzzle challenge," she announced, spreading out the papers like a map to buried treasure. "Looks like we need to analyze and reconstruct the original spam message. Think of it as digital archaeology."

Aiden pored over the papers, his fingers twitching with anticipation. "Where do we start?" he asked, scanning the jumbled data.

"Look for patterns, for anomalies. Ask yourself why someone would send this message." Elsa's guidance was a beacon. "Motivation is key. Was it a mischief? A demonstration of power? Or something more sinister?"

They leaned over the documents, shoulder to shoulder, their shared concentration forming an invisible bubble around them. Elsa watched as Aiden's gaze swept over the page, his features tightening with focused intensity.

"Could they have known what they were starting?" Aiden mused, tracing a line of code as if it were a thread in a vast and intricate tapestry.

"Maybe, maybe not," Elsa replied. "But intention doesn't always align with outcome. That's why we must tread carefully – with foresight, but also with the incredible gift of hindsight."

Together, they pieced through the puzzle, a dance of minds in which Elsa's expertise fused with Aiden's fresh perspective, creating a synergy that transcended time and technology.

Aiden's fingers sped over the scattered printouts, his movements almost a blur as he arranged and rearranged the snippets of code. "What if the sender was trying to connect, like in a weird pen pal sort of way?" he posited, his voice filled with the kind of wonder that only a 14-year-old on the brink of discovery could muster.

Elsa leaned back in her chair, the ghost of a smile playing across her lips as she watched her son. The sight of him – so alive with questions, so untainted by the cynicism that often clouded her vision – was a balm to the dull ache of fatigue that perpetually haunted her. "That's one possibility," she conceded, reaching out to tap a line of code on his sheet. "But consider the broader implications – privacy invasion, unsolicited contact. It sets a … precedent."

"Like opening Pandora's box?" Aiden's gaze lifted from the papers to meet Elsa's, the analogy having stuck with him.

"Exactly." She nodded, impressed with his intuition. "Unfortunately, once it's been opened, it can't be closed again."

They resumed their work, poring over the digital relics with forensic precision. Elsa shared bits of arcane knowledge, explaining the significance of each command and symbol while Aiden absorbed it all, hungry for every morsel. His theories grew more sophisticated with each passing hour, branching into discussions about the evolution of cyber ethics.

"Okay, hypothetical break time," Elsa declared after some time, her voice cutting through their intense focus. She stood, stretching limbs stiff from hours spent hunched over their makeshift workspace.

Aiden looked up, a hint of reluctance in his eyes, but he complied, pushing away from the table and joining Elsa as she walked a few steps to the side.

"Think about it this way," Elsa began, her words slow and deliberate as she sought the right metaphor to bridge the gap between her world-weary knowledge and his youthful optimism. "Imagine you're building a house, your dream home. You have all these amazing ideas – a library with floor-to-ceiling shelves, a kitchen filled with the latest gadgets, rooms that respond to your every need."

"Sounds lit," Aiden interjected, a grin spreading across his face.

"It does," Elsa agreed, letting the ghost of her own dream house flit through her imagination. "But what happens if you're so focused on the cool features that you forget to lay down a solid foundation?"

Aiden's expression sobered as he considered the question. "The house would eventually collapse, right? All those fancy things wouldn't matter then."

"Exactly." Elsa placed a hand on his shoulder, grounding herself in the moment. "Technology is a lot like that. We can build incredible things, push boundaries, create connections. But without a strong ethical foundation, without considering the potential harm, it can crumble under its own weight."

"Like spam leading to bigger trust issues online?" Aiden's understanding was quick, the connection immediately clicking into place.

"Right again," Elsa said, pride swelling within her. "Innovation is mesmerizing, seductive even. But oversight, responsibility – they're the foundation that keeps the whole structure stable."

Aiden nodded. They stood together in silent accord, the early computers around them a testament to human ingenuity – and a reminder of the vigilance needed to guide such power wisely.

"Let's finish the puzzle," Aiden suggested after a pause.

"We will," Elsa assured him, feeling an unexpected surge of hope. "And we'll make sure our house has the strongest foundation possible."

Aiden's fingers paused over the tablet screen, a frown creasing his brow as he absorbed the gravity of Elsa's metaphor. His mother had always been the gatekeeper of digital wisdom, but now, amid the whirring tape drives and clacking keyboards of the 1970s computer lab, her words resonated deeper than ever before.

"Mom, I want to be part of that foundation," he said with uncharacteristic gravity. "I mean, I know I'm just a kid, but maybe I could learn ethical hacking? Help build something that doesn't just ... collapse."

Elsa observed him – her son, no longer a boy lost in video games and social feeds, but a young man awakening to the responsibility nestled within their code-infused legacy. She smiled faintly, appreciating the symbiotic growth between them. Aiden's idealism tempered her cynicism, while her experience lent depth to his enthusiasm.

"Ethical hacking is about protecting people, Aiden. It's a big responsibility to take on, but someone with your heart and drive is the perfect candidate. It's about using your skills to make sure technology serves us, not the other way around." Her voice, usually laden with fatigue, vibrated with conviction.

"Sounds like being a digital superhero," Aiden quipped, a spark of his typical humor returning.

"Without the cape, and a lot more coffee," Elsa retorted with a chuckle, grateful for the levity.

Together, they turned their attention back to the ChronoPuzzle. Nearing its completion, they were confronted by an intricate sequence that defied easy decoding. The spam message, an artifact from the dawn of digital communication, now stood as a cipher challenging them both.

"Ugh, it's like this part is in another language," Aiden groaned, squinting at the jumbled text on the screen.

"Try looking at it from a different perspective," Elsa suggested gently. "Remember how you solved that level in 'Quantum Quest' by viewing the maze from above?"

"Right! The solution was literally a change in viewpoint." Aiden's posture shifted, his mind racing with possibilities. He began rotating the virtual puzzle, examining the scrambled words from multiple angles.

"Think about the person who sent this," Elsa encouraged him. "What were they trying to achieve? Sometimes understanding the creator's intent can help unravel the creation."

"Manipulation? Attention?" Aiden muttered, piecing together the psychological underpinnings of the first spam. "They wanted to be seen, to break through the noise."

"Exactly." Elsa nodded, watching as Aiden's fingers flew across the screen with renewed vigor. "Deconstructing their goals helps us construct our defense."

The characters on the screen aligned, yielding to Aiden's determination and Elsa's guidance. As the final pieces clicked into place, Elsa leaned back, observing her son's triumph.

"Creative problem-solving," she mused aloud. "It's an essential skill, not just for puzzles like this, but for life – especially when it intersects with technology."

"Life's just a big puzzle, isn't it?" Aiden grinned, eyes alight with accomplishment.

Elsa's smile was weary but genuine as she replied, "And we're all figuring it out one piece at a time."

Aiden's hands drifted over the tablet with precision as he dragged the last cluster of digital fragments into alignment. The screen flickered, and a message from decades past revealed itself whole once more.

"Got it!" Aiden exclaimed, his voice echoing slightly in the lab filled with retro technology. He turned to Elsa, seeking confirmation in her eyes that he had done well.

"Nicely done," Elsa said, her smile reaching her tired eyes as she peered over his shoulder at the reconstructed text. "You've just put together the first puzzle piece of digital deception."

Aiden puffed up with pride, his chest swelling in the way that only a teenager's can when they've felt the sweet victory of achievement. "So this ... this is what started it all? The spam wars, the phishing scams?"

"Indeed," Elsa replied, nodding solemnly. She guided him to sit on one of the lab's swivel chairs, its orange upholstery worn by time.

"Anyone can learn to code, but figuring out why people do what they do ... that's the tough part, right?" Aiden surmised, leaning forward, elbows resting on his knees. "Exactly," Elsa affirmed, crossing her arms as she leaned against the chassis of an old mainframe computer. "Technology – it's neutral, a tool. But in the hands of people, it reflects our virtues and vices."

"Like a mirror?" Aiden asked, head tilted slightly as he pondered the analogy.

"More like clay," Elsa corrected. "It takes the shape of the hands that mold it. When we create without considering the consequences, we risk crafting something harmful."

Aiden nodded slowly, absorbing her words. "So, we should build tech like we're shaping a better future, not just a cooler present."

"Thoughtful as always," Elsa said, her tone warm with parental affection. "Remember, every line of code you write, every system you design, touches lives, shapes society."

"Like Grandma Janet's work with ARPANET?" Aiden inquired, his gaze drifting to the terminals they had passed earlier.

"Janet believed in connection, in a web that would unite us. And in many ways, it has," Elsa said, pausing as memories flickered across her face. "But every web can ensnare as well as support. We must be vigilant weavers."

"Vigilant weavers," Aiden repeated, rolling the phrase around his tongue. "I like that. It's like being a hero in a game, but the stakes are real."

"More real than you can imagine," Elsa murmured, "and sometimes, the choices are harder than any challenge you've faced."

"Then I'm glad I have you as my guide, Mom," Aiden said, reaching out to squeeze her hand. His touch was light, mindful of her chronic pain, yet full of love.

Elsa squeezed back, anchoring herself in the moment with her son. "Together, we'll navigate this timeline – and any other that might come along – fighting for a world where technology uplifts, not undermines."

"Team Winters to the rescue," Aiden quipped, a playful twinkle in his eye.

"Team Winters," Elsa echoed, allowing herself the luxury of hope, however fleeting. Together, amid the ghosts of computing's dawn, they shared a quiet resolve to honor the past by protecting the future.

Lingering at the threshold of the bustling university computer lab, Aiden took one last sweeping glance over the mainframes and flickering green screens. "This ... was incredible, Mom. I mean, it's one thing to read about this stuff or see it in old movies, but being here? It's like touching history."

Elsa watched her son with exhaustion and contentment. The weight of their temporal trespass hung on her like a heavy coat, yet the spark in Aiden's eyes was enough to fend off the chill of time travel's toll on her body. "I'm glad you got to see it firsthand," she said, her voice a soft intrusion amid the clacks of keyboards and murmurs of data-driven discourse. "It's not just history, Aiden. It's our history."

"Facts," he replied, his voice bouncing with youthful verve. He fiddled with his tablet, a futuristic anachronism in his hands. "It makes me feel closer to Grandma, too, knowing she was part of all this." The reverence in his tone was almost tangible as he pocketed the device.

Elsa nodded, feeling the lineage of their family knit tighter with each shared experience. "She'd be proud of you, you know. You're carrying on her legacy in ways she couldn't have imagined."

"Thanks, Mom," Aiden said, cheeks flushing with a mix of pride and embarrassment. His gaze lingered on the ChronoCipher, its sleek surface incongruous against the retro tech surrounding them. "And thanks for guiding me. There's so much more I wanna learn."

"Learning is a lifelong quest," Elsa replied, her eyes reflecting the resolve that fortified her weary spirit. "And I'll be with you every step of the way. But remember, with great knowledge comes great responsibility. Especially when it comes to shaping the digital world."

"Spider-Man reference?" Aiden teased, a grin unfurling across his face.

"Very astute, Mr. Winters," Elsa quipped, allowing herself a momentary lightness. "Now, let's head back before we cause any more temporal ripples."

They approached the ChronoCipher, its interface awaiting their command. Elsa reached out, fingers moving over the controls with practiced ease. The device came alive with a low buzz, its core emitting a pulsating glow that cast shadows across their faces.

As the air around them began to shimmer with the energy of impending transition, Aiden glanced up at his mother. "Ready for the next round?"

"Always," Elsa affirmed, though fatigue pulled at her limbs. She looked at her son, his eagerness a beacon that guided her through the fog of chronic pain.

With a synchronous nod, they stepped into the ChronoCipher's embrace. The lab and its relics of computing's infancy faded away, leaving only the certainty of their bond and the uncharted possibilities of the future. Elsa's thoughts drifted toward the horizon of time, where vigilance and moral fortitude would be their compasses in navigating the ever-evolving digital seascape.

"Vigilant weavers," she whispered to herself, the phrase a silent vow.

Chapter 4

Creating the digital twin (2028)

The kitchen table groaned under the weight of Janet Winters' weathered journal and the sleek, enigmatic ChronoCipher. Elsa sat slumped in her chair, her fingers absently tracing the wood grain as she watched Aiden flip eagerly through the yellowed pages. The excitement in his eyes was a stark contrast to the weariness in her own.

"Mom, check this out!" Aiden's voice cut through her fatigue. He stabbed a finger at a densely scribbled entry. "Grandma Janet wrote about the ethical dilemmas she struggled with during the early stages of developing the internet."

Elsa leaned forward, her brow furrowing as she scanned the cramped handwriting. The words seemed to leap off the page:

> *Today, we stand at a crossroads. The very network we are creating to connect humanity could be twisted into a tool of control and surveillance. Who will bear the responsibility if our open doors are exploited by those with malicious intent? Can we truly build a digital future that upholds privacy and freedom, or are we doomed to compromise our values in the name of progress?*

Elsa's voice trailed off. The questions hung heavy in the air, echoing her own doubts about the role of technology in their lives. How many times had she grappled with similar dilemmas, weighing the potential benefits against the risks?

And now, here they were, trying to unravel the consequences of those choices. Her mother's words carried an uncanny foresight, as though she had anticipated the challenges that would confront future generations.

Aiden, oblivious to Elsa's introspection, continued to chatter excitedly. "It's like Grandma knew the vibe was serious, even back then. She was trying to do the right thing, but it wasn't always obvious what that meant."

Elsa nodded slowly, her gaze still fixed on the journal entry. The weight of her mother's legacy settled heavily on her shoulders. *How can we navigate*

DOI: 10.1201/9781003501626-4

this digital landscape responsibly? What would you have done, Mom, in my place?

As she pondered these questions, a contemplative silence descended upon the room. The ghosts of the past seemed to whisper through the pages, urging them to learn from history's hard-won lessons. Elsa knew that the path forward would be fraught with difficult choices, but perhaps, armed with her mother's wisdom, they could find a way to balance progress and ethics in this brave new world.

Elsa turned to Aiden. "You see, honey, your grandmother understood that creating an open network was like leaving the front door unlocked in a big city. It invites both opportunity and danger."

Aiden leaned forward, his brow furrowed in concentration. "You mean, like how anyone could come in and take stuff if you're not careful?"

"Exactly," Elsa nodded. "She was a visionary, always seeing not just what the internet could become, but also what it might unleash. Just like we have to be mindful of who we let into our home, we need to be cautious about who has access to the digital spaces she dreamed of building."

She reached out and gently traced the lines of code in Janet's journal, a wistful smile playing on her lips. "Your grandmother knew that with great power comes great responsibility. She wanted to create something that would connect people, but she also feared the potential for misuse."

Aiden's eyes widened as he considered the implications. "So, it's like in my favorite game, where you have to choose between unlocking a powerful weapon or protecting the innocent villagers. There's always a trade-off."

Elsa chuckled softly, amazed at how easily Aiden could translate complex concepts into relatable gaming analogies. "That's right, Aiden. Every decision we make in the digital world has consequences, just like in your games. We have to weigh the risks and benefits carefully."

Aiden's gaze drifted to the ChronoCipher, its sleek surface gleaming under the kitchen lights. A sudden thought struck him, and he turned to Elsa with an excited glint in his eye.

"Mom, what if we used the ChronoCipher to create a digital twin of Grandma? We could talk to her, ask her about what she was thinking back in the day and how she handled all these ethical dilemmas!"

Elsa's heart skipped a beat at the suggestion, longing and apprehension washing over her. The idea of speaking to her mother again, even in digital form, was both thrilling and terrifying. She hesitated, her mind racing with the emotional implications of bringing a virtual version of Janet to life.

Could I handle seeing her again, hearing her voice, knowing it's not truly her? Elsa wondered, her hand instinctively reaching for the locket that held her mother's picture. *And what if the digital twin can't capture the essence of who she was, the warmth and wisdom with which she guided me through so many challenges?*

Aiden, sensing his mother's hesitation, reached out and placed his hand on hers. "I know it's a lot to process, Mom. But think about how much we could learn from her, how much closer we'd feel to her memory."

Elsa met her son's earnest gaze, seeing in his eyes the same curiosity and determination that had driven her mother to push the boundaries of what was possible. Perhaps, in truly confronting the past, they could find the guidance they needed to navigate the future.

With a deep breath, Elsa squeezed Aiden's hand, a tentative smile forming on her lips. "You're right, Aiden. Let's do it. Let's bring Grandma's digital twin to life and see what she has to teach us."

Aiden's face lit up, a grin spreading as he quickly leaned over the ChronoCipher. "Okay, what do we do? How does it work?"

Elsa took a deep breath, steadying herself. Her fingers hovered over the glowing interface as she read the new instructions that had appeared as if on cue. "Integrate data from personal artifacts, written records, and historical timelines to create an interactive AI model."

"Artifacts? Like the journal?" Aiden asked, already flipping open the leather-bound book that had become their guide. He carefully laid it next to the ChronoCipher, the worn pages illuminated by the soft glow of the device.

"Yes," Elsa said, nodding. "The journal, her notes, anything we have that ties back to her thoughts and work. The ChronoCipher can use it to reconstruct her ... personality, her voice."

"And memories?" Aiden's voice was quieter now, the weight of what they were doing finally settling over him.

"To some extent, yes," Elsa said. "But it won't be perfect. It'll be fragmented, like a puzzle with missing pieces. It'll only know what's recorded. Let's also see if there is anything in Grandma's journal that could help us make this happen."

Elsa took a deep breath, her fingers trembling slightly as she reached for the ChronoCipher. The sleek, metallic device hummed softly in her hands, its surface cool to the touch. Aiden leaned in closer as Elsa carefully connected the device to her laptop.

"Okay," Elsa said, her voice steady despite the nervous energy coursing through her. "According to the journal, we need to input the data from these specific entries." She pointed to a series of complex equations and code snippets scattered across the worn pages.

Aiden nodded eagerly, his fingers already flying across the keyboard. "I've got this, Mom. Just read them out to me."

As Elsa recited the cryptic lines, Aiden's brow furrowed in concentration, his gaze locked on the screen. The room fell silent, save for the soft clicking of keys and the occasional beep from the ChronoCipher.

Suddenly, its LED lights started pulsing with an ethereal blue glow. The air seemed to crackle with energy as a hum filled the room, growing louder with each passing second.

As if on cue, the ChronoCipher let out a low whir, and a projection flickered to life above it. Lines of data spiraled outward, pulling in handwritten entries from Janet's journal. Schematics, equations, and fragments of old documents merged into the digital vortex. Aiden watched in awe, his breath catching as the ChronoCipher began piecing together the foundation of a digital mind.

"This is wild," Aiden whispered. "It's like she's coming back to life."

Elsa's stomach tightened. The thought of hearing her mother's voice again – of seeing her, even in fragmented form – was almost too much to process. Memories flooded back: Janet at her desk, muttering to herself as she sketched out network designs; her sharp laugh when she cracked a particularly tricky problem; the fierce determination in her eyes when she spoke of the internet's potential. But those memories were tinged with something else – an edge of distance, of decisions made in pursuit of ideals that often left family second.

"Mom?" Aiden's voice broke through her thoughts, grounding her.

She nodded, her voice steady but low. "Let's finish this."

The ChronoCipher pulsed again, and the projection shifted. A shimmering silhouette began to form – indistinct at first, like a watercolor painting coming into focus. The details sharpened: a figure in a crisp shirt and jeans, her hair pulled back in a no-nonsense bun. Then, the voice came.

"Well, isn't this something?" The tone was warm but firm, with a spark of humor that sent a shiver down Elsa's spine. "I didn't think I'd be making an appearance quite like this."

Aiden froze, his eyes wide. "Grandma Janet?"

The digital Janet turned, her gaze sharp and intelligent. "That's what you call me now, huh? Interesting. Aiden. It is so good to see you again. My, you've certainly grown into quite a handsome young man!"

Elsa's breath stopped. It was her mother – not entirely, but close enough. The cadence, the mannerisms – it was all there, painstakingly reconstructed. The room felt smaller, the air heavier, as Elsa stepped forward.

"Mom … " Elsa's voice wavered. "It's really you."

Janet tilted her head, a faint smile playing on her lips. "As much as it can be, given the data you've fed into this machine. You've done well to get this far."

Elsa's heart raced as the screen flickered, static giving way to a hazy, shadowed figure and, slowly, the image sharpened, revealing the unmistakable features of Janet Winters. Elsa gasped, tears pricking at the corners of her eyes as she stared at her holographic mother.

She looks just like I remember her, Elsa thought, her chest tightening with a bittersweet mix of love and loss. The same warm smile, the same knowing glint in her eye …

Aiden, meanwhile, leaned forward in his chair, his face illuminated by the screen's glow. "Wi-i-i-ld," he breathed. "It's really you, Grandma. Well, kind of."

He reached out tentatively, his fingertips grazing through the holograph as he tried to touch his grandmother's face. Janet's eyes seemed to focus on him, a gaze filled with the reserved warmth he remembered as a child.

Elsa watched the interaction with both wonder and apprehension. Part of her longed to reach out as well, to feel the comfort of her mother's presence once more. Yet another part held back, acutely aware that this was a simulation, a ghost in the machine.

Can a digital twin really capture the essence of a person? Elsa wondered, her gaze searching the face on the screen for answers. *Or will it just be a pale imitation, a shadow of the woman I loved?*

As if sensing her daughter's turmoil, Janet's expression softened, a gentle smile playing at the corners of her mouth. "Elsa," she said, her voice achingly familiar, "I know this must be strange for you. But I'm here, in whatever form I can be. And I'm so proud of the woman you've become." Tears slipped down Elsa's cheeks as she nodded, a watery smile spreading across her face. "Thanks, Mom," she whispered, her voice thick with emotion. "I've missed you so much."

Aiden glanced between the screen and his mother. "What do we do now?" he asked in a hushed tone.

Elsa took a deep breath, wiping the tears from her face. "Now," she said, her gaze locking with Janet's, "we listen and learn. We let Grandma guide us through the past, so we can protect the future."

Aiden couldn't contain his excitement. "We're trying to understand ARPANET and internet history, everything you worked on. There's so much we don't know … "

Janet's digital twin raised a hand, her projection flickering slightly. "I'm sure there is. Let me start with this: what we built wasn't just about technology. It was about vision, about believing in a future where connection could bridge divides. But … " Her smile faded, her tone shifting to something more somber. "Every creation has its shadows. I always hoped you'd be ready to face them when the time came."

Elsa swallowed hard. "What shadows, Mom? What aren't we seeing?"

Janet began, her voice taking on a lecturing tone. "We were so focused on the potential benefits of a connected world that we didn't fully consider the risks. Privacy violations, cybercrime, the spread of misinformation," the digital Janet listed, counting off on her fingers. "But perhaps the most insidious was the erosion of trust. When everything is connected, it becomes harder to know who or what to believe."

Aiden's eyes widened, his tablet clutched forgotten in his hands. "Is that why you left working in tech?" he asked.

Janet sighed, her gaze distant. "In part, yes. I saw firsthand how the technology I helped create could be misused. It was a heavy burden to bear."

Elsa's heart clenched at the weariness in her mother's voice. She carried this weight alone for so long, she thought, a pang of guilt piercing through her. If only I had known sooner ...

"But why didn't you tell anyone?" Elsa asked, her voice barely above a whisper. "Why keep it a secret all these years?"

Janet's eyes met Elsa's, a sad smile tugging at her lips. "I was afraid," she admitted, her voice raw with honesty. "Afraid of the consequences, of what people would think. But most of all, I was afraid of failing you and Aiden."

Elsa's breath caught in her throat, tears welling in her eyes once more. "You could never fail us, Mom," she said fiercely, her hand reaching out instinctively to touch the screen. "You did what you thought was right. That's all anyone can do."

Janet's smile widened, her eyes shining with pride. "You're so much stronger than I ever was, Elsa," she murmured, her voice thick with emotion. "You and Aiden both. That's why I know you'll be able to handle the truth, no matter how difficult it may be."

Janet hesitated. "I wish I could tell you everything, but there's a catch," she said, her voice tinged with regret. "My full capabilities, including access to critical information, are locked behind a ChronoPuzzle. It's a safeguard I put in place to ensure the knowledge wouldn't fall into the wrong hands."

Aiden's eyes lit up. "Another puzzle?" he asked, leaning forward eagerly. "We can solve it, Mom! Bet. It's like one of those escape room challenges, right?"

Elsa remained silent, her brow furrowed as she absorbed her mother's words. The prospect of unlocking the ChronoCipher's secrets was tantalizing, but a nagging sense of apprehension tugged at her thoughts. *What if the information is too dangerous?*, she wondered, her gaze drifting to Aiden's excited face. Can I really put him at risk, even for the sake of the greater good?

Elsa met Janet's gaze, her own eyes filled with both trepidation and resolve. *Mom always believed in facing hard truths,* she reminded herself. "We'll solve it," she said finally, her voice steady. "If this is the only way to unlock what you know, then we'll do it."

Aiden's grin was electric. "Yes! Let's go, Grandma – what's the first clue?"

Janet tilted her holographic head slightly, as if contemplating how best to guide them. "The first clue lies in my journal," she said, her voice carrying a hint of amusement. "A single phrase: *'Beginnings and endings are threads woven into time.'* Find the passage that resonates with this, and you'll uncover the key."

Elsa picked up the worn leather journal, its edges frayed from years of use. Her fingers traced the cover, and for a brief moment, she was a child again, watching quietly as her mother wrote feverishly by the glow of a desk lamp. She took a deep breath and flipped through the pages, scanning the familiar handwriting.

"Here!" Aiden exclaimed, pointing to a passage near the middle. "*'The anchor of ARPANET is not in its wires or protocols, but in the trust that bridges beginnings and endings.'* That has to be it, right?"

Elsa squinted at the passage, her fingers brushing the faded ink. "It's possible," she murmured. "But the question is: what does it mean? An anchor ... trust bridging beginnings and endings ... " Her voice trailed off as her mind pieced together fragments of memory and knowledge.

Janet watched with an enigmatic smile. "You're on the right track," she encouraged. "Think of what an anchor does – not just in the physical sense, but in time and space."

Elsa and Aiden exchanged a glance, their mutual determination sharpening their focus. Aiden leaned closer, his fingers poised over his tablet. "An anchor in time and space ... could it be a specific event? Or a key point in ARPANET's development?"

"Perhaps," Elsa said, flipping back to the beginning of the journal. "If we consider ARPANET's foundation, its 'anchor' could be the first successful connection or an early milestone."

Aiden's eyes lit up. "The first message sent over ARPANET! Wasn't it something basic, like 'LO,' before the system crashed?"

"Exactly," Elsa said, her voice gaining momentum. "That moment was both a beginning and an ending – an anchor for everything that came after."

The ChronoCipher hummed, its glow intensifying as Elsa and Aiden worked. A new interface appeared before them, displaying a fragmented timeline interspersed with glowing nodes. The words *"Connect the Threads"* hovered above the display.

"Looks like we need to reconstruct the timeline," Aiden observed, his fingers moving instinctively toward the holographic display. "But some of these nodes don't seem to fit."

Elsa leaned in, studying the glowing points. "It's testing us," she said. "We need to figure out which events are pivotal and which are distractions – false leads meant to throw us off."

"Let's start with the first message," Aiden suggested, selecting one of the nodes. As he connected it to another, the ChronoCipher emitted a soft chime, signaling progress.

As they pieced the timeline together, Janet offered occasional insights, her voice a guiding presence. "Remember," she said, "every connection tells a story. Pay attention to the threads – what they reveal, and what they conceal."

Elsa and Aiden worked in tandem, their collaboration seamless. Each correct connection illuminated a new fragment of Janet's journal on the ChronoCipher's interface, revealing hidden annotations and musings.

"Look at this," Elsa said, pointing to one entry. " 'The beauty of ARPANET lies in its simplicity. The danger lies in its trust.' "

"Like the first spam message," Aiden said. "It was just a joke, but it showed how fragile the system was."

"And how human nature plays into it," Elsa added. "Technology might evolve, but people's tendencies – to push boundaries, to exploit vulnerabilities – remain constant."

The final node clicked into place, and the timeline flared to life. Events cascaded across the screen, forming a coherent narrative of ARPANET's early days. Janet watched with approval, her expression one of quiet pride.

"You've done well," she said. "This timeline is more than just a record of the past – it's a map to understanding the challenges ahead. And now, you're ready for the next step."

A new prompt appeared on the ChronoCipher: *"Set the Temporal Anchor: November 2, 1988."*

Elsa's breath caught. "That's the day the Morris Worm was released," she whispered. "The first major cyberattack."

Aiden's excitement faltered, replaced by a touch of apprehension. "Are we ready for this?" he asked, looking to his mother for reassurance.

Elsa placed a hand on his shoulder, her grip firm and steady. "We are," she said, her voice resolute. "Together, we can face whatever comes next."

Janet smiled faintly, her image flickering as the ChronoCipher prepared to transport them. "Remember," she said, her voice echoing as the portal began to form, "every choice you make shapes the future. Be vigilant, and trust in each other."

The shimmering portal grew brighter, its energy filling the room with the familiar low hum. Elsa and Aiden exchanged a final glance, their resolve solidified by the lessons they had learned and the bond they had strengthened.

"Catch you when we get back, Grandma," Aiden grinned at the holograph. Elsa could only manage a small smile at her mother's ghost before, hand in hand, they stepped into the portal, leaving behind the comfort of their kitchen and the guiding presence of Janet's digital twin. The room fell silent, the ChronoCipher's glow dimming as it waited for their return.

The kitchen stood empty, but the echoes of their determination lingered – a testament to the Winters family's unwavering pursuit of truth, no matter the cost.

Journal entry – Elsa – January 16, 2028

I wasn't quite prepared ... scratch that ... I could never have been prepared to see my mother again in such a life-like way. It was almost too much to bear. So many memories came flooding back. Mixed, bittersweet emotions. Mom's cluttered desk, the glow of her computer screen almost permanently on her face, the ARPANET logo. Her dedication in teaching me to code.

Me feeling totally in-sync with her when we worked together. Me watching from the shadows as she muttered to herself and ran her hand through her hair in frustration in those moments I was not allowed to interrupt her. Me coming in to show her my new doll, only to receive an absent-minded pat on the head as her fingers clacked away on the keyboard and her eyes never left the screen. Moments of complete warmth and love, moments of dismissal.

I always knew that Mom's work was important, but it was only as an adult that I grasped on some level why it was. What I haven't understood until now was the weight that she carried for all those years. I had no idea. Her work was her life's purpose but she struggled with the pressures of compromise and balance. She took on the responsibility so deeply – perhaps a trait that I have inherited, and one that I see emerging in Aiden. She understood, even in those early days that her legacy would live on in the digital realm, and that this legacy could have two sides and lasting impact for good or bad.

Chapter 5

The worm in the system (1988)

The world materialized in a whirlwind of green phosphor and the acrid scent of ozone. Elsa blinked rapidly, her eyes adjusting to the dim light of a cramped office. Stacks of dog-eared coding manuals crowded every surface, their spines a mix of faded primary colors. Crumpled balls of paper littered the floor, a sea of discarded ideas.

"No way," Aiden whispered, his eyes wide as he took in the outdated computer setup. An IBM PC XT squatted on the desk, its bulky CRT monitor glowing faintly. "Is that ... a floppy disk drive?"

Elsa nodded, a faint smile on her lips. "Welcome to 1988, kiddo. Back when 640K of RAM was more than anyone would ever need."

"The IBM PC XT was one of the first personal computers. Back then, this was cutting-edge technology. And yes, floppy disks were how we stored and transferred data – kind of like the USB drives you're used to, but with way less space."

She moved carefully through the chaos, her joints protesting after the temporal jump. A handwritten note caught her eye – a scribbled algorithm that made her breath catch. This was it. The birth of the worm.

"Mom, check this out!" Aiden called, already hunched over the keyboard. His fingers tapped across the keys with the comfort of a digital native, even on this ancient machine. "The processing speed is so slow. How did anyone get anything done?"

Elsa watched her son, a bittersweet ache in her chest. His enthusiasm was so pure, untainted. She thought, not for the first time, how much easier it would be to shield him from the darker sides of technology.

"We made do," she said aloud, her voice nostalgic. "And sometimes, we made things we shouldn't have."

Aiden looked up, curiosity etched on his face. "What do you mean?"

Elsa sighed, running a hand through her hair. How could she explain the precipice they were standing on? The moment before the digital world changed forever.

DOI: 10.1201/9781003501626-5

"Let's just say," she began carefully, "that good intentions don't always lead to good outcomes. Especially when it comes to code."

She moved to join Aiden at the computer, the familiar green glow of the monitor both comforting and ominous. Here, in this cluttered office, a small piece of software was about to change everything.

"Want to see something cool?" Elsa asked, forcing a lightness into her voice.

Aiden grinned, scooting over to make room. "Always."

Elsa hesitated. She couldn't shake the sense that pressing a few keys could unleash something dangerous. However, she also believed that studying past events could help create a brighter future.

Elsa's fingers trembled slightly as she rested them on the keyboard. She leaned in close to Aiden, her voice barely above a whisper.

"We've arrived at the scene of the crime."

Aiden's eyes widened, excitement and apprehension flickering across his face. "Crime? What crime?"

Elsa gestured around the chaotic office, her gaze lingering on the scattered papers and dog-eared coding manuals. "Look closely, Aiden. What do you see?"

As Aiden scanned the room, Elsa's mind raced. She saw more than just clutter; she saw the blueprint for disaster. Hastily scribbled notes, lines of code crossed out and rewritten, empty coffee cups littering every surface. It's the workspace of someone working too fast, too recklessly.

"It's ... messy," Aiden offered, his brow furrowing. "Like, really messy. Even messier than my room."

Elsa couldn't help but chuckle, despite the tension coiling in her stomach. "True. But it's more than that. This mess, it's a warning sign. When you're coding something this important, this potentially powerful, you need to be meticulous. Careful."

"This," she said softly, more to herself than to Aiden, "is what happens when brilliance outpaces caution."

Aiden leaned in, his voice dropping to match hers. "Mom, you're low key freaking me out right now. What's about to go down? Is it that worm you mentioned earlier?"

"Something big, kiddo. Something that's going to change the way we think about the internet forever." She paused, then added with a faint smile, "Let's just say, it's going to be a very bad day for a lot of system administrators."

"Ready to meet the man of the hour?" she asked Aiden as she reached for the ChronoCipher.

Aiden nodded, eyes wide. "Bet! Let's do this."

With a practiced gesture, Elsa activated the device. The air shimmered, and suddenly, a young man materialized before them – Robert Tappan

Morris, looking haggard and intense, his fingers clacking at breakneck speed over a keyboard.

"Whoa," Aiden breathed. "He looks ... normal. I mean, not like some evil mastermind."

Elsa watched the holographic Morris work, her expression softening. "That's because he wasn't, honey. Just a brilliant mind without enough foresight."

The ChronoCipher's projection expanded, filling the room with ghostly lines of code. Elsa's eyes darted across the display, her tech-savvy brain already dissecting the worm's architecture.

"Look there," she said as she pointed at an area of code. "See how he's building in safeguards? He truly believed this wouldn't cause harm."

Aiden squinted at the code, a frown creasing his usually smooth features. "But something goes wrong, right? Otherwise, we wouldn't be here."

Elsa nodded. "Exactly. One small oversight, that's all it takes."

As they watch, the holographic Morris leaned back, a triumphant smile on his face. Elsa felt a pang of empathy, knowing the chaos that was about to unfold.

"Mom?" Aiden's voice was quiet. "Is this how it always is? Good intentions turning bad?"

Elsa pulled him close, her mind racing through the ethical minefield of tech innovation. "Not always, sweetie. But it's why we have to be so careful. Every line of code can change the world – for better or worse."

She took a deep breath, steadying herself against the familiar chronic ache in her joints.

"Morris's intention was actually quite noble," she explained, her voice taking on the measured tone she used for complex topics. "He wanted to measure the size of the internet – to understand its scope and growth."

Aiden's brow furrowed deeper, his fingers tapping rapidly on his thigh as he processed the information. "But why make something so dangerous?" he asked, genuine confusion in his voice. "Couldn't he have just ... I don't know, sent out a survey or something?"

A bittersweet smile played across Elsa's lips. "If only it were that simple," she said, her exhaustion momentarily masked by amusement. "The internet was still young then, constantly changing. A worm that could replicate and spread seemed like the perfect tool."

Aiden's eyes widened with understanding. "Like how my AvatarQuest game spreads through friend invites?"

"Similar concept, but with much higher stakes," Elsa nodded. She paused, her expression growing more serious as she watched Morris. "The problem is, experimentation and recklessness often look very similar from the outside."

Elsa's mind drifted to her own past, times when her coding experiments skirted ethical lines. "It's a blurred line, Aiden," she admitted, her voice soft.

"Sometimes, in the pursuit of knowledge or progress, we push boundaries without fully grasping the consequences."

Aiden studied his mother's face, sensing the layers of emotion beneath her words. "Is that why you always drill me about 'coding responsibly'?"

Elsa managed a smile, though it didn't quite reach her eyes. "Exactly. Because one day, you might be the one making these decisions. And I want you to be ready to make the right choices."

"Watch closely," Elsa whispered, her eyes fixed on the figure of Morris.

The spectral Morris typed furiously. Aiden leaned forward, fascinated by the intricate lines of code materializing before them.

"He looks so sure of himself," Aiden murmured, his own hands twitching as if longing to join in the coding.

Elsa nodded. "That's often how it starts. The thrill of creation, the certainty that you're on the verge of something groundbreaking."

As they watched, Morris's virtual expression shifted. His eyes widening in dawning horror. The code on the screen began to pulse an angry red, spreading like wildfire across the projected network map.

"Mom, what's happening?"

Elsa's throat tightens, recognizing the moment everything went wrong. "This is it, Aiden. This is the moment. He's realizing the worm isn't behaving as intended. It's replicating far faster than he anticipated."

Morris's panic was now palpable, his frantic keystrokes a desperate attempt to regain control. Aiden unconsciously mirrored the programmer's distress, his own hands clenching into fists, his eyes searching the projected code around them for a way out, a way to solve the problem, stop the worm.

"Can't he just … I don't know, hit delete or something?"

Elsa shook her head. "Once it's out there, Aiden, it takes on a life of its own. That's the danger – and the responsibility – that comes with creating something this powerful."

They watched in silence as Morris's futile efforts play out before them, a stark reminder of how quickly innovation can spiral into chaos. *How quickly his triumphant smile turned to panic,* Elsa thought with a silent shake of her head.

Elsa's eyes narrowed, her years of experience allowing her to spot the critical error in a heartbeat. She pointed to a specific line of code glowing on the holographic display.

"There," she said. "Do you see it, Aiden? The replication function – it's missing a crucial limiter."

Aiden leaned in, squinting at the ethereal digits. "A limiter?" He paused, and Elsa could almost see the wheels turning in his young mind. "Like in games when they cap how many times you can use a power-up?"

"Exactly. Without that cap, the worm just keeps making copies of itself, over and over, flooding the entire network."

She paused again, rubbing her temple as a wave of fatigue washed over her. The constant temporal shifts were taking their toll, but she would push through as she always did, knowing the importance of this lesson.

Aiden ran a hand through his hair, a nervous habit he'd inherited from his grandmother. "Wait, so you're telling me that one tiny oversight caused all this chaos?"

Elsa nodded solemnly. "In coding, as in life, the smallest mistakes can have the biggest consequences. One misplaced character, one unchecked assumption ... " She trailed off, lost in thought for a moment.

Aiden's mind raced, connecting this historical moment to his own experiences. "It's like when a meme goes viral, isn't it? But way more serious."

"That's ... actually a pretty apt comparison," Elsa admitted, impressed by her son's insight.

The air around them suddenly crackled with energy, and Elsa instinctively reached for Aiden's hand. The ChronoCipher pulses, its screen flashing with rapidly changing coordinates.

"Hold on tight," Elsa warned, her voice taut with anticipation. "We're about to – "

Their surroundings blurred, melting away in a dizzying swirl of light and color. When the world solidified again, they found themselves standing in a bustling computer lab, surrounded by rows of bulky monitors and the insistent whirring of cooling fans.

Aiden blinked rapidly, adjusting to the new environment. "No way," he breathed, taking in the scene. "Are we – "

"MIT's computer science department," Elsa confirmed, her eyes darting from screen to screen. "November 3rd, 1988. Ground zero for the Morris Worm's impact."

Around them, chaos unfolded in real time. Frantic researchers huddled around terminals, their faces bathed in the sickly glow of CRT monitors. Snippets of panicked conversation fill the air:

"It's replicating too fast!"

"The network's grinding to a halt!"

"Has anyone reached Morris?"

Aiden's hand subconsciously tightened around his mother's. "This is next level," he murmured.

"This is the moment the world realized how vulnerable our interconnected systems really were," she explained softly. "A wake-up call that came too late for many."

As they watched, a young researcher slammed his fist on a desk in frustration. "We need to pull the plug!" he shouted. "Disconnect everything before it spreads further!"

Aiden's eyes widened. "Wait, they're going to shut down the entire internet? Can they do that?"

"Not the entire internet," Elsa corrected. "But a significant portion of it. Sometimes, to stop the bleeding, you have to apply a tourniquet."

She paused, her gaze distant as she processed the scene before them. "This is why what we're doing is so important, Aiden. History has a way of rhyming, if not repeating. We need to understand these moments to prevent even worse catastrophes in our time. Let's see what else we can learn here before the ChronoCipher whisks us away again."

The chaos intensified as Elsa and Aiden watched helplessly as the digital carnage unfolded. Both mother and son itched to step in and help. But, alas, they remained only spectators in the holographic past. In a nearby lab, a frantic researcher yanked cables from a mainframe, her face knotted with panic. Across the room, a bank of monitors flashed red, each screen a mosaic of error messages and warning signals.

"Look at the network map," Elsa whispered. She pointed to a large display where glowing green lines connected cities across the United States. As they watched, the lines turned an angry crimson with the worm's relentless spread.

Aiden leaned in, his eyes wide. "It's like a digital wildfire."

Elsa nodded, her expression grim. "And just as destructive. This was the internet's first true crisis – a major wake-up call for cybersecurity."

Her voice dropped, taking on a tone of reflection. "You know, I was just a kid when this happened. I remember my mom – your grandmother – being glued to her computer for days, trying to help contain the damage."

Aiden turned to her, curiosity piqued. "What did she do?"

Elsa's lips quirked in a half-smile. "She was part of the team that reverse-engineered the worm. It was like solving a malicious puzzle, racing against time." Her eyes grew distant, lost in memory. "I think that's when I first realized the power of code – both to create and destroy."

As they spoke, another system crashed nearby, the sharp sound of a computer powering down cutting through the air.

"Mom?" Aiden's voice was tinged with concern.

Elsa shook her head, refocusing. "I'm okay. Just … remembering. And realizing how far we've come, yet how vulnerable we still are." She squared her shoulders, determination replacing the momentary weakness. "Come on, let's see what else we can learn here. As we know, every bit of knowledge is a shield for the future."

Aiden's eyes widened as he absorbed the scene unfolding before him. The holographic display from the ChronoCipher pulsed with an eerie red glow, mimicking the spread of the Morris Worm across countless systems. His fingers twitched, instinctively reaching for a controller that wasn't there.

"This feels like a sci-fi disaster movie," he murmured. "Like, you know that part in 'Cyber Apocalypse 3' where the AI takes over and all the screens go crazy? Except this is real."

He took a step closer to the projection, squinting as if trying to see through the chaos. "Mom, look at how fast it's spreading. It really is like a digital wildfire."

Aiden's hand traced the path of the worm's destruction through the hologram. "Wait, so each of these points is a real computer? With real people behind it?"

He turned to Elsa, his expression shifting from excitement to concern. "What happened to all their stuff? Their work, their games, their ... everything?"

As he spoke, Aiden's fingers drummed rapidly against his leg, a nervous habit that betrayed his growing unease.

"It's not just about the computers, is it?" he said softly, more to himself than to Elsa. "It's about all the people affected. All because of one mistake."

"You're right, Aiden. It's never just about the computers. Behind every flickering pixel, there's a human story."

She pointed to a cluster of red nodes pulsing angrily on the projection. "See those? That's probably a university research center. Years of data, countless hours of work – gone in an instant." Her finger moves to another sector. "And there? Could be a small business, maybe a startup. Their entire financial future, wiped out because their systems crashed at the wrong moment."

Elsa's shoulders slump slightly, the fatigue of her condition momentarily visible. She took a deep breath, steadying herself. "It's like dropping a stone in a pond, honey. The ripples keep going, affecting more than we can see. Lost productivity, missed deadlines, broken trust ... "

She turned to Aiden, her eyes softening as she saw the concern on his face. "This is why I've always taught you to think three steps ahead when you code. Innovation is beautiful, but unchecked, it can be devastating."

Aiden nodded slowly, his brow furrowed in thought. "So, coding isn't a game."

"Exactly," Elsa replied. "The digital world we build affects the real one in ways we can't always predict. That's the weight we carry as creators."

Elsa shifted into storyteller mode.

"It started as an experiment. A curious mind, a few lines of code, and a simple goal: to measure the size of the internet. Robert Tappan Morris was a bright young programmer when he designed a self-replicating worm to spread across ARPANET. But he made a mistake. His worm didn't just copy itself once per machine; it copied itself over and over again, endlessly. And as we have just witnessed firsthand, it wasn't long before systems at universities, research labs, and even military institutions began slowing down, freezing and then crashing."

Aiden's eyes widened. "So, it really was one small mistake that crashed everything?"

"Exactly," Elsa continued. "By the time the dust settled, the worm had infected around 6,000 machines – about 10% of the internet at the time.

Universities had to disconnect, businesses lost millions, and the US government was forced to take cybersecurity seriously for the first time."

Aiden leaned forward, intrigued. "What happened to Morris?"

"He became the first person ever convicted under the Computer Fraud and Abuse Act," Elsa said. "He never intended to cause harm, but the world suddenly realized that even well-meaning code could spiral out of control. That's why cybersecurity isn't just about defense – it's about responsibility. Every programmer, every creator, has to think ahead because even a small vulnerability can bring entire systems to their knees."

She reached out, squeezing Aiden's shoulder gently. "But it's also our responsibility to learn from these moments. To build safer, more resilient systems. To protect the human stories behind the code."

Aiden's fingers tapped restlessly against his leg, his eyes darting between the holographic chaos and his mother's weary face.

"But Mom," he started, "it sounds like Morris didn't mean for this to happen, right? He was trying to do something good, wasn't he?"

Elsa's eyes met her son's. She recognized the struggle in his expression – the same one she's grappled with countless times throughout her career.

"That's the thing, sweetheart," she said. "Intentions and outcomes don't always align. Morris wanted to measure the internet's size, to understand it better. But … "

Aiden cut in, his words tumbling out in a rush. "But it all went wrong. I get that. What I don't get is … do good intentions make bad outcomes okay?"

"That's the million-dollar question, isn't it?" she mused, a wry smile tugging at the corner of her mouth. "In the world of tech, and in life, really, it's rarely that simple."

She began to pace, her movements careful and measured to manage her chronic pain. "Think about it like this: If you're building a treehouse and accidentally drop a hammer that breaks someone's window, your good intentions won't fix the glass. The damage is still done."

Aiden nodded slowly, his fingers now drumming against his tablet. "So … it's not just about what we mean to do, but what we actually end up doing?"

"Exactly," Elsa nodded. "Intent matters, absolutely. It's what separates accidents from malicious acts. But accountability? That's nonnegotiable. Innovation without caution can be catastrophic."

She gestured toward the holographic display of Morris's code, still pulsing with ethereal light. "Look at this worm. One unchecked variable, one moment of oversight, and it brought systems across the country to their knees."

Aiden leaned in, studying the code with newfound intensity. "So it's not enough to just … create cool stuff? We have to think about *all* the ways it could go wrong?"

"Bingo," Elsa confirmed, a hint of her trademark dry humor creeping into her voice. "Welcome to the not-so-glamorous side of innovation, kiddo. It's all fun and games until your code accidentally crashes ARPANET. I mean internet."

She watched as Aiden's expression shifted. It reminded her painfully of Janet, of late nights poring over code and debating the ethics of each new breakthrough.

"Mom?" Aiden's voice pulled her from her reverie. "Is this why you always say coding is like having a superpower?"

"Exactly. With great power comes great – "

" – responsibility," Aiden finished, grinning. "Okay, now you're just quoting Spider-Man again."

"Hey, good advice is good advice, even if it comes from a guy in spandex," Elsa quipped, ruffling his hair. As they shared a laugh, she felt a glimmer of hope. Maybe, just maybe, the next generation will learn from the mistakes of the past.

Aiden's laughter faded, replaced by a look of intense concentration. He chewed his lower lip, a habit Elsa recognized as a sign he was wrestling with a complex thought.

"But Mom," he said slowly, fingers now drumming on his knee, "if we always worry about what could go wrong, wouldn't that, like, stop us from making anything cool? I mean, social media's got problems, but I wouldn't want to live in a world without it."

"It's a balancing act, kiddo. We can't let fear paralyze us, but we can't charge ahead blindly either."

Aiden nodded, his gaze drifting back to the holographic display of Morris's code. "So ... we have to be like game devs? Think about all the ways players might break the game, and then build in safeguards."

"That's a great analogy," Elsa said, impressed. "Cybersecurity is a lot like that. We're always trying to stay one step ahead of the hackers. On the bright side, every major error or cyberattack is a learning curve for cybersecurity – pushing development and safety in the end. The Morris Worm was the push that was needed for the development of firewalls and stronger password management."

As if on cue, the ChronoCipher emits a soft chime. The holographic display shifted, lines of code rearranging themselves into another complex network.

Aiden leaned in to closer observe the new behind-the-scenes display in front of them. "Is this ... the internet? Like, the old internet?"

Elsa nodded, her expression growing serious. "ARPANET, to be precise. And it looks like we've got a new challenge on our hands."

The ChronoCipher's surface flickered, and a new message materialized in glowing blue text: "**Unravel the Worm: Accountability in Action.**"

Elsa's forehead creased, her fingers instinctively reaching for a keyboard that wasn't there. "Looks like we're going to get our hands dirty with Morris's code after all," she muttered, a mix of excitement and apprehension in her voice.

Aiden's eyes lit up. "We get to hack the hack? That's lit!" He pauses, catching his mother's raised eyebrow. "I mean, uh, for educational purposes only, of course."

Elsa couldn't help but chuckle. "Your enthusiasm is noted, young padawan. But this is serious business." She gestured at the holographic display, where lines of code now swirled in a dizzying dance. "We need to reverse-engineer this worm, find its fatal flaw, and implement a kill switch."

"Kill switch?" Aiden echoed, his voice a mix of curiosity and concern. "Like in my racing games when the car goes out of control?"

"Exactly," Elsa nodded, her eyes never leaving the code. "But instead of a car, we're dealing with a digital entity that's replicating out of control across thousands of systems."

Aiden leaned in, squinting at the code. "So... we're looking for the part that makes it spread?"

"That's right. And once we find it, we need to figure out how to stop it without causing even more damage."

As they begin to dissect the code, Elsa couldn't help but reflect on the importance of the task. Here they were, mother and son, working to undo a mistake that shaped the future of cybersecurity. She had spent her career cleaning up digital messes, after spending her childhood watching her mother do the same, and now she was teaching her son to do the same.

"Mom?" Aiden's voice pulled her from her thoughts. "I think I found something sus in this part of the code. It's like ... there's no off switch?"

Elsa leaned in, her exhaustion momentarily forgotten as she focused on the section Aiden pointed to. "Good eye, kiddo. That's exactly the kind of oversight we're looking for. Now, let's see if we can fix it ... "

The holographic code shimmered before them, a complex latticework of glowing blue lines pulsing with an eerie, artificial life. Elsa's fingers danced through the air, manipulating the projection as if conducting an orchestra of light.

"See how this section loops back on itself?" She traced a spiraling pattern in the code. "That's the replication sequence. It's elegant, but ... "

Aiden leaned closer, "But it doesn't stop, does it? It's like when I set up an auto-clicker in Minecraft without a fail-safe. It just keeps going until the game crashes."

Elsa nodded. "That's right. Now we need to find a way to interrupt this loop without destabilizing the entire structure."

As they worked, Elsa couldn't help but think of her mother's warnings. Janet had always emphasized the delicate balance between innovation and responsibility, ad nauseam, Elsa had sometimes felt as a child. Now, staring at the code that nearly brought the early internet to its knees, those lessons felt more vital than ever.

Aiden's voice broke through her thoughts once again. "What if we inserted a conditional statement here?" He pointed to a junction in the code. "Like, if the number of replications exceeds a certain threshold, it stops?"

Elsa considered her son's proposal for a moment, her tired eyes brightening. "That's ... brilliant, Aiden. Let's try implementing it and see what happens."

As they began to modify the holographic code, Elsa felt a strange assortment of emotions wash over her – hope for the future, pride in her son, and a bittersweet longing for her mother's guidance in this moment of generational bridge-building.

Aiden's fingers flew across the holographic interface, his movements becoming more confident with each line of code he adjusted. "Like this?" he asked, glancing up at Elsa for approval.

She nodded, a small smile tugging at the corners of her mouth. "You're getting it. Now, let's focus on these vulnerable protocols. See how they're left wide open?"

As Elsa highlighted the weak points in the system, she couldn't help but marvel at how quickly Aiden was grasping these complex concepts. It reminded her of her own childhood, those late nights spent coding with Janet, the thrill of solving digital puzzles.

"It's kind of like leaving your base undefended in Fortnite, isn't it?" Aiden mused, his eyes never leaving the pulsing lines of code. "You're just asking for trouble."

Elsa chuckled softly.

As they worked together, seamlessly building upon each other's ideas, Elsa felt a warmth spreading through her chest, providing a fleeting relief from the persistent pain she rarely spoke of. She watched Aiden's face, illuminated by the soft glow of the holographic display, and saw not just her son, but the future of ethical hacking ... a perfect blend of innovation and responsibility.

Suddenly, Aiden paused, tilting his head to the side. "Mom, check this out. The worm ... it's using some really basic passwords to get into these systems."

Elsa leaned in, her eyes widening as she scanned the code. "You're right, Aiden. Good catch. These are practically default passwords – 'admin,' '123456,' 'password.' It's like leaving your front door wide open."

"But why would anyone do that?" Aiden asked in disbelief. "Didn't they know better?"

"Back then, not really. Nothing like this had ever happened before in internet history. I'm sure most people had never even considered it a possibility that anything could go wrong at all. Even today, with all our knowledge and experience, people still often prioritize convenience over security. Or they just don't realize the risks. It's a hard lesson many have had to learn. And yet it still comes as a shock every time it happens."

"Okay, so they were noobs. How do we make sure people take this stuff seriously now? I mean, if even big companies and universities can mess up like this ... "

Elsa took a deep breath, considering her words carefully. "It's about fostering a culture of accountability. Everyone, from individual users to big corporations, needs to understand the impact of their actions in the digital world."

As they continue to work, Elsa couldn't help but wonder how different things might have been if Janet's warnings had been heeded earlier. Would they still be here, fixing the mistakes of the past? Or would they be facing an even more daunting future?

Elsa leaned back in her chair, wincing slightly as her muscles and joints protested. "You know, reverse engineering isn't just about taking things apart to see how they work," she began, her voice taking on the measured tone she often used when explaining complex concepts. "It's also about understanding the thought process behind the creation. In cybersecurity, we use it to find vulnerabilities, but also to learn from others' mistakes. As developers, we have an ethical responsibility to anticipate how our creations might be misused."

"But how can you possibly predict everything that could go wrong?" Aiden asks, his voice tinged with frustration. "It seems impossible."

Elsa sighed, "You can't. Not entirely. But you can try. It's about considering the worst-case scenarios, building in safeguards, and always, always prioritizing security and user safety over flashy features or quick profits."

As she spoke, Elsa wondered if she was burdening Aiden with too much, too soon. But looking at his determined face, she realized that this was exactly what he needed to understand. The weight of responsibility that comes with the power to create and shape the digital world. Every line of code is a choice, a responsibility.

Aiden nodded in understanding. He turned back to the holographic display, studying it with newfound intensity. "Okay, so if we're gonna fix this, we need to think like Morris, but also … better than Morris."

As they delved deeper into the worm's architecture, the complexity of the code seemed to grow exponentially. What initially appeared as a straightforward replication algorithm now revealed layers of intricate subroutines and branching logic.

Aiden's brows knitted as he muttered to himself, "It's like trying to solve a Rubik's cube that keeps adding new sides." He glanced at Elsa, a mix of determination and frustration in his eyes. "How do we even begin to unravel this?"

Elsa leaned in, her eyes scanning the code. "Let's break it down piece by piece. We've identified the replication sequence, now we need to – "

Her words cut off abruptly as the holographic display flickered, a new layer of code materializing before them. The pulsing green lines twisted and morphed, forming an intricate, almost fractal-like pattern.

Aiden's eyes widened, his hand freezing mid-gesture. "Whoa, what just happened?"

Elsa's expression tightened. "Encryption. Morris must have built in a safeguard to protect the core functionality of the worm."

Aiden's fingers twitched, itching to interact with the hologram. He reached out, but his hand passed through the iridescent code, unable to manipulate it. "It's like hitting a boss level we're not ready for," he muttered in the frustrated tone typical of a boy his age.

He stood up abruptly, pacing the small space of Morris's cluttered office. His sneakers crunched over scattered printouts as he moved, hands running through his hair in agitation.

"This doesn't make sense," Aiden said, his voice rising. "If Morris was smart enough to encrypt part of the code, why didn't he think through the consequences? Why didn't he think this through?"

The words burst out of him. In his mind, he couldn't reconcile the image of a brilliant programmer with someone who could make such a catastrophic oversight.

Elsa watched her son, her eyes softening with understanding. She leaned back in her chair, wincing slightly as she shifted to a more comfortable position. The familiar ache in her joints reminded her of countless late nights spent debugging her own code.

"Aiden," she said gently, her voice cutting through his frustrated pacing. "Come here for a second."

He stopped, turning to face her with a questioning look. Elsa patted the chair next to her, inviting him to sit.

As Aiden settled beside her, Elsa took a deep breath. "You know, when I was about your age, I accidentally crashed my high school's entire network trying to set up a chat system."

Aiden's eyebrows shot up. "For real?"

Elsa chuckled, nodding. "Oh yes. I sure did. I was so sure I had it all figured out. But I didn't account for how the system would handle multiple simultaneous connections. One little oversight, and suddenly no one could access their files for a week."

She tilted her head toward him, her voice taking on a conspiratorial tone. "Your grandmother was furious. But you know what she told me after she calmed down?"

Aiden shook his head, intrigued despite his lingering frustration.

"She said, 'Elsa, the only coders who never make mistakes are the ones who never try anything new.' " She smiled slightly. "Learning through trial and error isn't just normal, it's essential. Even for geniuses like Robert Morris."

As she spoke, Elsa's fingers absently traced patterns on the arm of her chair, mimicking the flow of code. "The trick is to learn from those errors, to build in safeguards and fail-safes. That's how we grow, both as coders and as people."

Aiden nodded slowly, his shoulders relaxing. "I guess even the greats have their off days, huh?"

"Exactly," Elsa said, her eyes twinkling. "Now, let's take another look at that encryption. Sometimes a fresh perspective is all you need for a breakthrough."

Journal entry – Janet – April 20, 2000

Elsa, my innovative, brilliant little ELIZA Kid, has learned a critical lesson today. A phone call came through from the school letting me know that their systems had completely crashed – and my daughter had admitted (turned herself in, essentially) that she was to blame. Needless to say, I was furious. And, I will admit, a little proud. As I calmed down on the drive to pick her up from the principal's office, I realized how proud I was of her, my not-so-little girl for growing into a young lady who would live honestly, truthfully. Take responsibility for her actions, for her mistakes.

I kept my furious face on as I walked into the office, until I saw how Elsa was clearly beating herself up. I saw her humiliated, heavy demeanor, slouched shoulders and dipped head. Eyes, hidden behind her bangs, focused only on her shoes. And I realized that this needed to be a teaching moment for her, rather than a scolding.

At an educated guess, the school will be locked out for at least a week. She really did a proper job of messing up! Yet, I have never seen such a prodigy as my daughter. Coding is in her blood. More natural to her than anything in the world.

On the way home, I told her how proud I was of her, and that it was only true innovators who risked such outcomes. Her big eyes raised and a small smile on her face, and in that moment, she was my little girl again under the grunge. She would not make the mistake again of innovation without proper planning, consideration for all of the potential outcomes. Something I still wrestle with every day of my career.

Aiden's expression tightened as he studied the holographic display of the worm's code. Suddenly, his eyes lit up. "Wait, Mom! What if we approach this like a boss battle in Cyber Siege?"

Elsa tilted her head, intrigued. "Go on."

"In the game, when you face a tough encryption, you don't just brute force it. You look for patterns, weaknesses in the algorithm." Aiden's hands moved animatedly as he explained. "What if we analyze the worm's behavior, find its recurring patterns, and use that to predict the encryption key?"

Elsa's eyes widened, a smile spreading across her face. "Aiden, that's brilliant! We could create a probability matrix based on the worm's known behaviors."

Her fingers flew across the holographic interface, refining Aiden's idea into actionable code. "If we combine this with a frequency analysis of the encrypted segments ... "

Aiden watched in awe as his mother's expertise transformed his gaming-inspired notion into a sophisticated decryption method. He thought, "She's like a code wizard, turning my clumsy idea into something insane."

As the new algorithm ran, Elsa turned to Aiden, her eyes shining with pride. "This is exactly the kind of creative thinking that pushes technology forward. You saw a connection that I might have missed."

The hologram flickered, then burst into a cascade of decrypted code. Aiden's jaw dropped. "We did it!"

Elsa smiled as she high-fived her son. "And there it is," she said softly, pointing to a specific line. "The missing replication cap. Such a small thing to cause so much chaos."

Aiden leaned in, studying the code. "It's hard to believe one line could change everything like that."

"That's the power and danger of code, sweetie," Elsa replied. "One small change can ripple out to affect millions. It's why we always have to be mindful of the potential consequences of our creations."

Aiden's face beamed with pride, his eyes darting between the holographic display and his mother's face. "So, what now? Do we just ... delete that line?"

Elsa shook her head, a small smile playing on her lips. "Not quite. Implementing a kill switch is delicate work. We need to neutralize the worm without causing further damage to the systems it's infected."

She began typing at a dizzying speed. Aiden watched her practiced precision intently, trying to follow her logic. He found it almost impossible to keep up with her pace.

"See, we're not just stopping the replication," Elsa explained, her voice taking on the warm, patient tone she used when teaching. "We're also adding a self-destruct sequence to the existing instances of the worm."

Aiden's features tensed in concentration. "Like a boss fight's final phase in a game? When you beat it, everything it spawned disappears too?"

Elsa chuckled, the sound filled with both amusement and a hint of relief at their progress. "You catch on quick, kiddo."

As she worked, Elsa felt a mix of emotions. Pride in Aiden's growing understanding, relief at finding a solution, and a bittersweet admiration for the ingenuity behind the worm, despite its destructive impact.

"*If only all our tech challenges could be solved with this kind of teamwork,*" she thought, glancing at Aiden's eager face. "*Maybe there's hope for bridging the generational divide in cybersecurity after all.*"

Elsa's fingers paused over the keyboard. "Alright, Aiden. This is it. Are you ready to make history ... or rather, unmake it?"

Aiden nodded. "I'm down! Let's do it."

Together, they input the final line of code. Elsa took a deep breath, her finger hovering over the execution key. "Here goes nothing," she muttered, and pressed enter.

For a moment, nothing happened. Then, the holographic display erupted into a flurry of activity. The pulsing red lines representing infected nodes began to falter and change.

"Look!" Aiden exclaimed, pointing at the map. "It's working!"

Elsa leaned forward, her eyes scanning the display intently. One by one, the infected nodes on the ARPANET map started turning green. It began slowly at first, then picked up speed, spreading like a benevolent version of the worm they'd just neutralized.

"It's beautiful," Elsa whispered, watching the transformation. She felt a rush of emotions – relief, triumph, and a touch of melancholy. This was the kind of moment her mother would have reveled in. "Your grandmother would have loved this."

Aiden sighed and wrapped his lanky arm around Elsa's shoulders. "She would have. So, we just saved the early internet?"

Elsa smiled, "In a manner of speaking, yes. But remember, we're observers here. We're learning from history, not changing it."

As the last red node turned green, Elsa couldn't help but think about the long road ahead in cybersecurity. "*One crisis averted,*" she thought, "*but how many more are waiting in the future?*"

The holographic map faded, replaced by glowing text. Elsa read aloud: "**Lesson: Innovation Demands Responsibility.**"

Aiden's expression shadowed. "What's that supposed to mean, exactly?"

"It means that when we create something new, especially in technology, we have to think about all the ways it could be used – or misused."

Elsa leaned back, feeling a twinge in her lower back. She massaged it absently. "That's the eternal struggle in our field, kiddo. We have to balance progress with protection. It's not easy, but it's necessary."

Aiden nodded, his eyes darting between the fading holographic display and his mother's face. He chewed his lower lip for a moment, a habit Elsa recognized as a sign he was piecing together another complex thought.

"Mom," he started, "so this was the moment when cybersecurity became necessary, right?"

"That's a perceptive question, Aiden," she replied, her fingers drumming lightly on her thigh as she organized her thoughts. "In many ways, yes. The Morris Worm was a wake-up call for the entire tech world."

She paused, gesturing to the fading image of chaos they had just witnessed.

"Before this, the early internet – ARPANET – was like an open frontier, a Wild West of innovation. It was full of possibility, but with very few rules or protections in place. The Morris Worm changed that. It was a wake-up call, forcing everyone to see just how vulnerable our digital systems were.

"The Morris Worm wasn't malicious in intent – it was an experiment gone wrong – but it demonstrated how a single piece of flawed code could wreak havoc on interconnected systems. Entire networks went down, critical data was disrupted, and researchers and companies were left scrambling to recover."

She turned back to the terminal. "It wasn't just about fixing bugs or patching systems. It was about realizing that this incredible technology we were building could be both a tool and a weapon. The worm forced the world to recognize, for the first time, the critical importance of cybersecurity in a connected digital world."

Aiden nodded. "It's kinda crazy to think that something so messed up could actually lead to progress," he mused, absentmindedly fidgeting with the sleeve of his hoodie.

"That's often how it goes in technology, and in life. Sometimes it takes a crisis to push us forward." She leaned against the wall, wincing slightly as her muscles ached. "Think about it like this: before a major security breach, people might ignore warnings about weak passwords or outdated software. But after an attack? Suddenly, everyone's scrambling to upgrade and protect themselves."

As she spoke, Elsa's mind drifted to her own experiences. The countless late nights poring over code, searching for vulnerabilities before they could be exploited. The heated debates with colleagues about ethical hacking and responsible disclosure. Each crisis had pushed her to learn more, to innovate, to stay one step ahead of those who would abuse technology.

Aiden leaned forward. "Mom," he said, his voice steady and reassuring, "we're learning from this. That's what matters."

"We need to prepare for whatever comes next," Elsa mused. "The history of cybersecurity is a constant game of cat and mouse. We fix one vulnerability, and hackers find another."

Aiden's eyes lit up with excitement. "So we're like time-traveling white hat hackers? That's so cool!"

As if on cue, the ChronoCipher buzzed to life, its holographic display flickering into existence once again between them. Aiden leaned forward, his eyes widening as he read the glowing text:

"What You Fix Today, They Will Break Tomorrow."

Elsa inhaled sharply. "That's … ominous," she murmured.

Aiden turned to his mother, a determined glint in his eye. "We'll figure it out, no matter how tough it gets. I mean, we already took down the Morris Worm, right? Whatever comes next, we got this."

Elsa studied her son, marveling at the blend of youthful enthusiasm and growing maturity in his face. She could see echoes of her own passion for problem-solving blending with Janet's innovative spirit.

"You're right, Aiden," she said, her voice soft but firm. "But remember, in cybersecurity, the stakes are higher than any game. We're not just protecting data; we're protecting people's lives and livelihoods."

Aiden nodded. "I get it, Mom. It's like ... it's not just about winning. It's about keeping everyone safe in the digital world."

"You know," she mused, her eyes distant, "your grandmother used to say that the best firewalls are built by those who can think like hackers. I never fully appreciated what she meant until now."

Aiden leaned in, curiosity piqued. "What do you mean, Mom?"

Elsa's fingers absently tapped a rhythm on her leg, as if typing out code. "It's about anticipation, Aiden. It's a chess game where the board keeps changing."

She paused as a new thought struck her. "But what if – "

Suddenly, the ChronoCipher emitted a high-pitched whine, cutting off Elsa's words. The device's surface rippled like disturbed water, its usual steady glow flickering erratically.

"Mom?" Aiden's voice held a note of alarm. "What's happening?"

Elsa's hands flew over the device, her aching joints momentarily forgotten as adrenaline surged through her. "I don't know," she muttered, her fingers moving rapidly across the interface. "It's like it's picking up some kind of temporal interference."

The air around them began to glisten, reality seeming to bend and warp. Elsa's heart raced as she realized they might be about to face a challenge far beyond anything they'd encountered so far.

As Elsa worked feverishly on the ChronoCipher, holographic numbers and coordinates flashed across its surface, a dizzying array of data resolving into a clear destination.

"The 1990s," Elsa breathed, her eyes widening. "It's taking us to the dawn of the World Wide Web."

Aiden's face lit up with excitement. "Bussin! That's when the internet really took off, right?"

Elsa nodded. "Yes, but it's also when things got ... complicated. The rise of social engineering, the birth of the dark web. It's where the digital wild west truly began."

The ChronoCipher's portal began to form a swirling vortex of light and data. As it stabilized, Elsa could see fragments of the era beyond – chunky desktop computers and dial-up modems, the iconic sound of early internet connections.

Aiden stepped closer to the portal, his hand reaching out instinctively. "Mom, look! Is that – "

"Don't touch it yet," Elsa warned, gently pulling him back. She studied the portal intently, her mind racing. "We need to be prepared. The 90s weren't just about technological advancement. It's when people started realizing the power – and danger – of information in the digital age."

Elsa took a deep breath, squaring her shoulders. "Ready?"

Aiden nodded, his eyes shining with determination. "Let's do this."

Together, they stepped into the glowing portal, their silhouettes merging with the fading light of the past as they plunged into the digital frontier of the 1990s.

As the light of the portal enveloped them, Elsa felt the familiar mix of exhilaration and trepidation course through her.

Chapter 6

Social engineering and the dark web's genesis (1990s)

The muffled whir of a computer fan filled the air as Elsa and Aiden materialized in the dimly lit office. The space was cluttered with relics from a bygone era – rotary phones, bulky monitors, and stacks of floppy disks teetered precariously on every surface.

"Okay, but first things first," Aiden said, picking up a rotary phone with a puzzled expression. "How do you even use this thing?"

"Really?" Elsa chuckled, rolling her eyes. "You'll figure it out. Now, pay attention. We've got work to do."

As they explored the room, Elsa couldn't help but feel a twinge of nostalgia. This was the world she'd grown up in, where technology was rapidly evolving and opening new doors – but also creating new dangers.

"Welcome to the 1990s," she said with a wry smile. "This was when cybersecurity took a turn for the deceptive."

"Deceptive?" Aiden asked.

"That's right," Elsa nodded, her gaze distant as she recalled her own experiences from that time. "This was when hackers began shifting their focus from brute-force attacks to something much more subtle and insidious – human manipulation. By exploiting human trust, these hackers could breach even the most secure systems. It was an art of deception that changed the landscape of cybersecurity forever."

Her fingers clacked across a keyboard, bringing up images of newspaper headlines detailing high-profile hacks and data breaches from the era. Aiden leaned in, soaking up the information like a sponge.

"This era represents the dawn of modern cybersecurity challenges," Elsa added.

Shaking his head in disbelief, Aiden murmured, "I never realized how deep this rabbit hole goes."

"Mom, check this out." Aiden pointed to a shadowy projection on the wall, depicting a hacker manipulating a company employee over the phone.

DOI: 10.1201/9781003501626-6

Elsa and Aiden watched in awe as "Ghost of the Wires", a notorious master of deception, appeared before them. The shadowy figure spoke into a phone, his voice oozing charm and urgency.

"Hello, this is Mike from IT," the hacker began, posing as an employee of the company he was targeting. "We're experiencing a serious issue with our servers, and I need your help to resolve it right away."

Elsa observed Ghost of the Wires' tactics closely, her eyes narrowing as she analyzed his every move. Aiden, on the other hand, leaned in closer, as if he were watching a movie.

"Of course, happy to help," replied the unsuspecting employee on the other end of the line. "What do you need?"

"Thank you so much," Ghost of the Wires continued, feigning relief. "I'm going to need your login credentials to access your computer remotely. We need to act quickly to prevent any data loss."

"Sure, no problem," the employee said, without a moment's hesitation. He rattled off his username and password, completely unaware that he had just handed over the keys to his company's digital kingdom.

"Got it," Ghost of the Wires confirmed, his voice dripping with satisfaction. "You've been a huge help. I'll take it from here."

As the call ended and the projection faded, Aiden stared at the empty space in disbelief. "No way," he muttered, shaking his head. "That guy just dropped his password like it was nothing. How could he be so easy to play?"

"That's the power of social engineering," Elsa explained. "By using psychological principles like urgency, empathy, and authority, hackers can exploit human trust to gain access to sensitive information and secure systems."

"Urgency?" Aiden asked, his expression clouded with thought.

"By creating a sense of urgency, Ghost of the Wires made the employee feel like the situation was too critical to question his authority or motives. It's a tactic that preys on our instinct to act quickly in times of crisis," Elsa elaborated.

"Empathy, because he pretended to be grateful for the help?" Aiden guessed.

"Exactly," Elsa confirmed. "By expressing gratitude and vulnerability, the hacker connected with the employee on an emotional level, making it easier for him to manipulate the situation. Most humans have the instinct to help in situations where they can offer it."

"And authority ... that one's obvious. He pretended to be an IT technician, someone the employee would naturally trust to handle this kind of issue," Aiden concluded.

"Right," Elsa nodded. "Hackers like Ghost of the Wires understand that people are often the weakest link in any security system. By targeting those vulnerabilities, they can bypass even the most sophisticated defenses."

Aiden looked around the outdated office, taking in the rotary phones and stacks of floppy disks. "It's kinda scary to think about," he admitted, his voice barely above a whisper. "But I guess understanding these tactics is the first step in learning how to defend against them, right?"

"That's exactly right, Aiden. And together, we're going to make sure you're prepared for anything."

Elsa leaned against a dusty desk, illuminated by the dim glow of a CRT monitor. "You know, Aiden, Ghost of the Wires wasn't just some fictional character. He was inspired by real-life hackers like Kevin Mitnick." She gestured to the outdated office around them.

"Who's Kevin Mitnick?" Aiden asked curiously.

"Mitnick was one of the first hackers to truly understand the power of social engineering," Elsa explained, her expression distant as she recalled memories of her early days in cybersecurity. "He bypassed technical defenses by exploiting human trust and manipulating people into giving him access to confidential information. He was a genius in a sense, of course when it came to coding, but he also had a deep understanding of human nature and psychology. For him, it was all about the thrill of accessing forbidden information, getting in where he shouldn't be."

"Wild," Aiden muttered with a shake of his head. "Did this guy ever get caught? Or was he too smart for that? How did people find out who he was?"

"Yup. He was caught a couple of times, actually. Mitnick ended up spending around four years in prison overall and faced a three-year ban from using any computers, cell phones, modems, or any device that gave him access to the internet."

"But how did they catch him?" Aiden asked, fully invested in this story.

"Eventually, they traced one of his hacks back to a modem near his home, and the FBI managed to trace him to his apartment. Took them two weeks!"

"So he made a mistake, then, in a way. Allowing himself to be traced. Interesting."

"Yes. Even geniuses are not invulnerable to error. It was reported that throughout his hacking career, he managed to break into some of the most secure computer systems ever developed at the time. He became quite the celebrity in the hacking community. Although, later he seemed to turn a corner and use his skills for the better – he wrote a couple of books helping people understand how to protect themselves against cybercrime, and went on to run a successful cybersecurity company."

"Huh," Aiden said thoughtfully. "So not such a bad guy in the end, then. Just shows how anything can be turned to good."

"Indeed," came a voice from behind them. Both Elsa and Aiden jumped at the unexpected intrusion, and turned to see Janet Winters materializing before their eyes.

"Grandma? How ... ?" Aiden stammered, momentarily forgetting that it was only a digital version of his grandmother.

"Hello, dear," Janet said with a warm smile, her eyes flicking between Elsa and Aiden. "It seems I've been summoned here to share my insights on this pivotal moment in cybersecurity history."

"Your experiences could certainly provide valuable context, Mom," Elsa admitted, her face reflecting surprise and relief at seeing her mother's likeness.

"Very well, then," Janet began, her voice adopting a professorial tone. "During this time, we witnessed an evolution of hacking methods. It marked the dawn of an age where social engineering would become a prominent weapon in the arsenal of cybercriminals."

"By understanding this shift," Elsa added, "we can better protect ourselves and others from falling victim to these tactics."

"Exactly," Janet agreed. "My experiences during the ARPANET days taught me that trust, once a cornerstone of our digital world, could also be its greatest vulnerability."

Aiden, his curiosity piqued, asked Janet, "So, what else was going down during this time? I mean, besides the whole social engineering thing?"

"Ah," Janet replied thoughtfully, "you're asking about the early seeds of the dark web."

"Dark web?" Aiden echoed, his eyes widening. "That sounds intense."

"Indeed. It was a time when the internet was still young, and the potential for both good and evil was immense, and perhaps still largely unrecognized."

Elsa closed her eyes, as if seeing the past unfold.

"Timothy C. May was a key figure in the cypherpunk movement, and one of the earliest voices advocating for privacy on the internet," Elsa continued. "He and others saw what was coming – governments and corporations tightening their grip on information, building systems of surveillance that could one day track, monitor, and control entire populations. To them, cryptography wasn't just about securing messages; it was about resisting control, about ensuring that personal freedoms weren't eroded by digital authoritarianism."

Aiden listened intently as Elsa's words wove a tapestry of secrecy and rebellion. "What is the cyberpunk movement? Never heard of it!" he asked. "Sounds hardcore!"

Elsa chuckled. "Not cyberpunk, Aiden. Cypherpunk."

"Oh, My bad," Aiden laughed.

"I'll tell you more about them in a minute. Have patience, my son!" She smiled.

Elsa leaned back, her gaze growing distant, as if watching the past unfold. "May, along with other cypherpunks like Eric Hughes and John Gilmore, believed that privacy was a fundamental right, not a privilege granted by those in power. They weren't just theorizing; they were actively building the tools that would enable anonymous communication, untraceable digital transactions, and secure online interactions. They saw encryption as the great equalizer – something that could empower individuals against powerful institutions."

Aiden raised an eyebrow. "But why were governments so against it? Wouldn't encryption help everyone?"

Elsa sighed. "That was the battle. The people in charge – governments, intelligence agencies, law enforcement – feared that strong encryption would make their jobs harder. They argued that it would allow criminals, terrorists, and bad actors to operate in secrecy. In the 1990s, this turned into a full-blown war over cryptography. The US government even tried to regulate encryption like a weapon, banning the export of strong cryptographic algorithms under the same laws that controlled military-grade arms. At one point, the NSA wanted to force companies to build 'backdoors' into encryption so they could still access private communications."

Aiden's eyes widened. "Wait, they actually wanted to make encryption weaker on purpose?"

"Exactly," Elsa nodded. "But the cypherpunks fought back. They believed that if encryption had backdoors, then no one would truly be safe – not journalists, not dissidents in oppressive regimes, not everyday people who just wanted privacy. May was radical in his views. He wrote something called the Crypto Anarchist Manifesto, predicting a world where digital money, encrypted communication, and anonymous transactions would challenge traditional power structures. To some, it sounded like paranoia. But today? He wasn't far off. Cryptocurrencies, encrypted messaging apps, and privacy tools are everywhere – just like he envisioned."

Aiden leaned forward, fascinated. "So, encryption wasn't just a tool – it was a revolution?"

Elsa smiled. "That's exactly how they saw it. A revolution not fought with guns or protests, but with mathematics and code. And while the cypherpunks won many battles – giving us the secure technology we rely on today – the fight for digital privacy is far from over."

"They were also known as 'crypto anarchists.' In the early days of the internet, there was no such thing as the dark web. But people who understood encryption – people like May and Phil Zimmerman, who created Pretty Good Privacy – were laying the foundation for something new. They didn't just want encrypted emails – they wanted the ability to be invisible. To be free. But what they didn't foresee was that as the internet grew, so did the shadows. The desire for anonymity began to outpace the safeguards.

"People like Roger Dingledine, Nick Mathewson, and Paul Syverson – three names that shaped the very foundation of what we now call **the dark web** – understood that privacy wasn't a luxury. It was a necessity.

"Not just for activists or criminals, but for anyone who wanted to control their own digital footprint. It wasn't until the mid-1990s that Tor started taking shape," Elsa continued.

"What's Tor?" Aiden interrupted.

"Tor – The Onion Router – was the first step in creating a truly anonymous internet. Tor allowed people to surf the web without anyone knowing who they were or where they came from. It used layers of encryption, like the layers of an onion, to mask users' identities."

Aiden's eyes widened. "So, Tor was the beginning of the dark web?"

Elsa nodded. "Yes. But it wasn't just the creation of Tor – it was its purpose. Tor was created to protect people, to allow nonconformists and activists in oppressive regimes to communicate without fear. It was a tool for freedom. But then, as soon as Tor was available to the public, people began to see its darker potential.

"Hackers – criminals – saw it as a way to hide, to evade law enforcement." She leaned forward, her voice dropping to a whisper. "In 2002, Tor was officially launched. The first dark web marketplaces began to emerge soon after – hidden platforms where stolen data, illegal drugs, and weapons could be bought and sold, all under the radar of the authorities.

"The first and most notorious of these marketplaces was The Silk Road," Elsa said. "It wasn't just a marketplace for illegal goods – it was a platform for free trade. It was anarchic, revolutionary. Ross Ulbricht, the founder, believed he was creating a system that liberated individuals, allowing them to trade freely, without interference from governments. He became Dread Pirate Roberts, the digital Robin Hood who took on the authorities."

Aiden frowned, trying to make sense of this strange new world. "But it wasn't just freedom – it was crime."

Elsa's eyes softened. "Yes, but it was more complicated than that. For some people, the dark web became a form of resistance. A rejection of the government's surveillance, the corporations' control. For others, it was a refuge from society's rules – an opportunity to disappear."

"But the criminals – " Aiden started.

Elsa raised a hand. "Yes, the criminals saw an opportunity too. And soon enough, the Silk Road wasn't just selling stolen identities – it was selling everything. Drugs. Weapons. Even human trafficking. Tor made it possible to hide, and that was all they needed."

"You're losing me, Mom. How does this connect to me? To us?"

Elsa sighed, her mind momentarily drifting. "Because, Aiden, this isn't just about hacking or code. It's about us.

"The vulnerabilities on the dark web mirror those in us. People use the internet for freedom, but freedom can also become an addiction. The very thing we use to escape the world can become the thing that imprisons us. The same vulnerabilities we all carry – the need for connection, for belonging, for escape – are the things hackers use to manipulate us." She paused, meeting his gaze.

"The dark web is a shadow, Aiden. It reflects the shadows within all of us. The internet, like our minds, is filled with both light and darkness. It's our job to understand both."

Aiden clenched his fists, his expression tense as he struggled to reconcile these conflicting ideas. "So, how do we know if it's worth it? What's the right balance?"

Elsa glanced over at her mother, hoping she would take it from there. Janet hesitated before answering. "That is an ethical question that has no easy answer. It will always be a delicate dance between freedom and security."

The ChronoCipher began to glow, the familiar pulsating light signaling the start of a new challenge. As they watched, the device projected the image of a hacker manipulating a company employee over the phone.

"Decode the Trust Hack: Learn the Psychology of Social Engineering," the ChronoCipher commanded, its voice echoing ominously through the room.

"Remember Psychology, Aiden," Elsa explained thoughtfully. "Hackers like Ghost of the Wires use tactics like urgency, empathy, and authority to manipulate people into giving them what they want."

As they spoke, the ChronoCipher projected the scene further, showing the hacker's charm and calculated authority as he effortlessly extracted sensitive information from his unsuspecting victim.

Aiden murmured, his eyes widening as he watched. "It's like watching someone hack the human mind. What's our challenge, then? To learn how to recognize and work against these techniques?"

"Indeed," Elsa confirmed, her voice steady and resolute. "We need to be able to see through the smoke and mirrors if we're ever going to stand a chance against threats like this."

Together, mother and son turned their attention back to the ChronoCipher, determined to rise to the challenge and unlock the secrets of social engineering – for their own sake, and for the future that awaited them all.

Elsa's eyes narrowed as she studied the ChronoCipher's display, watching intently as a series of simulated social engineering scenarios began to unfold before them. Aiden leaned in beside her, his youthful curiosity quickly giving way to concern as he realized the devious nature of the challenges they faced.

"Alright, Aiden," Elsa started, her voice steady and focused. "We need to analyze these situations and identify the red flags that indicate manipulation. Let's start with this first scenario: pretexting. Something Mitnick was well-known for."

As they watched the simulation, a virtual con artist posed as a utility worker, attempting to gain access to a secure facility by exploiting the sympathy of an unsuspecting employee.

Aiden narrowed his eyes, focusing intently as he tried to figure out what made this interaction stand out from any other legitimate request.

"Mom, I think I see it," Aiden said hesitantly, pointing at the screen. "The worker says they're responding to an emergency, but they don't have any identification or proof. The employee shouldn't let them in without verifying who they are, right?"

"Exactly," Elsa affirmed, pleased with her son's growing awareness. "Now let's move on to the next one: baiting."

In this scenario, a hacker left a seemingly harmless USB drive in a public space, waiting for an unsuspecting victim to pick it up and plug it into their computer out of curiosity. Aiden's eyes widened as he realized the potential consequences of such a simple action.

In another scenario, an individual picked up a USB drive labeled "Confidential" from the ground outside an office building.

When they plugged it into their computer, malware spread throughout the network undetected. Aiden shook his head, astonished by the simple yet effective baiting technique.

"Sheesh, that's slick," Aiden whispered, shaking his head. "I never would have thought twice about picking up a random USB drive. Isn't it crazy how just a little curiosity can lead to such wild consequences?" Aiden mused aloud, his fingers tapping nervously on his tablet.

"Curiosity is human nature, but we must learn to be cautious and verify things before we act," Elsa explained, her face solemn.

"Unfortunately, many people don't," Elsa sighed. "That's why it's important to approach anything unfamiliar with caution and skepticism." She paused, taking a moment to emphasize the gravity of their lesson. "Remember, Aiden, trust is a powerful weapon – and it can be used against you just as easily it can protect you."

Aiden nodded solemnly, absorbing his mother's wisdom as they moved on to the final scenario: phishing.

"Phishing is when someone tries to obtain sensitive information by pretending to be a trustworthy entity," Elsa explained. "For example, an attacker might send an email that appears to be from your bank, asking you to click a link and enter your account details."

"Those emails can be very convincing," Aiden said with a wry smile, recalling how he'd almost fallen for a scam himself not long ago – a "special offer" for a video game he'd been wanting for a while.

"Exactly. But now you know better, right? You won't be falling for anything like that anytime soon, I don't think," Elsa said with a reassuring smile.

"Definitely not," Aiden replied, his determination shining through. "I won't let anyone trick me like that again."

"Good," Elsa said, her voice softening with pride. "Now let's finish this puzzle and show the ChronoCipher what we've learned."

Together, they crafted counter-responses to each social engineering scenario, navigating the complex web of deception with growing confidence. And as they did, Aiden couldn't help but feel grateful for the priceless gift his mother was giving him – not just the knowledge to recognize manipulation, but the strength to resist it and protect both himself and others from harm.

"Mom, check this one out," Aiden pointed to a projection where a hacker was posing as a delivery person, convincing a receptionist to grant them access to the company's secure area. "Just by wearing a uniform and carrying a package, they got right through the front door."

"Always question what you see, Aiden," Elsa advised. "Appearances can be deceiving, especially in the world of social engineering." Aiden's attention shifted to the next scenario, where a caller impersonated a grandchild in distress, asking for money to be wired immediately. The elderly victim readily complied, only realizing they'd been scammed when it was too late.

"For real?" Aiden whispered, his stomach twisting in knots at the thought of someone taking advantage of a vulnerable grandparent. "I can't believe people would sink that low."

"Unfortunately, Aiden, there will always be those who exploit trust and kindness for personal gain," Elsa said with a shake of her head. "That's why it's so important to stay skeptical in situations like these."

As they watched the projections, Elsa couldn't help but feel a pang of guilt for the times she'd allowed her own trust to be manipulated. She knew all too well that the consequences of falling for a social engineering attack could be life-altering.

"Mom," Aiden said quietly, sensing his mother's inner turmoil. "I know we can't change the past, but I'm glad you're teaching me all this now. It'll help me protect myself and others in the future. I can't wait to tell my class about this."

Elsa looked down at her son, his earnest expression filling her heart with love. She squeezed his shoulder gently and smiled.

The ChronoCipher hummed to life, casting its eerie glow over the dimly lit office. Elsa, Aiden, and Janet watched as another scene materialized before them. This time, they found themselves in a bustling corporate office, where employees typed furiously on clunky keyboards, the sharp clatter of keys echoing throughout the room.

"Look at this one," Elsa said, pointing to a projection of a woman sitting at her desk, staring intently at her computer screen. "She just received an email from her boss asking for an urgent money transfer to a vendor."

Aiden leaned in closer, scrutinizing the details of the message. "Except that's not really her boss, is it?"

"Nope," Elsa nodded. "It's a hacker posing as her boss. They're using the employee's trust in authority to manipulate her into sending the funds to their account."

As they watched, the woman hesitated for a moment before entering the transfer information, her fingers hovering uncertainly over the keyboard.

"Can't she tell it's fake?" Aiden asked, frustration in his tone.

"These emails can be very convincing, as you know" Elsa explained, her eyes narrowing as she studied the holographic projection. Aiden blushed at his own naivete just a few weeks prior that had almost had him entering credit card details into an unverified, and fake, website.

"Especially if the attacker has done their homework and knows enough about the company and its employees to mimic the boss's tone and writing style."

Aiden clenched his fists, anger simmering beneath the surface. "I hate the thought of messed up people preying on others like this. It's just ... wrong."

Elsa placed a comforting hand on her son's shoulder. "I know, but that's why we're here – to learn how to recognize and combat these tactics."

Before Aiden could respond, the ChronoCipher shifted again, revealing a new scenario.

This time, they found themselves in a cozy living room, where a middle-aged man sat in front of a computer, his face etched with focused determination.

"Another phishing attempt, Mom?" Aiden asked, taking note of the man's puzzled expression.

"Indeed," Elsa confirmed. "This one is disguised as a charity donation request. The hacker is preying on the target's empathy and generosity to steal their financial information."

Aiden watched in dismay as the man clicked the link in the email, entering his credit card details into the fake donation form. He couldn't help but feel a surge of indignation at the thought of someone exploiting another person's kindness for personal gain.

Together, they continued to study the ChronoCipher's projections, each scenario offering valuable lessons in the subtle art of deception. And as they delved deeper into the world of social engineering, Aiden found himself more determined than ever to protect himself and others from the manipulative tactics that had plagued the digital realm since its inception.

Aiden shook his head in disbelief. "I've heard about scams like this happening today. People pretending to be from Microsoft or Apple and tricking people into giving up control of their computers. It's crazy to think that these tactics have been around for so long."

"Indeed," Elsa agreed. "The methods may evolve, but the principles behind them remain the same: exploit human trust and manipulate vulnerabilities in our psychology. That's why it's so important to stay vigilant and keep learning."

"Alright," he said with determination, "let's keep going. I'm ready to learn more about how to beat these scammers at their own game."

Aiden's fingers hovered over the ChronoCipher. After a moment, he tapped the correct sequence to defuse the simulated phishing attempt. The holographic image of an elderly man flickered, relief washing over his face as he hung up the phone.

"Nicely done, Aiden," Elsa said, watching her son with pride.

"Mom," Aiden said, his voice filled with both excitement and disbelief, "it's crazy to think that the same technology used to protect people like whistleblowers could also empower criminals."

Elsa nodded solemnly. "Yes, it's an ethical gray area. On one hand, anonymity can be a powerful tool for those who need to expose corruption or seek refuge from persecution. But, on the other hand, it can be exploited by those with malicious intent."

Aiden stared at the floor, processing what his mother had said. "So, can systems ever truly make up for human flaws? I mean, if we keep creating new technologies to solve old problems, won't we just keep making the same mistakes?"

"Perfection is impossible," Elsa admitted, her gaze focused on the shadows playing across the room. "But education and awareness are powerful tools for resilience. By teaching people about the risks, we can help them make informed decisions about how they interact with technology."

Aiden's eyes gleamed. "But how do we know where to draw the line? How do we balance openness with security?"

Elsa allowed herself a small smile, impressed by her son's insight. "That's the challenge, isn't it? It's a delicate dance, constantly adjusting our steps as the landscape shifts beneath us."

"Then why does it feel like we're always one step behind the bad guys?" Aiden asked, a hint of frustration returning to his tone.

"Because that's the nature of progress," Elsa replied. "We learn from our mistakes, we adapt, and we grow stronger. The key is to be aware of the risks – that way, we can make informed decisions about how we use technology."

Aiden considered his mother's words, his young mind grappling with the complexities of the world he had inherited. As they kept digging into the past, he knew he'd have to figure out how to balance the good and bad in people – how we can be amazing, but also mess everything up.

But for now, he had another challenge to face: decoding the ChronoCipher's next puzzle and proving that he could rise above humanity's flaws to protect the digital world he loved.

Elsa watched Aiden's frustration as he stared at the ChronoCipher, his fingers drumming impatiently on its metallic surface. She knew it was time to share a story that might help him understand the importance of vigilance and accountability.

"Before you were born, I faced an ethical dilemma in my work as a cybersecurity expert," she began, her voice soft but steady. "A client had asked me to break into their competitor's system and steal sensitive information. They claimed it was for 'research purposes,' but I knew it was wrong."

Aiden looked up from the device, his eyes wide with surprise. "What did you do?"

"I refused," Elsa said, her expression resolute. "I realized that my skills could be used for good or ill, and I chose to uphold my principles even if it meant losing potential clients. It wasn't easy, but it taught me that it's crucial to remain vigilant and accountable for our actions."

"Even when it means going against what others want?" Aiden asked, his brow furrowed in thought.

"Especially then," Elsa replied, placing a hand on his shoulder. "We can't control the actions of others, but we have the power to choose how we respond. By standing up for what's right, we can make a difference in the world – one decision at a time."

Janet drew closer, her eyes studying the swirling patterns on the ChronoCipher's display. "Elsa, Aiden, I believe this device has a deeper purpose than we initially realized. It may have been designed for something beyond our current understanding."

"Beyond our understanding? What do you mean?" Elsa asked, her expression clouded with concern.

"Consider how the ChronoCipher has guided us through history, revealing not only the technological advancements but also the ethical challenges that have come with them," Janet explained. "There are layers to this device that we have yet to uncover. But I cannot say more – my knowledge is bound by my original memories and experiences."

The air crackled with static as Elsa and Aiden materialized in a strangely familiar environment. They found themselves standing in the same dimly lit office from earlier, surrounded by rotary phones, outdated computers, and stacks of floppy disks. Aiden glanced around in confusion, gripping his tablet tightly.

"Mom, are we back where we started?" he asked, his voice laced with worry. "Did something go wrong?"

Elsa looked down at the ChronoCipher device, which seemed to be functioning normally. Her expression shifted, deep in contemplation of the possibilities. "I don't think so," she said slowly. "It might just be showing us a different aspect of this time period."

As they spoke, a cryptic warning appeared on the device's screen: **"Not All Shadows Can Be Seen; Some Grow as the Light Gets Brighter."** Elsa felt a shiver run down her spine. She knew that danger could lurk even in seemingly innocuous places, but what did this message mean? Was it a prophecy or a threat?

She reached for it, trying to discern what was happening, but it was too late – the device projected a fragmented memory, revealing a shadowy figure that seemed to hover in the air before them.

Before they could process this new phenomenon, the figure spoke with an eerie, distorted voice. "In the darkest corners of cyberspace, secrets are hidden, waiting to be uncovered. Tread carefully, for the path forward is filled with both enlightenment and peril, rewriting history to reclaim power," the figure said cryptically, its voice echoing through the room. "But only for those who can navigate the treacherous waters of deception and manipulation."

The figure vanished as abruptly as it had appeared, leaving behind an air of icy unease. Aiden looked to Elsa, his eyes wide with apprehension. "Is there something we need to be worried about, Mom, Grandma? Was that … the inventor of the ChronoCipher?"

Elsa frowned, her mind racing to make sense of the mysterious message. "I'm not sure, Aiden. But whoever it was, they seemed to be warning us about something."

Aiden's expression grew wary as he eyed the ChronoCipher, doubt creeping into his thoughts. "Do you think we can trust this thing? What if it's trying to manipulate us somehow?" He thought he saw a flicker of recognition in Janet's eyes, but it disappeared so quickly, he couldn't be sure.

Elsa placed a reassuring hand on his shoulder. "I don't know, Aiden. But we must continue our journey and uncover the truth behind these mysteries."

"Bet," Aiden agreed, his determination overcoming his fear. "We've come this far. We can't back down now."

"Indeed," Janet added. "Our journey is far from over, but remember to always question what you see and hear. The digital world is full of deception and misdirection."

Elsa mulled over her son's words, aware that the stakes were higher than ever before. "I don't have all the answers, Aiden," she admitted. "But from now on we need to question everything we encounter on this journey."

As they stood there, surrounded by the relics of a bygone era, Elsa couldn't help but reflect. The world had changed so much since her mother's time, and yet, in many ways, the underlying themes remained the same – trust, deception, and the delicate balance between progress and vulnerability.

Aiden let out a deep breath as he considered the implications of their mission. He was beginning to understand how complex and morally ambiguous the world of cybersecurity could be. While he had initially been excited to learn about the tools and techniques used by hackers throughout history, he now felt the weight of responsibility that came with this knowledge.

Even Janet appeared contemplative. "It is time for me to go now, but I have no doubt I will see you both again soon."

Elsa shared a troubled glance with Aiden before turning back to her mother's digital twin. "Thank you, Mom. We'll be cautious as we continue our journey."

"Mom, I'm starting to get why you and Grandma have been so passionate about cybersecurity," Aiden said, his eyes shining with newfound respect. "There's so much more to it than just coding and hacking."

"That's right, Aiden. And now it's our turn to carry on the legacy Grandma started – together."

"Mom, do you think the world would be better off without the internet?" Aiden asked suddenly, a hint of worry in his voice.

Elsa sighed, pausing to consider her answer. "That's a difficult question, Aiden. The internet has brought people together, connected us in ways that were once unimaginable. But it comes with its pros and cons."

As they spoke, Janet appeared next to them once again. As they looked at her in surprise, Janet chuckled. "Even I didn't think I'd be back *this* soon! Aiden, your question is one that many people have grappled with over the years," she said gently. "But remember, the internet didn't create these vulnerabilities – it merely exposed and amplified them."

"Moments like these," Elsa added, "the rise of web browsers, search engines, and the first online marketplaces – they all helped shape the world we know today, but as we know by now, they also presented new challenges for those working to protect innocent people from digital threats."

As Aiden listened to their explanations, he couldn't shake the feeling that something was off. He knew we couldn't reverse tech progress, but it was wild to think about how much of human history had been shaped by straight-up lies and manipulation.

Aiden said hesitantly, "Even with everything we've learned so far, can we really make a difference? Can we prevent future attacks and protect people from these threats?"

Elsa squeezed Aiden's hand tightly, her eyes searching his face for reassurance as much as offering it. "I don't know, my love," she admitted. "But we can try."

Aiden stared at the swirling vortex of the time portal, its iridescent lights reflecting off his wide eyes. He clenched his fists, taking a deep breath as he tried to steady himself. "Why can't people learn from their mistakes, Mom? We've seen how these things keep happening, but it just feels like nothing changes," he said, frustration evident in his voice.

Janet spoke once more, "Remember, both of you must remain vigilant. Not everything will be what it seems, and sometimes the greatest challenges lie in the shadows we cannot see."

Aiden nodded, his expression resolute. Despite his frustrations, he knew that giving up was not an option. As scared as he was about the unknowns that lay ahead, he found comfort in his mother's steadying presence and Janet's wise words.

Elsa felt as though the past and present had collided in that moment. There was no clean divide between the two – no boundary between the ethical and the exploitative.

"Just as we've seen with the dark web," Elsa said, "the gaps in our defenses reflect the gaps in our self-awareness. The more we understand those weaknesses – our human tendencies to trust, to want control, to feel the need to connect – the more we can protect ourselves, not just digitally, but in life."

"Alright," he said, steeling himself. "I'll try to remember that. Let's do this, Mom."

With a final glance at Janet, they stepped forward into the portal, the swirling lights enveloping them as they embarked on their next adventure.

Journal entry – Elsa – January 24, 2028

The last few days have been a relentless blur. Endless searches, encrypted leads, and sleepless nights have pulled us deeper into the hidden layers of the dark web. The complexity of what we're confronting is overwhelming. This isn't merely about tracking criminal networks. It's something much larger – a shadow that has been growing over the digital world for decades.

At first, I thought it was just about data: stolen identities, money laundering, illegal trade. But now I see that the real threat lies deeper. It's not just technology's vulnerabilities that we're contending with – it's human nature itself. The digital world has become a mirror to our desires, fears, and weaknesses. Vulnerabilities I thought I had overcome long ago have resurfaced, reflected back at me in this twisted landscape of anonymity and manipulation.

There is something almost poetic about how the internet has evolved. What was once a tool of connection has become a breeding ground for division and deceit. The very architecture of the web – its openness, its promise of endless access – has exposed the rawest parts of human behavior. Our need for validation, our hunger for control, our fear of exclusion – all of these have been encoded into the structure of online life.

The implications are chilling. This investigation has forced me to confront the truth that hacking is no longer confined to breaking into systems. It's about infiltrating the human mind – exploiting thoughts and behaviors, manipulating perceptions. Social engineering is perhaps the most dangerous threat of all. It operates on psychological triggers: trust, curiosity, fear, and greed. It feeds on our impulses, turning our own instincts against us.

The dark web isn't just a network hidden from view. It is a manifestation of our collective shadows – a repository of both our ambitions and our worst fears. The more I learn, the clearer it becomes that technology is not inherently the problem. It is merely a tool, shaped by those who wield it. What truly makes us vulnerable is how easily we can be deceived by promises of power, control, or belonging.

I have seen this manipulation unfold both in the physical world and online. And yet, despite these dangers, I still believe in the power of technology to connect and protect. The key is knowledge. Awareness is the first line of defense. If we can understand the patterns of deception, the tactics of those who prey on the vulnerable, we can resist.

Aiden is beginning to grasp this as well. I can see the weight of these realizations in his eyes. He is learning that cybersecurity is more than coding or firewalls – it's about human behavior. Protecting people means understanding them, their needs and fears, and building resilience against those who would exploit them.

This journey has already reshaped how I see both myself and the world we inhabit. It's not just about finding and neutralizing threats. It's about holding a light to the darker parts of ourselves. Only by confronting those shadows can we hope to build a future where trust and security coexist.

For now, the ChronoCipher remains our guide. Its mechanisms seem to understand the stakes better than we do. The next step on this path feels heavier than the last, as though we are approaching a pivotal moment. I can only hope that Aiden and I have the strength to face what lies ahead.

The stakes are higher than I ever imagined.

We're not just fighting hackers. We're fighting the echoes of our own darkness.

Chapter 7

The dawn of the web and its ripples (1993)

Aiden's eyes widened as the ChronoCipher hummed to life, its glowing display casting a pulsating light on the room's outdated technology. As the device's inner mechanisms whirred and clicked, it seemed to be calculating their next destination with intense precision.

"1993," Elsa announced, reading the date from the ChronoCipher's screen. "The birth of the World Wide Web."

As the familiar sensation of time travel washed over them, Aiden clung to his mother's hand, grateful for her unwavering support. Together, they stepped into the swirling portal, ready to face the challenges that awaited them in 1993 and beyond.

The air crackled with static electricity as Elsa and Aiden materialized in the packed conference hall, their arrival masked by the buzz of excited chatter. Elsa instinctively steadied herself, her hand grasping Aiden's shoulder as she blinked away the disorientation of time travel.

"I've never seen anything like this," Aiden whispered, his eyes wide as he took in the sea of boxy computer monitors and shoulder-padded suits. "It's like we landed in one of those old movies you like, Mom."

Elsa smiled, despite the familiar ache settling into her joints. "Welcome to 1993, kiddo. The year the world changed forever."

They shuffled through the crowd, Elsa's practiced movements belying her exhaustion as she guided Aiden toward an open spot near the back. The air hummed with anticipation, reminding Elsa of the countless hackathons she'd attended in her youth. But this was different. This was history.

A hush fell over the room as a bespectacled man took the stage. Elsa leaned close to Aiden, her voice low but intense. "That's Tim Berners-Lee. In about two minutes, he's going to introduce something that will reshape humanity's future."

Aiden nodded, his fingers twitching as if longing for a touchscreen. "The World Wide Web, right? We learned about it in Tech History class, but seeing it for real is ... "

DOI: 10.1201/9781003501626-7

"Mind-blowing?" She watched her son's face, seeing the same wonder she'd felt decades ago reflected in his eyes. For a moment, her cynicism faded, replaced by a bittersweet nostalgia for simpler times.

As Berners-Lee began to speak, Elsa felt a familiar tightness in her chest. Pride in humanity's potential for innovation? Fear of the challenges to come? Or maybe just the weight of knowing too much about where it all led.

She nudged Aiden gently, her voice barely above a whisper. "Pay attention, sweetheart. This moment right here? It's going to change everything. The way we communicate, the way we learn, the way we see the world ... it's all about to shift."

Aiden nodded, his gaze fixed on the stage. "It's like watching the first player log into an MMORPG, isn't it? The start of a whole new virtual world."

Elsa chuckled softly, marveling at her son's ability to frame complex concepts through the lens of gaming. "Just remember, this 'game' doesn't have reset buttons or cheat codes. The consequences are very real."

As Berners-Lee continued his presentation, Elsa found herself torn between the electric atmosphere of innovation and the nagging voice of experience.

Aiden's eyes widened as Berners-Lee demonstrated the first webpage. "Mom," he whispered, excitement bubbling in his voice, "how does it actually work? Like, how does the information travel?"

Elsa leaned in, her tired eyes brightening with a spark of enthusiasm. "Think of it like a massive library, kiddo. The web is full of documents, and each one has a unique address. When you type in that address, your computer sends a request across the internet – like a librarian fetching a book."

"But how does it know where to go?" Aiden asked, pressing for clarification.

"That's where protocols come in," Elsa explained, her hands moving in small, precise gestures. "HTTP – Hypertext Transfer Protocol – is like a universal language that computers use to talk to each other. It's the rulebook that makes sure everyone's on the same page."

Aiden nodded slowly. "So it's kind of like ... the chat system in a game? Everyone follows the same rules to communicate?"

"Exactly," Elsa smiled, impressed by his intuition. "And just like in your games, there's a lot more going on behind the scenes than what you see on the surface."

As the presentation concluded, the crowd surged forward, buzzing with questions and excitement. Elsa gently guided Aiden to a quieter corner of the hall,

"There's something else you need to understand about the web," she began, her tone growing more serious. "What we just saw? That's only the tip of the iceberg."

Aiden tilted his head, curiosity alight. "What do you mean?"

Elsa paused, considering her words carefully. "Imagine the web as an ocean. What Berners-Lee showed us is like the surface – easily visible, accessible to everyone. But there's a whole world beneath that surface. We call it the deep web."

"The deep web?" Aiden echoed. "Is that like … the dark web we just learned about?"

Elsa shook her head, "Not quite, though that's a common misconception. The deep web is simply any part of the internet that isn't indexed by search engines. Think of it like … the VIP areas in your favorite MMO. You need special permissions or knowledge to access them."

Aiden's eyes lit up with understanding. "Oh! Like private servers or hidden quests?"

"That's a great way to think about it. The deep web includes things like your email inbox, online banking, or private social media accounts. It's not inherently good or bad – it's just hidden from casual browsing."

"Remember when I helped track down that cyberbullying ring at your school last year?" Aiden nodded, and Elsa continued, "The anonymity of the web made it easier for those kids to say cruel things. But that same anonymity also allowed me to infiltrate their network and shut it down."

"So … anonymity is both good and bad?" Aiden asked, his fingers absently tapping on his tablet.

"Exactly," Elsa replied. "It's a double-edged sword. I've used it to protect whistleblowers exposing corporate corruption. But I've also seen it weaponized by scammers and worse."

Suddenly, Elsa's watch beeped, and the ChronoCipher's interface flashed urgently. "Looks like we've got our next challenge, kiddo," she said, her voice taking on a more focused tone. "We need to map the layers of the web to move forward."

"Map the web?" Aiden repeated, excitement creeping into his voice. "Like, all of it?"

Elsa chuckled. "Not quite that ambitious. But we need to outline its structure, from the surface to the deepest layers. What do we know so far?"

Aiden's fingers flew across his tablet. "Well, we've got the surface web, which is everything we can Google. Then the deep web, which is all the stuff that needs special access. Is there more?"

Elsa nodded, her mind racing. "There is. But there are gaps in our understanding. We need to figure out how these layers interact, how information flows between them."

As they huddled together, brainstorming and sketching out ideas, Elsa couldn't help but marvel at the situation. Here she was, in 1993, teaching her son about a web that didn't yet exist, preparing him for a digital landscape that would shape his future.

Aiden's fingers danced across the tablet's surface, his eyes alight with inspiration. "What if we look at it like an iceberg?" he suggested, quickly sketching out a rough diagram. "Like you said earlier, Mom, the surface web is just the tip, and everything else is hidden beneath."

Elsa leaned in, a smile tugging at her tired features. "That's brilliant, Aiden. You're really grasping the concept." She pointed to the bottom of his sketch. "Now, what do you think we'd find in the deepest, darkest part?"

As Aiden pondered, adding details to his diagram, Elsa felt a surge of pride mixed with a twinge of concern. Her son's natural affinity for technology was both a gift and a potential vulnerability in their mission.

"Mom," Aiden's voice pulled her from her thoughts, "have you ever been to the really deep parts of the web?"

Elsa's expression grew serious. "I have, and it's not a place to be taken lightly." She paused, choosing her words carefully. "There was this one time, early in my career ... "

Her voice trailed off, memories flooding back. "I stumbled upon a forum. At first, it seemed harmless – just people sharing tech tips. But as I dug deeper, I realized they were exchanging information on how to exploit security flaws in major systems."

Aiden's eyes widened. "Like, to steal stuff?"

"Worse," Elsa replied, her voice barely above a whisper. "They were planning to manipulate critical infrastructure. Power grids, water systems – things that could hurt a lot of people if tampered with."

"Wow," Aiden murmured. "What did you do?"

"I got out of there and made an anonymous report to the authorities. The forum was shut down a few weeks later – I never heard if any arrests were made. The problem is, once a forum is shut down, it inevitably reopens shortly after under a different name, a different web address, a different location. Where there's a will, there's a way."

She watched as understanding dawned on Aiden's face. "That's why what we're doing is so important, isn't it?" he asked, his usual exuberance tempered by the weight of this revelation.

As they returned to their mapping exercise, finishing each other's thoughts and building on each other's ideas, Elsa felt a glimmer of hope. Perhaps, with Aiden's fresh perspective and her hard-won experience, they could navigate this treacherous digital landscape and make a real difference.

Elsa squinted at the holographic display, her tired eyes straining to make sense of the intricate web of connections they'd mapped out. Aiden paced behind her, his sneakers squeaking on the polished conference room floor.

"We're missing something," Aiden muttered, running a hand through his hair. "It's like there's a piece of the puzzle that just won't fit."

Elsa nodded, feeling the familiar twinge of pain in her shoulders. "You're right. We've mapped the surface web, the deep web, but there's still a gap in our understanding of how they connect to the dark web."

Aiden groaned, flopping dramatically into a nearby chair. "This is impossible! How are we supposed to solve a puzzle about something that doesn't even exist yet?"

"Hey," Elsa said softly, turning to face her son. "Remember, the foundations are already here. We just need to think creatively about how they'll evolve."

Aiden's focus deepened, his thoughts clearly racing. "Okay, so ... anonymity is key in the dark web, right? But how does that work without compromising the whole system?"

As Elsa opened her mouth to respond, Aiden's eyes suddenly lit up. He leaped from his chair, nearly knocking it over in his excitement.

"Wait, wait! What if it's like ... like a game of digital hide and seek?" His hands moved rapidly as he spoke. "You're hidden, but you still need a way to connect with others who are also hidden. So you'd need some kind of ... I don't know, secret handshake or something?"

Elsa felt a smile spreading across her face. "Aiden, that's brilliant! You're talking about encryption and anonymity networks. They act like a series of secret handshakes, allowing users to connect without revealing their true identities or locations."

Aiden grinned, his earlier frustration forgotten. "So it's protective because it keeps people safe from surveillance or persecution, but it's also dangerous because bad guys can use it to hide?"

"It's both a blessing and a curse," Elsa nodded.

As they worked to incorporate this new insight into their map, Elsa couldn't help but marvel at Aiden's ability to see connections she might have missed.

Elsa leaned back in her chair, her tired eyes scanning the completed ChronoPuzzle. The web of interconnected nodes and layers they'd mapped out seemed to pulse with potential, each line a digital artery carrying information across time and space.

"We did it," Aiden breathed. He turned to his mother, eyes bright despite the late hour. "But what does it all mean?"

Elsa ran a hand through her hair, buying time to organize her thoughts. "It means, kiddo, that we're standing at a crossroads. This web we've mapped? It's going to change everything."

"Like how smartphones changed everything for my generation?" Aiden asked, his fingers absently tracing patterns on his tablet screen.

"Exponentially more," Elsa replied, her voice soft but intense.

As they began packing up their equipment, preparing to leave this pivotal moment in 1993, Elsa asked, "Ready for the next jump, kiddo?"

He nodded eagerly, his lanky frame vibrating with anticipation. "Bet! Where are we heading next?

Elsa chuckled, shaking her head. "You'll see soon enough. Remember, we're not just sightseeing. Each stop has a purpose, a piece of the puzzle we need to solve."

The air around them began to shimmer, the conference hall fading at the edges. Elsa felt a familiar tug in her chest, the mix of excitement and apprehension for the unknown challenges ahead.

"Hold tight," she instructed, reaching for Aiden's hand. As their fingers interlocked, the world dissolved into a kaleidoscope of light and data streams.

In the split second before they vanished completely, Elsa caught a glimpse of Tim Berners-Lee on stage, still explaining his world-changing invention. The image seared into her mind, a poignant reminder of the relentless march of progress and the ethical tightrope they all walked in the digital age.

Then, with a flash and a rush of displaced air, Elsa and Aiden were gone, leaving behind only a faint electrical charge and the echoes of a pivotal moment in technological history.

Journal entry – Aiden – January 29, 2028

I think I'm finally starting to get why Mom's always so obsessed with her job. It's like, mad important stuff. No cap, she's pretty much a genius. I never thought coding could be such a flex. It's kinda awesome watching her figure out all these crazy problems and even helping her out sometimes. We make a solid duo, like a tag team. Honestly, it's kinda fun.

I never really thought about how gaming connects to real life and all the sketchy stuff that happens online. But now, I'm kinda seeing it, and I know Mom totally gets it. She's out here, doing all this behind-the-scenes stuff to protect people. Honestly, after this whole mission thing wraps up, I might wanna be a part of that too. Feels like something I could get into.

Chapter 8

Family legacy unveiled (2000s)

The ChronoCipher's ethereal glow faded like a dying star, leaving Elsa and Aiden in the dim twilight of their living room. It was still raining, rivulets streaming down the windows. Elsa blinked, her eyes adjusting to the familiar surroundings. The air hung heavy with the scent of ozone and something older – the musty aroma of time itself.

"We're back," Aiden whispered.

Elsa nodded, her gaze sweeping across the room. Janet's journal lay sprawled open on the coffee table, its pages seeming to whisper secrets. Above it, fragments of holographic data shimmered like fireflies, casting dancing shadows on the walls.

"It's like we never left," Elsa murmured, her joints aching as she lowered herself onto the couch. She wondered if time travel would ever feel routine. Probably not – and that was probably a good thing.

Aiden flopped down beside her, his lanky frame nearly vibrating with nervous energy. "Mom, did you see how the data streams converged when we – "

"Breathe, kiddo," Elsa interrupted gently, placing a hand on his arm. "Let's process for a minute."

As Aiden took a deep breath, Elsa's mind raced. *We've barely scratched the surface,* she thought. *And every answer just leads to more questions.*

"What do you think Grandma Janet was trying to tell us?" Aiden asked, his fingers already twitching toward his ever-present tablet, eager for answers.

Elsa sighed, choosing her words carefully. "I think … she was trying to protect something bigger than herself. Sometimes, when you're dealing with complex systems – whether they're computer networks or human organizations – you have to make difficult choices."

She paused, studying the holographic data swirling above them. It's beautiful, in a way, she mused. Like constellations made of pure information.

"But why would she leave vulnerabilities on purpose?" Aiden pressed.

DOI: 10.1201/9781003501626-8

"Your grandma was brilliant, but she was also idealistic. Maybe she thought future generations – people like us – would be able to fix what she couldn't."

Aiden nodded slowly, his eyes lighting up with understanding. "Like ... leaving cheat codes in a game, but for the good guys?"

Elsa chuckled. "Something like that. Though I think Janet would have a thing or two to say about comparing ARPANET to a video game."

As they lapsed into contemplative silence, Elsa's gaze drifted back to the journal. "*What other secrets are you hiding, Mom?*" she wondered. *And are we ready for what comes next?*

Elsa's fingers traced the worn edges of Janet's journal, her mind awash with conflicting emotions. She let out a slow, measured breath, trying to ease the tension building in her shoulders.

"You all good, Mom?" Aiden's voice cut through her reverie, tinged with concern.

She managed a wan smile. "Just ... processing. It's a lot to take in, you know?"

Aiden nodded, his eyes bright with enthusiasm. "Hundred percent. But isn't it amazing? We're like, decoding history in real time!"

Elsa couldn't help but chuckle at his unbridled excitement. "You sound just like I did at your age," she mused, a wave of melancholy washing over her.

"Really?" Aiden perked up, leaning forward. "What were you like back then?"

Elsa's mind drifted back, memories surfacing like long-buried code. "Oh, I was a real piece of work. All attitude and algorithms."

"Tell me more," Aiden urged, settling in for a story.

Elsa hesitated, weighing the value of sharing her past against the potential risks. But looking at Aiden's eager face, she realized this could be a teachable moment.

"Well," she began, her voice taking on a storyteller's cadence, "picture this: It's the year 2000. I'm 16, and the internet is this wild, untamed frontier ... "

As Elsa's words hung in the air, the ChronoCipher hummed to life, its holographic interface shimmering in its familiar ethereal glow. Suddenly, the room around them dissolved, replaced by a vivid projection of Elsa's teenage bedroom.

Aiden's eyes widened in wonder. "Unreal," he breathed, spinning around to take it all in.

Elsa felt a rush of nostalgia, her hand instinctively reaching out to touch a desk that wasn't really there. "This is ... uncanny," she murmured, her voice tight with emotion.

The room was a perfect snapshot of the early 2000s, filled with relics of a bygone digital era. Aiden moved closer to examine the chunky desktop computer in the corner, its fan whirring softly.

"Is this what passed for cutting-edge back then?" he asked, a hint of amusement in his voice.

Elsa laughed, the sound tinged with both fondness and embarrassment. "Hey, don't knock it. That beauty could run Napster like nobody's business."

She watched as Aiden explored the space, marveling at how accurately the ChronoCipher had recreated her past. Every detail was perfect, from the stack of floppy disks on her desk to the tangle of cords beneath it.

"It's strange," Elsa mused, more to herself than to Aiden. "Being here, seeing all this … it makes me realize how far we've come."

Elsa's gaze drifted to the computer screen, where her AIM profile glowed with an overly enthusiastic array of glitter graphics and a quote from "The Matrix." She couldn't help but chuckle at her teenage self's attempt at digital coolness.

"God, look at that profile. I thought I was so edgy," she said, shaking her head. "But you know what? That girl had no idea how vulnerable she was every time she logged on."

Aiden leaned in closer to the screen, squinting at the flashy display. "It's kinda cute, though. In a retro way."

"Cute, maybe. But also naïve," Elsa replied. She reached out, her fingers ghosting through the holographic keyboard. "I remember thinking the internet was this amazing playground where I could be anyone, do anything. I had no concept of digital footprints or data mining."

The room filled with the opening chords of "Teenage Dirtbag," and Elsa felt a wave of wistfulness wash over her. She closed her eyes for a moment, letting the music transport her back in time.

"You good, Mom?" Aiden asked, concern evident in his voice.

Elsa opened her eyes, offering him a small smile. "Yeah, just … remembering. It's strange to think how much of my life has been defined by technology, even back then."

She walked over to the wall, gesturing to the posters. "Buffy, Linkin Park, 'The Matrix' … they all seemed so revolutionary at the time. But looking back, I can see how they were already hinting at the digital revolution that was coming."

As she spoke, a familiar ache settled in her joints. She flexed her fingers, brushing the discomfort aside with practiced resilience.

"You know, Aiden," she said, turning back to her son, "I think this is why I push so hard for digital ethics now. Because I remember what it was like to be young and trusting in a world that was just learning how to exploit that trust."

As they looked around the room, the door opened and a young Elsa settled into the chair in front of the chunky beige desktop, its fan whirring loudly. The glittery AIM profile cast a soft glow on her face, illuminating her teenage features.

Elsa's breath caught at the sight of her younger self. *How surreal.*

"Mom! Is this you?" Aiden exclaimed with wide eyes. "W-i-i-ld!" He couldn't quite wrap his head around seeing his mother as a teenager, living and breathing right in front of his eyes.

"Oh, look," the young Elsa murmured, a new email notification popping up. " 'ILOVEYOU' with a heart emoticon. How sweet."

Without hesitation, her teenage self clicked on the email. Instantly, the screen flickered, and a cascade of error messages flooded the display.

"No, no, no!" young Elsa's voice rose in panic as she frantically clicked the mouse. "What's happening?"

The computer's drive began to make a sickening grinding noise. Pop-up windows multiplied across the screen, each one a harbinger of digital doom. In the background, "Teenage Dirtbag" continued to play, an oddly upbeat soundtrack to the unfolding disaster.

"Mom?" Aiden's voice cut through the memory. "Is this … ?"

Elsa nodded grimly. "The ILOVEYOU virus. One of the most devastating cyber attacks in history, and I walked right into it."

As they watched, the AIM client started sending messages to all of Elsa's contacts, spreading the virus further.

"I remember the pit in my stomach," Elsa said softly, her hand unconsciously moving to her abdomen. "That moment when you realize you've made a terrible mistake, but it's too late to take it back."

The scene before them dissolved into chaos as teenage Elsa tried desperately to regain control of her computer.

Aiden's eyes widened, a mix of fascination and empathy playing across his expressive features. He ran a hand through his tousled hair, unconsciously mirroring his grandmother's nervous habit.

"You were me back then," he said softly. "Curious. Trusting."

Elsa turned to look at her son, surprise evident in her eyes. She hadn't expected such insight from her usually boisterous teenager. Aiden's gaze remained fixed on the holographic scene, his fingers twitching as if longing to reach out and help his younger mother.

"I mean," Aiden continued, his words tumbling out faster now, "I totally get it. It's like when I almost clicked on that sketchy link in Discord last month. You know, the one promising rare Fortnite skins?" He shook his head, a rueful smile tugging at his lips. "If you hadn't warned me about phishing … "

Elsa reached out and squeezed Aiden's shoulder, a surge of pride and protectiveness washing over her. She marveled at how her son could see past the outdated technology to the universal human experience beneath.

"You're right, kiddo," she said, her voice warm. "The tools change, but the vulnerabilities? Those stay pretty much the same."

Elsa's gaze drifted back to the holographic scene, her younger self frozen in a moment of panic. She sighed, her fingers absently tracing the outline of her ever-present pain relief patch.

Aiden leaned in, his expression tense. "But Mom, you always say the internet's like … like a Swiss Army knife. Useful, but dangerous if you're not careful."

Elsa nodded. "True. But back then? We were kids with a new toy, no instruction manual." She gestured at her teenage self. "Look at me, diving headfirst into the digital ocean without a life jacket. The ILOVEYOU virus, or the Love Bug as it was also known, preyed on the innocence of humans looking for love and connection – a simple email attachment, a 'love letter for you', was all it took to crash infinite systems, cause immense data losses and billions of dollars in financial losses."

"How did it work? And who released it?" Aiden asked, trying to process the amount of damage done by a seemingly innocent little message.

"The worm was released by a Filipino college student as part of a school project, if you can believe that. Once opened, it was designed to infiltrate Microsoft Outlook, scanning users' email address books and sending itself to every contact on that list."

Aiden simply shook his head. "But why would he do this? What was the point?"

"I read somewhere that his goal was to provide free internet access to those who could never afford it by stealing login details. I guess he saw himself as some kind of digital savior, a Robin Hood, if you will. And, he got away with it. He later expressed regret at the damage done, claiming he had no idea it would spread that far."

"You mean he didn't get arrested or anything, even after causing so much carnage?" Aiden asked, eyebrows raised so high they almost touched the ceiling.

"Nope. He was not. At the time, there were no laws against designing malware in the Philippines."

"No freaking way!" Aiden exclaimed dramatically. "Seriously? No cap?"

"No cap!" Elsa chuckled. "This was really the moment in internet history that shocked big tech globally into doing something serious about cybersecurity. To this day, it remains one of the effective strains of malware in history."

As if on cue, the holographic Elsa clicked frantically, trying to undo the damage. Aiden winced in sympathy.

She paused, lost in thought. *I was so eager to connect, to explore. Just like Aiden is now. How do I protect him without stifling that spark?*

Journal entry – Elsa – May 4, 2000

Oh. My. Goodness. What a day! It's been an absolute disaster, and I can't stop crying. Jeez. All I did was click on a lousy, sketchy email – I thought it was from a boy. It's so lame. And now everyone I know has had their computer infected, and everyone they know. I couldn't stop it. I posted on Myspace to try and warn everyone, but it was too late ... I am humiliated.

I think I'm going to have a panic attack. I need to take a chill pill. See you later ...

Okay, I'm back. I can't believe that happened. Mom says it's an important lesson that I've learned the hard way. Thanks, Mom. Like I didn't realize that. Apparently it's called the Love Bug ... some kind of virus. I never want to be caught like that ever again – I am going to fight these douchebags for the rest of my life. I swear! I might be ashamed now, but I am not going to take this lying down. Absolutely not. Not just for me. I am going to do everything in my power to protect the innocent people that are affected by these monsters. It will be my life's mission!

"Mom?" Aiden's voice pulled her back to the present. "You alright?"

Elsa blinked, realizing she'd been silent for a moment too long. "Yeah, just ... thinking. This whole trip down memory lane? It's a reminder. We need to be careful, but we can't let fear paralyze us."

Aiden nodded, his fingers drumming a rapid rhythm on his knee. "So ... what's next? We've seen your past, but what about Grandma Janet's?"

Elsa reached for Janet's journal, its worn leather cover a stark contrast to the holographic displays surrounding them. "Good thinking, kiddo. Let's see what other secrets this holds."

As Elsa flipped through the pages, Aiden leaned in, his eyes widening at the complex diagrams and dense notations. "Incredible, it's like trying to read alien hieroglyphics!"

Elsa chuckled. "Your grandmother had a unique way of – " She stopped abruptly, her finger hovering over a page titled "*The Unseen Compromise.*"

Aiden's brow furrowed. "Mom? What is it?"

Elsa swallowed hard, her voice barely above a whisper. "I think I've found something, Aiden."

As they read together, Aiden's expression shifted from curiosity to confusion. "Wait, what? Intentional vulnerabilities? Why would Grandma Janet do that?"

Elsa's eyes scanned the page, her heart heavy. "Military pressure. They wanted ... backdoors, essentially."

Aiden's face scrunched up in disgust. "But that's like ... leaving your house unlocked on purpose! It goes against everything you've taught me about cybersecurity!"

"I know, honey," Elsa sighed, running a hand through her hair in the family way. She's struggling too, Aiden realized. This isn't just tech stuff for her. It's family.

"Your grandmother was brilliant, but she was also human," Elsa continued, her voice a mix of admiration and disappointment. "She had to make impossible choices."

Aiden bit his lip, processing. "So ... what do we do with this information?"

Elsa looked at her son, seeing not just a tech-savvy teenager, but a young man grappling with complex ethical dilemmas. "We learn from it, Aiden. We use it to make better choices, to build stronger, safer systems."

As they bent their heads together over the journal, the room hummed with the weight of legacy and the promise of redemption.

Aiden's fingers traced the faded ink of Janet's handwriting, his eyes widening as he deciphered a pattern in the seemingly random notations. "Mom, look at this," he breathed, excitement rippling through his voice. "These numbers, they're not just data points. They're ... coordinates?"

Elsa's eyes sharpened as she examined the markings, but her thoughts drifted for a moment. "Aiden, this reminds me of something from tech history. Have you heard of Ken Thompson?"

"Ken Thompson? Yeah, the Unix guy, right?"

"Exactly. In 1984, he gave a speech called *Reflections on Trusting Trust*. He'd created a hidden backdoor in the Unix operating system through its compiler. The scariest part? Even if someone reviewed all the source code, they wouldn't find it. The compiler was designed to hide the vulnerability when it was compiled – completely undetectable."

Aiden blinked. "That's insane. He hacked his own system ... to prove a point?"

"Exactly," Elsa said. "His point was simple but powerful: *If you don't understand a system entirely, it can be used against you.* That's why this ... what your grandmother did ... isn't just some theoretical problem. It's real and incredibly dangerous."

Aiden took a deep breath, his eyes narrowing in thought. "So Grandma Janet was under pressure to build something like that. But maybe she left clues for someone like us to find."

Elsa leaned in, her analytical mind kicking into overdrive. "You're right. And these symbols ... they're not part of any programming language I know." A flicker of tension played at the edges of her mouth as she pieced it together. "They're markers. Signposts."

"Breadcrumbs," Aiden whispered, the realization dawning on him. "Grandma Janet left us a trail to follow."

Elsa's eyes misted over, a complex cocktail of emotions swirling within her. "She knew. She knew someone would come along to fix what she couldn't."

Aiden looked up at his mother, determination etched across his young face. "Us. She was waiting for us, wasn't she?"

Elsa nodded, her voice thick with emotion. "Your grandmother always believed in the power of future generations. She used to say, 'The best firewalls are built by those who've seen the flames.' "

"But why not just fix it herself?" Aiden asked, his fingers still tracing the intricate patterns in the journal.

Elsa sighed, her mind racing through the complexities of Janet's situation. "Sometimes, honey, the very constraints that bind us can become the catalyst for innovation. Janet couldn't openly defy her superiors, but she could leave a path for those who came after."

Aiden's eyes lit up with understanding. "Like ethical hacking! We learn the vulnerabilities to patch them, not exploit them."

"Exactly," Elsa smiled, pride swelling in her chest. "Your grandmother was playing the long game, trusting that someday, someone would come along with the knowledge and the courage to finish what she started."

Elsa's fingers traced the elegantly scrawled words in Janet's journal, her heart racing as she read aloud: "I fear the shadow we cast will grow beyond our control. I hope those who come after will fortify what we have left exposed. Follow the crumbs."

Aiden leaned in, his eyes wide. "Mom, it's like she knew we'd be here."

Elsa nodded, her throat tight. "She did, in a way. Your grandmother always thought ahead."

As the weight of Janet's words sank in, Elsa felt a complex brew of emotions churning inside her. Pride in her mother's foresight mingled with a gnawing anxiety about the magnitude of the task before them.

"What do you think she meant by 'shadow'?" Aiden asked, his thoughts circling the word, trying to unravel it.

Elsa took a deep breath, choosing her words carefully. "I think she saw the potential for the technology she helped create to be misused. The internet, AI, all of it – they're incredible tools, but in the wrong hands ... "

"They become weapons," Aiden finished, his voice barely above a whisper.

"Exactly," Elsa said, squeezing his shoulder. "But in true Janet style, she didn't just leave us warnings. She left us a roadmap."

As they pored over the journal, decoding Janet's cryptic notes, Elsa found herself oscillating between awe at her mother's brilliance and a creeping sense of inadequacy. "Can we really do this, Aiden? Can we live up to her legacy?"

Aiden looked up, his eyes shining with determination. "We have to try, Mom. Grandma believed in us. We can't let her down. Grandma knew what she was doing, we have to trust her. She won't let us down either. Also, we have digital Grandma to help us!"

Elsa nodded, swallowing hard. The responsibility felt overwhelming, but Aiden's unwavering faith bolstered her resolve. Together, they bent over the journal, ready to follow Janet's breadcrumbs wherever they might lead.

Elsa's fingers traced the faded ink of her mother's handwriting, a bitter-sweet smile tugging at her lips. "You know, Aiden, I always thought of Mom as this infallible genius. The Oracle of ARPANET, they called her. But now … "

She trailed off, her eyes fixed on a particularly cryptic passage. Aiden leaned in, curiosity piqued. "What's going on, Mom?"

Elsa sighed, running a hand through her hair. "It's just … she made compromises. Big ones. She knew the vulnerabilities she was building into ARPANET, but she did it anyway."

"Maybe she didn't have a choice," Aiden offered gently.

"There's always a choice," Elsa muttered, more to herself than to her son. She stood up abruptly, pacing the room. "God, I can't decide if I'm more impressed by her foresight or frustrated by her compliance."

As if in response to her turmoil, the ChronoCipher began to hum, its surface pulsing with an eerie blue light. Elsa and Aiden exchanged a wary glance.

"Mom?" Aiden's voice wavered slightly. "What's it doing?"

Elsa approached the device cautiously, her muscular exhaustion moment-arily forgotten. "I'm not sure, but I think … I think it's presenting us with a new challenge."

The ChronoCipher's display flickered to life, revealing another complex array of symbols and code. Elsa's eyes widened as she recognized elements of advanced encryption algorithms interwoven with what appeared to be DNA sequencing.

"Well," she said, a hint of her old dry humor creeping into her voice once again, "looks like your grandma's left us quite the puzzle to solve. Ready to dive in, kiddo?"

Aiden nodded eagerly, already pulling up a chair. As they began to tackle the new challenge, Elsa couldn't shake the feeling that they were standing on the precipice of something monumental – for better or worse.

The ChronoCipher's hum intensified, its crystalline surface now pulsating with an urgent, otherworldly glow. Suddenly, a beam of light shot out from its core, coalescing into a shimmering holographic message that hovered in the air before them:

"Face the Legacy: Mend the Past to Protect the Future."

Elsa's breath caught in her throat. "What on earth … ?"

This time Janet's digital twin appeared more vibrant, more complete, her eyes blazing with an intensity that made Elsa take an involuntary step back.

"Mom?" Elsa whispered, her voice a mix of awe and trepidation.

The holographic Janet turned to face them, her gaze sharp and focused. When she spoke, her voice carried a clarity and conviction that sent shivers down Elsa's spine.

"The time has come," Janet announced, her tone brooking no argument. "The vulnerabilities I left behind must be addressed. The future of our digital world hangs in the balance."

Elsa's thoughts raced, a whirlwind of emotions threatening to overwhelm her. She glanced at Aiden, seeing her own mix of excitement and apprehension mirrored in his eyes.

"I don't understand," Elsa said, fighting to keep her voice steady. "How are we supposed to mend the past? And why now?"

Janet's hologram smiled, a familiar glint of challenge in her eyes. "Because now, you have the tools and the knowledge to do what I couldn't. The clues I left behind in my journal were always meant for you, Elsa. You and Aiden."

Janet's holographic form flickered, her expression softening as she gazed at Elsa and Aiden. "To understand what must be done, you must see what was concealed," she said, her voice carrying the weight of decades of secrecy. "Trust that the solutions you seek are within you."

Elsa's heart raced, her mind struggling to process the implications of her mother's words. She took a deep breath, steadying herself. "What exactly was concealed, Mom? And how can we possibly find solutions to problems we don't even fully understand?"

As Janet's projection began to respond, Aiden stepped forward, his eyes alight with curiosity. "Is this about the vulnerabilities in ARPANET? The ones you were pressured to include?"

Elsa watched her mother's hologram closely, noticing a flicker of pain cross her face. It was strange, she thought, how lifelike this digital twin was, capturing even the subtlest of her mother's expressions.

"Yes, Aiden," Janet confirmed, her voice tinged with regret. "But it's more than that. The compromises I made ... they've cascaded through time, creating weaknesses in our digital infrastructure that we never anticipated."

Elsa felt a surge of frustration. "Why didn't you just fix it yourself? Why leave it to us?"

Janet's hologram turned to face her daughter directly. "Because I realized that the future of technology couldn't be shaped by one person's vision alone. It needed to evolve, to be guided by new perspectives, by those who would inherit the digital world we created."

As Elsa processed this, she felt a mix of pride and trepidation. Her mother had trusted her – trusted them – with this monumental task. But could they really live up to such expectations?

"How do we even begin?" Elsa asked, her voice barely above a whisper. But Janet faded away with a faint smile.

The ChronoCipher suddenly whirred to life, its gears spinning and lights pulsing in an intricate dance. A holographic display materialized in the air between Elsa and Aiden, filled with cascading lines of code and complex mathematical equations.

Elsa's eyes widened, her heart racing as she recognized fragments of her mother's handwriting interwoven with the digital script. "It's ... it's embedded in Mom's notes," she breathed, reaching out to touch the shimmering display.

Aiden leaned forward, a shadow crossing his face. "This isn't just an algorithm," he said quietly. "Look at the way it's built. The structure. The movement. It's like ... ." He hesitated, his voice dropping lower. "It's alive."

Elsa nodded, her mind already racing to decipher the puzzle before them. "Mom always said that the best encryption was one that could adapt, evolve. But this ... this is beyond anything I've ever seen."

As they studied the shifting patterns, Janet's hologram reappeared and spoke again, her voice carrying a weight of responsibility. "This is the Ethical Encryption, a safeguard I built into the very fabric of our digital world. It's not just about protecting data, it's about preserving the integrity of human choice in the face of advancing technology."

Elsa felt a chill run down her spine. "So decrypting this ... "

"Will give you the power to reshape the foundations of our digital infrastructure," Janet finished before dissolving into a cascade of pixels with a smile.

Elsa's fingers swept across the holographic interface, her eyes focused with sharp intensity. "The Vigenère cipher is just the outer shell," she muttered. "Something else is hidden deeper inside ... "

Aiden leaned in, his eyes darting across the shifting patterns. "Look, Mom! Some of these characters seem to flicker differently than the others. Could that be the steganography part?"

"Good catch, kiddo. Let's isolate those flickering characters and see what we're dealing with."

As they worked, Elsa's mind raced. *What if we can't solve this in time?* She forcefully pushed the doubts aside, focusing on the task at hand.

"It's like a digital onion," Aiden mused, his fingers flying over his tablet. "Each layer we peel back reveals another puzzle underneath."

Elsa chuckled, despite the tension. "Your grandma always did have a flair for the dramatic. I bet she'd love hearing you describe her work that way."

They fell into a rhythm, mother and son working in tandem. Elsa tackled the Vigenère cipher, her years of experience guiding her through the complex substitutions. Aiden, meanwhile, focused on isolating the hidden data within the flickering characters.

"Mom," Aiden said suddenly, his voice tight with excitement. "I think I've found something. Check out this pattern in the flickering bits."

Elsa leaned over, her eyes widening as she saw what Aiden had uncovered. "It's ... it's a map. No, wait. It's the structure of a network. The original ARPANET?"

Janet flickered to life again. "You're on the right track," she said, her voice filled with pride and urgency. "But remember, the true power lies not in the past, but in how you apply these lessons to the future."

Elsa nodded, her throat tight with emotion. "We won't let you down, Mom. We'll finish what you started."

As they delved deeper into the encryption, Elsa couldn't shake the feeling that they were racing against time. Somewhere out there, Lucien was working to unravel the same secrets. But here, in this moment, Elsa felt a surge of hope. Together, she and Aiden just might have what it takes to protect the digital future her mother had fought so hard to secure.

Aiden's fingers flew across the holographic keyboard. "Mom, check this out," he said, gesturing to a series of letters that seemed to pop out from the rest of Janet's notes. "These bold characters ... they're not random. It's like they're trying to tell us something."

Elsa leaned in, her eyes scanning the text. A pattern emerged, triggering a memory. "Wait a second," she murmured, her voice tinged with excitement. "I've seen this before. It's a keyword ... for the Vigenère cipher!"

As she spoke, Elsa's mind raced through possibilities. What if this was the key to unlocking her mother's hidden message?

"Can you decipher it?" Aiden asked, his eyes shining with curiosity.

Elsa nodded, her fingers already moving to input the keyword. "Let's see what Grandma Janet left for us," she said, a hint of nervousness in her voice.

As they worked together, applying the keyword to the cipher, letters began to materialize on the screen. Elsa felt her heart racing, wondering what secrets her mother had embedded in this complex encryption.

"Yes! It's working!" Aiden exclaimed, leaning forward eagerly.

The message slowly came into focus, revealing words that made Elsa's breath catch in her throat. She read aloud, her voice barely above a whisper, "The foundation is yours to rebuild."

Aiden looked at her, his expression a mix of awe and uncertainty. "What does it mean, Mom?"

Elsa sat back, her mind reeling with the implications. "It means," she said slowly, "that your grandmother left us more than just a puzzle. She left us a mission."

Elsa's fingers hovered over the keyboard, trembling slightly as she absorbed the weight of her mother's words. "Trust in the next generation to secure what she could not," she murmured, her voice a mixture of reverence and trepidation. "Your grandmother was brilliant, but she worked within constraints we can't even imagine. The early days of the internet were like ... building a house without knowing what kind of storms it might face."

"And now we're supposed to, what, renovate?" Aiden's hands fidgeting with nervous energy.

"Exactly," Elsa said, a hint of her dry wit creeping into her voice. "We're here to reinforce the foundation and patch the leaks."

Aiden's face lit up with understanding. "Like in Fortress Defender! When you have to upgrade your base defenses against new types of attacks!"

Elsa chuckled, grateful for her son's ability to bridge complex concepts with relatable analogies. "That's not far off, actually. Except the stakes are a bit higher than losing a game."

She turned back to the screen, her fingers attacking the keyboard as she pulled up additional data. "Look here," she said, pointing to a complex network diagram. "This is a simplified version of how data moves across the internet. Each node, each connection, is a potential vulnerability. But it's not just about patching holes. We need to anticipate future threats, build in safeguards that can adapt and evolve."

Elsa leaned back in her chair, wincing slightly as her muscles protested. She took a deep breath, her eyes flickering to the holographic display of encryption algorithms hovering above her desk.

"Alright, Aiden," she began, her voice taking on the tone of a seasoned professor. "Let's dive into the nitty-gritty of what we're dealing with here. The Vigenère cipher is like a polyalphabetic version of the Caesar cipher. Imagine a secret handshake that changes every time you use it."

Elsa couldn't help but smile, recognizing the same look of intense focus she often wore herself.

"But that's just the beginning," she continued. "Steganography is about hiding the very existence of the message. It's like … hiding a secret note inside a normal-looking picture."

"So it's not just about making the message unreadable, but invisible too?" Aiden asked, leaning forward.

"Exactly," Elsa confirmed, a hint of pride in her voice. "Your grandma was a master at layering these techniques. But here's the thing, kiddo – knowing how to build these walls also means knowing how to break them down."

Aiden's eyes widened. "Isn't that what ethical hacking is about?"

Elsa nodded. "It's about using our skills to find the weak spots before the bad guys do. We're like … digital locksmiths, testing the security to make it stronger."

As she spoke, Elsa couldn't help but reflect on her own journey. The thrill of cracking codes, the weight of responsibility, the constant dance between creation and deconstruction. It was a legacy she was now passing on to Aiden, for better or worse.

"But mom," Aiden said, his voice thoughtful, "isn't it dangerous? Knowing how to break into systems?"

Elsa felt a surge of maternal pride at her son's perceptiveness. "It's not just about *can we* do it, but *should we*? And if we do, how do we ensure it's for the right reasons?"

She paused, gathering her thoughts. "That's why ethics are so crucial in this field. We have to be the guardians, the protectors."

The ChronoCipher, previously dormant on the desk, exploded into life with a cacophony of discordant beeps and flashing lights. Its holographic display flickered erratically, distorting the air around it like a heat mirage.

Elsa's heart leaped into her throat. "Aiden, get back!" she commanded, instinctively stepping between her son and the malfunctioning device.

As if in response to her protective gesture, the ChronoCipher's chaotic display coalesced into a familiar, yet chilling shadowy form. Then, out of the ether, a shadowy figure materialized before them, his tall figure looming larger than life in the holographic projection.

"Well, well," his smooth voice filled the room. "Isn't this a touching family moment?"

Elsa recognized that voice and her mind raced. How had he infiltrated the ChronoCipher? What did he want? Her fingers twitched, longing for a keyboard, some way to counter this digital intrusion.

"Lucien Morvain," Janet said, her voice steady despite the looks of confusion and shock from Elsa and Aiden. "I see you still haven't learned to knock."

A ghost of a smile played on Lucien's holographic lips. "Oh, Janet. Always so quick with a quip. But I'm afraid your little encryption lessons won't be enough this time."

Aiden pressed closer to Elsa's side. She could feel him trembling slightly, but his voice was defiant when he spoke. "We'll stop you. Whatever you're planning."

Lucien's pale eyes fixed on Aiden, calculating and cold. "Ah, the next generation of Winter ingenuity. Tell me, boy, do you truly understand the flawed world your grandmother helped create?"

Elsa's mind whirled. So this was Lucien Morvain. She recognized that name. Her mother's archnemesis. An all-round nasty guy from the stories she'd heard – an evil genius in every sense of the word. The creator of the ChronoCipher. How much did Lucien know of their progress? How much should she reveal? She opted for a defensive strategy. "The only flaw here is your twisted vision, Lucien. Whatever you think you're going to accomplish, you're wrong."

Lucien's holographic form shifted, his impeccable suit rippling as he leaned toward them, his pale eyes boring into Elsa and Aiden. His voice, soft yet commanding, filled the room with an unsettling calm.

"Your family's naivety built this flawed world. It's time for someone with *true* vision to reconstruct it."

The words hit Elsa like a physical blow. She felt Aiden stiffen beside her, his hand gripping hers tightly. Her mind raced, trying to process the implications of Lucien's statement.

"Reconstruct?" Elsa challenged, her voice steadier than she felt. "You mean destroy. You can't possibly understand the complexities of what my mother – "

"Oh, but I do understand, Elsa," Lucien interrupted, his tone dripping with condescension. "I understand far more than Janet ever did. She saw the potential for connection, but failed to grasp the inevitable corruption that would follow."

Elsa's free hand clenched into a fist. How dare he speak about her mother like that? But beneath her anger, a seed of doubt took root. Had her mother's work truly been so flawed?

"You're wrong," Aiden piped up, his young voice cutting through Elsa's internal struggle. "Grandma Janet left us the tools to fix things. She believed in us."

Lucien's attention shifted to Aiden, his gaze softening in a way that made Elsa's skin crawl. "Such faith in family. It's ... admirable. Misplaced, but admirable."

Elsa stepped in front of Aiden protectively, her eyes narrowing as she faced Lucien. The exhaustion that had been weighing on her for years seemed to evaporate in an instant, replaced by a fierce determination.

"You can't fix the present by erasing the past," Elsa declared, her voice carrying the weight of her years as an ethical hacker. She thought of the ILOVEYOU virus, of countless vulnerabilities she'd patched, of the intricate web of human decisions that had shaped the digital landscape. "Our history, flaws and all, is what guides us forward."

Lucien's pale eyes glinted with amusement, a smirk playing at the corners of his mouth. He took a step closer, his movements fluid and predatory. "Oh, Elsa," he said, his voice a silky whisper that sent chills down her spine. "You still think in such linear terms. Watch me. Unless you can stop me."

The challenge hung in the air between them. Elsa's brain was a storm of possibilities, each one more urgent than the last, analyzing potential vectors of attack, considering what Lucien might do next. She felt Aiden shift behind her, and knew he was probably already formulating some brilliant counter-strategy.

"We will stop you," Elsa said, infusing her words with a confidence she didn't entirely feel. But as she spoke, she realized it wasn't just bravado. They had the ChronoCipher, Janet's breadcrumbs, and most importantly, each other. "Whatever you're planning, Lucien, you're not the only one who can think ahead."

Lucien's eyes narrowed, his focus shifting to the shimmering hologram of Janet Winters. With a flick of his wrist, he produced a sleek, obsidian device. "Your grandmother's digital likeness is impressive, Elsa. But like all things, it can be ... improved."

A beam of pulsing crimson light erupted from Lucien's device, enveloping Janet's hologram. The image flickered, lines of corrupted code rippling across her form.

"No!" Elsa lunged forward, fingers flying across the ChronoCipher's interface. I can't let him take control. Think, Elsa, think! She urged herself, recalling every encryption trick she'd ever learned.

Aiden's voice cut through her panic. "Mom, the journal! There might be a failsafe!"

Elsa's eyes darted to Janet's open journal. Of course. Mom always planned ahead. "Keep him talking, Aiden," she whispered, diving into the pages.

"What's your endgame here, Lucien?" Aiden challenged, buying time. "Rewrite history in your image?"

Lucien chuckled, his attention split between corrupting Janet's twin and addressing Aiden. "Oh, it's far grander than that, my boy. I'm not erasing history – I'm optimizing it."

As Elsa's fingers traced the journal's hidden codes, Janet's hologram spoke, her voice distorted but defiant. "You ... cannot ... control ... what you do not ... understand, Lucien."

Elsa's heart raced. Time was running out. She had to find the key before Lucien fully corrupted her mother's digital legacy – and with it, the power to reshape the past, present, and future.

Elsa's eyes widened as she deciphered a hidden pattern in Janet's journal. *Clever, Mom. Always three steps ahead.* She glanced up, catching Aiden's eye. "The ChronoCipher," she mouthed silently.

Aiden nodded imperceptibly, his hands already moving across the device's interface. Elsa turned her attention back to Lucien, buying more time.

"You're missing too many pieces, Lucien," she said, her voice steady despite her racing heart. "The ChronoCipher isn't just a tool. It's a legacy."

Lucien's smirk faltered for a moment. "A legacy of shortsightedness, perhaps. Your mother's work was ... incomplete."

That's it, Elsa thought. *Keep talking.* Out loud, she challenged, "And you think you can complete it? You don't even have all the data."

As she spoke, Aiden's fingers flew across the ChronoCipher, inputting a complex sequence of commands based on the patterns Elsa had uncovered.

Lucien's eyes narrowed. "I have more than enough to – "

Suddenly, Janet's hologram stabilized, the corrupted code receding. "Insufficient access," it announced in Janet's voice, now clear and strong. "Initiating recursive encryption protocol."

Lucien snarled, his device sputtering. "What have you done?"

Elsa allowed herself a small smile. "Like I said, it's a legacy. And it's not yours to claim."

In an angry red flash, Lucien faded into shadow, scowling with cold anger as he went.

"*We've bought ourselves some time,*" she thought, "*but we're far from safe.*" She turned to Aiden, her voice urgent. "We need to secure the remaining data and fortify the ChronoCipher. Fast."

Aiden nodded, already pulling up holographic schematics. "On it. But Mom, if Lucien gets his hands on even a fraction of this ... that guy is super sus. Gives me the ick in a major way."

"I know," Elsa said grimly. "He could rewrite history itself. We can't let that happen."

As they worked feverishly to safeguard Janet's remaining data, Elsa couldn't shake a chilling thought. *We're racing against time to protect time itself. And failure isn't an option.*

As her fingers moved with years of experience, sweat beaded on her forehead as she fought against the familiar ache in her joints.

"Aiden, I need you to run a recursive encryption on the temporal coordinates," she said, her voice taut with urgency. "Use the Vigenère-based algorithm we found in Janet's notes."

Aiden nodded, his lanky frame hunched over his tablet. "On it. But Mom, what if Lucien's already accessed part of the temporal matrix?"

Elsa's stomach churned. "Then we'll have to isolate and contain any compromised data streams. Can you – "

A sudden burst of static cut through the air and Lucien's voice emerged, distorted but unmistakable. "Your efforts are admirable, but futile. The future requires a steady hand, not sentimental attachments to flawed legacies."

Elsa's jaw clenched. "Aiden, keep working. I'll handle this." She turned to face Lucien's flickering image. "And what makes you think your hand is steadier than ours?"

As she engaged Lucien, buying time, Elsa's mind raced. We're so close. If we can just stabilize the temporal lock …

Aiden's excited voice broke through her concentration. "Mom! I think I've got it!"

Elsa spun back to the ChronoCipher, her heart pounding. The holographic display scintillated, lines of code coalescing into a complex, pulsing lattice.

"It's beautiful," Aiden breathed.

Elsa allowed herself a small smile, pride and love swelling in her chest. "You did it, kiddo. We did it."

As the ChronoCipher hummed once again with stability, Elsa felt a weight lift from her shoulders. They weren't out of danger yet, but in this moment, facing whatever came next alongside her brilliant son, she felt a flicker of hope she hadn't dared to embrace in years.

Elsa's fingers traced the intricate patterns of code her mother had woven decades ago. Her eyes stung with unshed tears as the full weight of Janet's legacy settled upon her.

"Mom?" Aiden's voice was soft, tinged with concern. "Are you all good?"

Elsa took a deep breath, her gaze still fixed on the pulsing lattice of light. "I think I am, honey. For the first time in a long time." She turned to face her son, a bittersweet smile playing at her lips. "I thought your grandmother had failed somehow. That she'd left us with an impossible mess to clean up. But now I see … "

Her voice trailed off as she struggled to find the words. Aiden stepped closer, his lanky frame radiating warmth and understanding beyond his years.

"What is it? What do you see, Mom?"

Elsa's tired eyes crinkled at the corners. "Hope, Aiden. I see hope. And trust." She gestured to the complex algorithm before them. "Your grandmother ... she knew she couldn't solve everything. But she believed in us – in the future – enough to leave us the tools to finish what she started."

Aiden nodded, his face lighting up with that familiar spark of enthusiasm. "Grandma didn't fail," he said, his voice firm with conviction. "She trusted us to finish what she started. And we will."

She reached out, ruffling Aiden's hair affectionately. As her son ducked away with a good-natured groan, Elsa turned back to the ChronoCipher, her resolve strengthened. *I understand now, Mom,* she thought. *And I won't let you down.*

Elsa's fingers flew across the holographic keyboard, her eyes narrowing with fierce concentration. The familiar ache in her joints faded to background noise as she immersed herself in lines of code.

A notification pinged, harsh and urgent. Elsa's breath caught as a familiar silhouette materialized in the corner of their digital workspace.

Lucien's voice, smooth as silk and cold as ice, filled the room. "How touching. The family that codes together, fails together."

Elsa instinctively moved to shield Aiden, her voice tight. "What do you want, Lucien?"

The holographic figure smiled, a predator's grin. "Oh, Elsa. I want what I've always wanted. A clean slate. A chance to rewrite the flawed code of human nature itself."

The air crackled with tension as Lucien's image flickered, revealing glimpses of intricate schematics. "While you've been playing family reunion, I've been busy. Care to guess how many identities I can steal in a nanosecond?"

Elsa's mind raced, calculating possibilities, each more horrifying than the last. "Lucien, whatever you're planning – "

"Is already in motion," he interrupted, his eyes gleaming with triumph. "Catch me if you can, ELIZA kid."

The hologram vanished, leaving Elsa and Aiden staring at the space where it had been, the weight of an unseen threat pressing down on them.

Elsa's fingers sailed across the holographic interface, pulling up streams of data and security logs. Her heart pounded as the implications of Lucien's threat became clear.

"Aiden," she said, her voice tight with urgency, "I need you to run a deep scan on the ChronoCipher's recent activity. Look for any anomalies, no matter how small."

As Aiden got to work, Elsa's mind raced. What was Lucien's endgame? She muttered to herself, "Identity theft on a massive scale ... but why include the deceased?"

Suddenly, a horrifying realization struck her. "Oh god, he's not just stealing identities. He's planning to rewrite them."

Aiden looked up, his young face etched with concern. "Mom, what does that mean?"

Elsa took a deep breath, trying to steady herself. "It means Lucien isn't just after financial gain or personal information. He's trying to alter the very fabric of our digital history. By manipulating both living and deceased identities, he could rewrite entire family lines, change records, erase, or create people at will."

The ChronoCipher hummed ominously, its display flickering with what looked like cascading lines of corrupted code.

"Mom, check!" Aiden pointed at the screen. "These patterns ... they're like, wild, like nothing I've ever seen before."

Elsa leaned in, her eyes widening. "That's because they're not just code, Aiden. They're timelines. Lucien isn't just hacking systems; he's hacking history itself."

As the gravity of the situation sank in, Elsa felt a mix of dread and determination. She turned to her son, her voice resolute. "We need to stop him, Aiden. Not just for us, but for everyone whose lives he's threatening to erase or rewrite. Are you with me?"

Aiden nodded, his jaw set with a determination that mirrored his mother's. "Bet, Mom. You know it. Where do we start?"

She gestured to the swirling data streams surrounding them. " We adapt, we learn, we stay one step ahead."

Elsa's fingers flew across the ChronoCipher's interface in a rush of adrenaline. "We start by tracing Lucien's digital footprint through time. If we can predict his next move, we might be able to cut him off."

The ChronoCipher pulsed, projecting a complex web of timelines and data streams. Elsa's brow furrowed as she decoded the patterns. "He's targeting key moments in technological history. Look here," she pointed to a glowing node, "the creation of the first computer virus. And here, the dawn of social media."

"Mom," Aiden's voice wavered slightly, "if we jump now, how do we know we won't get lost in time ourselves?"

Elsa paused, her hand hovering over the activation sequence. She turned to her son, seeing not just the eager teenager, but the weight of their family legacy reflected in his eyes. "We don't," she admitted, her voice soft but steady. "But sometimes, Aiden, the biggest risks carry the most important rewards. Your grandmother knew that. Now it's our turn. We adapt, we learn, we stay one step ahead."

With a final shared look of determination, Elsa activated the device. The room around them began to blur, reality itself seeming to bend and warp. As the familiar sensation of temporal displacement washed over them, Elsa's last thought before they plunged into the unknown was a silent promise: *We won't let you down, Mom. We'll finish what you started.*

The ChronoCipher's light engulfed them, and with a flash, Elsa and Aiden vanished, diving headlong into their most perilous adventure yet, the fate of digital history hanging in the balance.

Journal entry – Janet – December 1, 1973

Compromise. A word I loathe. But one that seems to have become a part of my daily existence as of late.

Compliance. Also a loathsome concept.

Yet, I find myself caught between the two. I take my work so seriously. Sometimes it feels like it's my whole existence – there must be something deeper to explore in that, but who has the time?

The pressure mounts daily, calls coming in from every side. It feels immense sometimes. How does one make the morally, ethically correct decisions when faced with such pressure? Do I deliberately leave these vulnerabilities here, or do I close them off? What is the right thing to do. Do I trust that future generations will solve the problems that I leave behind. Creating the prefect system is just not possible right now.

I can only hope that I will one day teach my children well enough, and that their passion and skill will guide them. I hope that they will not only be smart enough to follow my trail, but also to fix what I have left behind.

Chapter 9

The rise of social media, identity theft, and manipulation (2000s)

Elsa stepped through the temporal rift, her hand clasped tightly around Aiden's, and they emerged into the early 2000s – a time of burgeoning digital dreams just poised on the cusp of reality. The ChronoCipher had done its work seamlessly, depositing them amid a buzzing tech conference where the air vibrated with the hum of possibility.

Aiden let out a low whistle, his eyes widening as the novelty shimmered in the atmosphere. Booths adorned with bright banners and prototype displays stretched out before them, each vying for attention in a cacophony of innovation.

"Keep close," Elsa murmured, her gaze sweeping across the room with practiced caution.

They navigated through the throngs of attendees, each step a dance between curiosity and restraint. Aiden's nimble fingers itched to explore every gadget and interface on display, but he stayed anchored to Elsa's side, tethered by an unspoken understanding.

"Check out these people," Aiden said, gesturing toward a group gathered around a charismatic speaker who was detailing how their social media platform would connect friends and family across the globe. "They have no idea what's coming, do they?"

"Most visionaries don't," Elsa replied, her voice tinged with the weight of hindsight. She watched the entrepreneurs with tired but sharp eyes, noting the passion that fueled their pitches and the eager nods from their audience.

"Amazing, isn't it?" she replied, an edge of caution in her voice only detectable by those who knew her well. "A whole world connected at your fingertips."

"Isn't this what Grandma wanted?" Aiden asked, his face glowing with reflected light. "To bring people together?"

Elsa nodded, remembering her mother's idealistic dreams spun amid the hum of giant computers, dreams that now felt both realized and distorted. "Yes, she did," she said, "Remember – every share, every like, every friend request ... it leaves a digital footprint."

DOI: 10.1201/9781003501626-9

"Which is mad lit!" Aiden countered, still absorbed in the novelty. "It's like we're all part of this big story, writing it together."

Elsa's smile was wistful as she observed her son. He was a child of this new era, one where sharing equated to existence. Yet, beneath the veneer of global harmony, she sensed the undercurrents of exploitation, the data streams being diverted into invisible reservoirs. She hesitated to voice her fears, not wanting to cloud his vision but feeling the responsibility to guide him.

"Stories are powerful, Aiden," she finally said, her hand resting lightly on his shoulder. "But so is the pen that writes them, and in this case, the pen is hungry for more than just ink."

"Because of the data, right?" Aiden looked up at her. "That's what you're worried about?"

"Partly." Elsa pointed to a nearby poster with bold slogans about unity and progress. "These platforms become reflections of our lives. We must be cautious about how much of ourselves we give to them."

"Because once something's online, it's out there forever," Aiden concluded.

"Exactly," Elsa affirmed. "And forever is a long time in the digital world. Longer than any of us can truly comprehend."

They moved through the conference, Aiden soaking up the idealism of a connected future, while Elsa remained ever vigilant, her eyes scanning for the hidden snares within the glittering web of social media's rise.

Elsa led Aiden through the humming corridors of the social media giant's headquarters, a sprawling maze of glass and steel that seemed to pulse with the energy of a thousand conversations. They paused at an open-plan office area where young developers clustered around monitors, their discussions peppered with terms like "user engagement" and "click-through rates."

"Look at them," Elsa said, her voice barely above a whisper as she nodded toward a group animatedly debating over graphs and analytics. "They're not just building a platform; they're engineering society's digital heartbeat."

Aiden leaned in, watching as a developer highlighted a section of code on a screen, speaking excitedly about the potential for targeted ads. "It all seems so ... dynamic," he remarked, his eyes tracing the flow of data on the visualizations that adorned the walls.

"Dynamic, yes. But there's more beneath the surface." Elsa's gaze was steady, analytical. "These algorithms, they're designed to learn what keeps you clicking, what holds your attention. To these platforms, users are less about connection and more about retention."

"Retention?" Aiden echoed, turning to face her.

"Exactly," Elsa affirmed, tapping her temple. "They want your time. Your eyeballs on the screen. It's all about maximizing screen time because that translates to ad revenue. It's commodification of the most personal kind – your interests, your interactions, your data."

"Like selling bits of yourself without even knowing it? That's major sketchy," Aiden's voice was tinged with a growing edge of skepticism.

"Right again." Elsa gave him a small, approving nod. "It shifted from sharing to exploiting. Our desire to connect was harnessed to serve their profit margins. They made a marketplace out of our experiences."

Aiden absorbed her words, looking back at the developers who now seemed less like pioneers and more like merchants in a digital bazaar. "So when we share something online … "

"We're feeding the machine, and the machine is insatiable. We teach it how to keep us engaged, and it learns, evolves, becomes better at manipulating our behavior."

"Creepy," Aiden muttered, a shiver running through him despite the warmth of the bustling office.

"Knowledge is power, Aiden," Elsa replied, her hand finding its way to his shoulder once more. "But only if we understand how to use it – and how it can be used against us."

The modern corridors shifted and contorted before their eyes, and they found themselves in a large, dark room filled with hooded figures and screens.

The pulsating glow of multiple monitors cast a stark light on Elsa's face, her expression a blend of grim determination and clinical interest. She and Aiden huddled behind the reflective glass of an observation room, peering into the dimly lit den that had been repurposed as a hacker's lair.

"Welcome to the underbelly," Elsa whispered, her voice barely breaking the silence.

Aiden squinted, trying to make sense of the streams of code scrolling across screens, while shadowy figures tapped away at keyboards with predatory speed. The rhythmic clacking of keys was a sinister symphony, and his skin crawled with the realization of what transpired before them.

"Each keystroke is a trap being set," Elsa continued, "phishing campaigns designed to lure the unsuspecting."

Aiden watched, transfixed, as one of the hackers leaned back in their chair, swigging from a can of energy drink. With a few clicks, they launched a wave of emails masquerading as urgent messages from banks, social media platforms, even charities – a wicked lure for personal information.

"Identity theft," Elsa said, reading Aiden's horror-stricken face. "They feast on the data shared with trust, twisting it into keys that unlock lives."

Aiden felt a chill as he observed the casual cruelty, the ease with which these hackers deconstructed identities. He thought of friends and family, of his own digital footprints scattered across the web like breadcrumbs leading back to him.

"Can we stop them?" His voice was tight, the optimism that once laced his words now frayed with unease.

Elsa regarded him with a somber nod. "That's why we're here, Aiden. To understand, to learn, and ultimately, to act."

As they turned away from the voyeuristic view of the lair, Aiden's hands clenched into fists.

"Let's trace their steps, expose their tactics," Elsa said, tapping at her wrist device to activate the next ChronoCipher challenge. She was weary, but her eyes held a fire that belied her exhaustion. Aiden mirrored her resolve, ready to stand alongside his mentor in this temporal crusade.

Elsa led Aiden through the digital labyrinth of the early social media era, her fingers dancing across the ChronoCipher's interface. The air hummed with the energy of a time when the world was just waking up to the power of online connections.

"See this?" she pointed to a cluster of data on the screen, where names and birthdays were displayed alongside geotagged photos. "It's like leaving your house keys under the doormat. Hackers don't need to break in; we invite them."

Aiden leaned closer, his eyes scanning the screen. "But it's just basic info, right? What can they really do with it?"

"Everything," Elsa said gravely. "Impersonate you, reset your passwords, access your bank accounts ... Once they piece together your digital identity, they hold the strings to puppeteer your life."

She showed him a simulated profile, an amalgamation of shared snippets that revealed too much. Here, a birthday party photo with comments about the joy of turning eighteen – ripe for age-verification questions. There, a check-in at a favorite cafe – the answer to a security question, "Where is your favorite place to relax?"

"Users trust these platforms with their personal narratives," Elsa continued, "not realizing each post can be a piece of the puzzle to their undoing."

"They prey on human psychology, Aiden, creating traps that are disarmingly approachable."

"Like a game that plays you," Aiden muttered, a tinge of bitterness lacing his tone.

"Exactly," Elsa nodded, seeing the gears turn in her son's head. "We share without thinking, making their game all too easy."

Aiden's gaze lingered on the profiles, the emails, the false sincerity woven through every line.

"Can we beat them at their own game?" he asked.

Elsa met his gaze, pride mingling with the chronic ache that shadowed her movements. "We have to, Aiden. Not just for us, but for everyone who doesn't realize they're part of this game until it's too late."

As the ChronoCipher pulsed with their next challenge, Elsa and Aiden braced themselves. They were ready to dissect the mechanisms of deceit, to safeguard a future where sharing didn't mean surrendering security.

Elsa's finger hovered above the tablet's glowing surface, tracing the outer edge of a fraudulent email that had snared countless victims. Aiden leaned in, his eyes wide as he scanned the cunningly crafted message, a perfect imitation of an official communication from a popular social media platform.

"Mom, this looks so real," Aiden said, his voice tinged with disbelief. "How could anyone tell it's fake?"

"Details, Aiden. Always look for the details." Elsa tapped on the sender's email address, which upon closer inspection, deviated by a single character from the legitimate domain. "It's easy to miss at first glance, especially when you're not expecting deception."

She scrolled through a list of similar cases, a litany of digital duplicity. "Back in the early 2000s, phishing was just gaining traction. Scammers would set up fake login pages to mimic those of well-known sites. People would enter their usernames and passwords, thinking they were logging in securely."

Aiden's face fell, the lines of his youthful expression settling unhappily. "And once the hackers had that info … "

"They could access real accounts, impersonate the victims, wreak all sorts of havoc," Elsa finished for him. Her words were clinical, but her tone carried the weight of every hour she'd spent fighting these shadows.

"Catfishing, too," she continued. "Criminals would create false identities, lure people into relationships, and then exploit them for money or information. It's always been about trust – betraying it for gain."

"Was no one suspicious?" Aiden asked, struggling to fathom the ease with which people's trust was twisted.

"Many were, but it only takes a moment of distraction, a single lapse in judgment. And back then, awareness was lower; people were still learning the rules of this new digital landscape."

Aiden chewed on his lip, digesting the history of deceit laid bare before him. "So we've got to teach them, right? Show them how to spot these scams?"

"Exactly," Elsa affirmed. "We have to arm them with knowledge, make them question more than they accept at face value."

"Ready for another round?" Elsa asked without looking up.

"Born ready," Aiden replied, buoyed by a mix of excitement and resolve. He leaned in closer, eyes fixed on the flickering display.

The device projected their new challenge into the air between them, holographic text shimmering like a neon sign: "**Trace the Exploitation: Protect What Is Shared.**" Below the directive, a series of social media profiles materialized, each one meticulously detailed yet eerily hollow.

"Looks just like the real thing," Aiden noted, reaching out to swipe through the virtual interfaces, his fingertips passing through the images as if they were ghosts of the digital age.

"Appearances can be deceiving," Elsa murmured, scrutinizing the profiles. "That's the first lesson of cybersecurity."

Together, they sifted through the faux accounts, noting the subtle inconsistencies hidden amid posts of smiling faces and check-ins at trendy cafes. Elsa pointed out a profile with a disproportionately high number of followers compared to its engagement – a telltale sign of a fabricated identity.

"See the pattern?" she quizzed, her mind already three steps ahead.

Aiden nodded, his gaze sharpening as he caught on. "Yeah, this one here has been reposting the same articles across different platforms. It's like they're trying to build credibility quickly."

"Exactly. And look at the friend lists – all bots or inactive accounts." Elsa tapped on a profile picture, bringing up a slew of comments that were nothing more than generic platitudes.

"How can you tell they're bots?"

"Well, bots on social media often show clear patterns. They post repetitive or generic comments, like these ones. But some other things to look out for are unusually high activity at all hours, low or fake engagement – many followers but little real interaction. Their profiles may be newly created, with stolen or AI-generated images and vague or keyword-stuffed bios."

"I think I've seen a few of those on my socials lately," Aiden said.

"They're everywhere. Some studies estimate that almost 50% of interactions in comments online are bots. Another giveaway is that bots often repost the same content across multiple platforms, push divisive narratives, and hijack trending topics to manipulate public opinion. Some are designed to attack or discredit individuals, using coordinated efforts to amplify misinformation. While AI makes them more sophisticated, spotting them relies on recognizing these behaviors and verifying the authenticity of profiles, which is getting more and more difficult with the advancement of AI."

"This is wild. They're laying the groundwork for trust," Aiden realized, the gears in his mind whirring. "Building a network to spread misinformation ... or maybe worse."

"Right again," Elsa said, pride warming her tone. "These are the seeds of exploitation – fake accounts leading to phishing links, malware-laden downloads. Once a user's personal data is compromised, it's open season for identity theft."

The ChronoCipher beeped affirmatively as they identified each manipulation tactic, validating their analysis. Yet, with every success, Elsa's expression grew grimmer. She knew all too well the real-world consequences of these virtual traps.

"Remember, Aiden," she said, locking eyes with her son, "behind every one of these fake profiles could be someone's ruined credit, stolen savings, or a shattered sense of security."

The ChronoCipher's screen flickered, casting a blue glow over Elsa's focused face. A mosaic of digital profiles, each one more convincing than the last, filled the display. She leaned forward, her fingers poised above the keyboard – a conductor ready to orchestrate a symphony of code. Beside her, Aiden mirrored her posture, his youthful eyes scanning the puzzle with equal parts excitement and trepidation.

"Look for inconsistencies," Elsa instructed, her voice steady despite the thrumming of her pulse. "Hackers leave breadcrumbs – small errors that reveal the deception."

Aiden nodded, zooming in on a profile. "This one says he's from Ohio, but the timestamp of his posts is off. It's like he's in a different time zone."

"Good catch," Elsa praised. "Now, cross-reference that with the contact list. Any mutual friends popping up too frequently?"

"Here and here." Aiden's finger tapped the screen, connecting dots only he could see. "It's like a spider web, all leading back to the same few nodes."

"Exactly. Those are the anchor accounts – the hubs of the operation." Elsa's mind raced as she traced the lines of influence across the virtual landscape. The hackers had been clever, layering their traps beneath a facade of everyday interactions.

"Emails next," she said, pulling up a series of correspondences brimming with pleasantries and peril. Each one was a masterclass in manipulation – friendly tones masking malicious intent.

"Mom, this one's got an attachment claiming to be photos, but the file size is huge," Aiden pointed out, "Too big for just pictures, right?"

"Right again," Elsa confirmed. "It's likely a payload of malware, waiting to unleash chaos once it's downloaded."

As they sifted through scam messages riddled with urgency and offers too good to be true, Elsa felt Aiden's unease grow. She placed a comforting hand on his shoulder, grounding him in the reality of their mission.

"Remember, these patterns – they're not random. They're psychological warfare, designed to exploit trust and curiosity. And that makes our job both technical and empathetic. We must think like the hackers to stop them but never lose sight of the people at risk."

Elsa's fingers moved with practiced precision across the ChronoCipher's interface, each tap revealing another layer of the tangled web. Digital footprints shimmered on the holographic display, illuminated against a backdrop of cascading data streams. Beside her, Aiden leaned in, his gaze darting between the glowing projections, trying to keep pace with the complexity unfolding before him.

"Wait," Elsa murmured. Her hand hovered over a cluster of data points, freezing the projection in mid-shift. "Do you see this? Back when social media was still in its infancy, the doors were wide open – too open. It wasn't just a space to connect; it became a hunting ground."

Aiden followed her gesture, focusing intently on the profile floating in front of them. It was disturbingly convincing: a smiling face, warm comments, and an archive of photos chronicling a seemingly real life.

"They even mirrored the typos," Aiden noted, his voice tinged with unease. "I totally see how people fell for this."

Elsa exhaled sharply, brushing a stray strand of hair from her face. "Because trust is currency, and back then, no one realized how quickly it could be counterfeited. Hackers created fake profiles so precise, they could have fooled anyone. Friends, family, co-workers – they mimicked everything. Then they'd send messages, small and disarming at first, building rapport until ... " Her voice trailed off, heavy with implication.

"Until they struck?" Aiden guessed.

"Exactly," Elsa said, nodding. "At first, it was small-scale phishing – links disguised as photos, emails pretending to be from banks. But it didn't stop there. They started impersonating customer service agents, claiming they needed personal details to resolve nonexistent issues. Then they played on emotions – pretending to be a friend in trouble, begging for urgent help."

She expanded the holographic projection, revealing a spiderweb of interlinked accounts. "By the time social platforms caught on, they weren't dealing with one fake account. Hackers had scaled the operation – creating dozens, sometimes hundreds of profiles. It wasn't just about stealing identities anymore. They used these armies of fake personas to spread malware, manipulate public opinion, even sway elections."

Her voice tightened, the implications hanging heavy in the air. "And it all started so simply – by preying on trust."

The display shifted, highlighting a map of an early social media network riddled with red flags. Nodes representing users blinked erratically, showing where conversations had turned malicious, where innocent users were drawn into traps.

"They'd infiltrate entire communities," Elsa said, gesturing to a cluster of compromised profiles. "Imagine a trusted moderator of an online group being replaced overnight by an imposter. People wouldn't question it. Why would they?"

Aiden's face darkened as the scope of it all settled over him. "So, they could manipulate groups into anything – sending money, downloading viruses, even spreading lies."

"Exactly," Elsa said, her voice hardening. "And this isn't just the past. These methods laid the foundation for even more insidious attacks. The rise of deepfakes, bots, and algorithmic manipulation all trace back to this one thing: the exploitation of trust."

Aiden straightened, his young face disturbed. "It's like in those games I play," he said, his tone contemplative. "You start small, probing for weaknesses, and when you find one, you expand until the whole system collapses."

Elsa glanced at him. "Yes. And now you see why we're here. It's not just about stopping Lucien – it's about understanding the foundation he's standing on. If we don't, everything he's building will come crashing down on the rest of us."

The screen pulsed ominously, casting faint shadows across the room. Aiden reached out, his fingers brushing against the projection. "Then let's figure out his next move," he said firmly. "Before he makes it."

"And the best defense we have is awareness and skepticism. Never take a profile at face value. Question everything that feels off."

"Because once you click ... " Aiden trailed off.

"Everything can change," Elsa finished for him solemnly.

Elsa's finger moved toward the ChronoCipher's luminous display, the light casting an ethereal glow on her sharp features. She tapped a sequence, bringing up another holographic cascade of social media profiles, each one a puzzle piece in a larger scheme.

Aiden leaned closer, squinting as he traced the digital breadcrumbs of deception. Elsa watched his young face, once carefree and now furrowing with the weight of knowledge. Her heart ached, knowing she'd thrust him into this tangled web of past and future where innocence was a luxury they couldn't afford.

She could see Aiden processing her words, the lessons embedding themselves like code into his understanding of this digitized world. This was more than teaching; it was a rite of passage, a transfer of wisdom from mother to son, hacker to heir.

A memory flickered across Elsa's mind – the first time she had sat at her mother's bulky computer, fingers leaping across the keyboard, a child in awe of the boundless digital frontier. How different that world seemed now, tarnished by misuse and exploitation.

"Mom," Aiden spoke up, his voice tinged with newfound maturity, "it's kinda scary to think about how easily someone could pretend to be me ... or you."

"Scary, yes, but not insurmountable," Elsa replied, her voice steady despite the fatigue tugging at her edges. "We can build our defenses, arm ourselves with the right tools, and most importantly ... "

As Elsa imparted her understanding of this cyber realm's dangers, she felt a shift within her – a mixture of pride and sorrow. Pride for the strength and acumen she saw blossoming in Aiden, and sorrow for the fading vestiges of his childhood, slipping away with each lesson in caution.

"Anonymity once meant safety in numbers, a way to explore without judgment," Elsa mused aloud, more to herself than to Aiden. "Now, it's hiding both seeker and predator."

Elsa watched as Aiden scrolled through his social media feed, the vibrant display casting a soft glow across his contemplative face. She recognized that look – it was one she'd seen in her own reflection countless times: the dawning realization of something not quite right.

"Mom, I've been thinking … " Aiden's voice trailed off as he locked his tablet and met Elsa's gaze. "I've posted so much stuff online without thinking twice. What if my information is already out there being used by someone else?"

She took a breath, appreciating the gravity of his concern. "That's a valid concern," Elsa replied, maintaining gentle eye contact. "And it's why we need to be digitally literate. Understand what we're sharing, who might be collecting it, and how it can be used."

"What's the best way to be digitally literate, Mom?"

"First, secure your home. Your social media accounts, emails, and apps are like the locks on your door. If you're using the same key everywhere – a weak password – you're just asking for trouble. Use a strong, unique password for every account, and enable two-factor authentication. Think of it like adding a deadbolt to your front door – an extra layer that makes it harder for intruders."

"Second, don't leave your windows open." She tapped the side of her phone. "Every time you post personal details – your location, your habits, even small things like your favorite coffee shop – you're leaving clues. Imagine you're being watched through an open window. A stranger doesn't need your password if they can predict where you'll be and when."

"Third, don't believe every street sign." She glanced at him meaningfully. "Online, misinformation is like a fake road sign that leads you straight into a trap. AI-generated deepfakes, manipulated headlines, and bots disguised as real people are everywhere. Always double-check before you believe or share something. Cross-check sources, reverse search images, and question anything that makes you feel an extreme emotion – that's usually a sign someone wants to manipulate you."

She sat back and gave a small smile.

"And most importantly – stop, think, and act. Before clicking a link, responding to a message, or posting something, ask yourself: Who benefits from me engaging with this? Is this real, or is someone trying to steer me down the wrong path? or Who gains from my attention? Is this truth, or just a carefully crafter illusion?" She exhaled. "Staying safe online doesn't mean being afraid of the internet. It just means being aware – navigating it like a smart traveler in a city full of hidden dangers."

Aiden nodded, absorbing her words like a sponge. His fingers tapped an anxious rhythm on the tablet's edge, signaling his growing unease – a mirror of Elsa's own internal rhythms when faced with uncomfortable truths.

"Social media was meant to bring us together, make the world smaller … friendlier," Elsa continued, her voice a blend of warmth and solemnity. "But somewhere along the way, those platforms realized there was more money in mining our data than in nurturing our connections."

"Did you know that would happen?" Aiden asked, his eyes searching hers for answers.

Elsa hesitated, the weight of her past decisions pressing down on her shoulders. "Not at first," she admitted. "But once I saw the signs, I didn't do enough to stop it. My code – my work – it helped build these systems."

"Is that why you fight against them now?" The innocence in Aiden's question was a stark contrast to the complexity of the answer.

"Partly," Elsa said, a rueful smile touching her lips. "Guilt is a powerful motivator. But more than that, I want to fix what's broken – to make sure others don't fall into the traps that we set without even knowing it."

"Like me," Aiden said quietly, a reflective understanding crossing his features.

"Like all of us," Elsa corrected gently. "We're in this together, Aiden. And that's why we need to keep learning, keep teaching, and never stop questioning how our digital lives affect the real ones."

Together, they sat in the afterglow of the screen's light, bonded not just by blood but by a shared commitment to navigate the treacherous waters of an ever-evolving digital landscape.

As Elsa turned away from the glowing screen, her eyes adjusting to the dim light of the conference room, the ChronoCipher on her wrist flickered erratically. Its usual steady hum of quantum calculations skipped like a scratched disc, drawing both her and Aiden's attention.

"Is it supposed to do that?" Aiden asked, his voice tinged with concern as he leaned in closer.

"Never," Elsa replied tersely, her fingers moving swiftly over the device. She was about to initiate a diagnostic when the ChronoCipher stabilized, but not before releasing a burst of static that filled the room with a crackling tension.

Then, breaking through the electronic noise, Lucien's voice emerged, fragmented yet unmistakable. "Anonymity is just the beginning. Control comes when identity is fractured."

The words hung in the air like an ominous cloud, and Elsa felt a shiver run down her spine. Aiden looked at her, confusion etched across his youthful face. She knew he sensed the gravity of Lucien's message, though its full meaning was a puzzle yet to be deciphered.

"Lucien believes in peeling back the layers of a person until they're exposed," Elsa explained, keeping her gaze fixed on the ChronoCipher. "To him, every secret we keep online is a thread he can pull to unravel our lives."

"Fracture our identities?" Aiden questioned, piecing together the implications.

"Exactly." Elsa nodded, her mind racing. "He wants to break down the very concept of a unified self. When we're scattered and unsure, that's when people like him can rewrite who we are."

"We won't let him," Aiden stated, more to himself than to Elsa. His resolve was a mirror of her own determination – a shared legacy of resistance against those who would exploit the vulnerabilities of an interconnected world.

"Come on," Elsa said with renewed focus, the ChronoCipher returning to its normal operation. "We have work to do."

She paused, staring into the luminous glyphs swirling on the device's screen, as a sickening realization took root. Anonymity wasn't the endgame; it was merely the cover of darkness under which more insidious deeds could flourish. Elsa turned to Aiden.

"Lucien isn't just meddling with time," she said, her voice low but piercing. "He's planning something grander, more dangerous."

Aiden watched his mother, waiting for clarity. She rarely looked this way – like a storm cloud about to burst.

"Think about it," Elsa continued, connecting the dots out loud. "What's the one thing that ties us to our actions and history? Our identity. And if someone can steal that, manipulate it ... "

"Then they could control what everyone believes happened," Aiden finished, his own eyes widening with understanding.

"Exactly." Elsa paced, her movements sharp and deliberate. "If he orchestrates a large-scale identity theft, using the ChronoCipher, he could rewrite history in his image. He could erase missteps, fabricate events, even insert himself into power structures where he never belonged."

"Like digital forgery, but on a historical scale," Aiden muttered, horrified by the scope of Lucien's ambition.

"History is written by the victors," Elsa quoted grimly. "And Lucien intends to claim victory by authoring the past."

The implications hung between them, a heavy shroud of possibility that made the room feel smaller, the air denser. They were up against a mastermind who sought not only to change history but also to become its architect.

Suddenly, the ChronoCipher whirred, its panels illuminating with an urgent flicker.

"Another puzzle," Aiden said, his voice barely above a whisper.

"More than that," Elsa replied, her finger hovering over the console. "It's a clue to his next move."

As they leaned in, examining the cryptic challenge, the room seemed to tilt, reality itself stretching thin. The ChronoCipher's display began to distort, edges blurring, colors bleeding into each other in a dizzying kaleidoscope.

Elsa reached out, steadying herself against the console. "We need to solve this before Lucien bends history beyond recognition. We have no time to – "

But her warning was cut short. Without warning, everything went black. The ChronoCipher shut down, plunging them into darkness. They stood, hearts pounding, enveloped by a silence so complete it felt like an entity in its own right.

"Mom?" Aiden's voice was small, a beacon of humanity in the void.

Elsa opened her mouth to respond, but the words refused to come. In the pitch black, every sound amplified, she heard it – a faint, mechanical hum, growing steadily louder, resonating with the promise of dangers unseen and timelines unraveling.

The ChronoCipher was rebooting, but to what end?

The hum crescendoed into a symphony of electronic life, and with a sudden burst of blinding light, the ChronoCipher snapped back to existence. Elsa shielded her eyes as the room re-materialized around her. Aiden, his face lit by the glow of the machine's interface, gasped at the revelation on the screen.

"Mom, check it out!" His finger trembled as he pointed to the timestamp etched into the corner of the display: 2010s.

Elsa's heart raced. "Lucien's already there," she whispered, dread knotting in her stomach. The data on the screen cascaded like a waterfall of ones and zeroes, forming images and headlines that painted a stark picture of the decade: the rise of the dark web, the anonymity it promised, and the surge of cybercrime that followed.

"Bitcoin ... Ethereum ... " Aiden read aloud, his voice tinged with disbelief. "Mom, these weren't just currencies, right? They were perfect for ransomware and money laundering."

"Anonymity became currency, Aiden." Elsa's words were heavy with regret. She had seen the signs, even back then, of how technology could be twisted. And now Lucien was somewhere within those shadowy corridors, plotting.

"Control comes when identity is fractured," Elsa recalled Lucien's fragmented message, the words chilling her more than the cold air of the temporal void they'd just escaped.

"Fractured identity ... " Aiden echoed, his curiosity getting the better of him. He stepped closer to the ChronoCipher, his fingers dancing across the touchscreen with an urgency born of both fear and fascination.

"Wait, what's this?" He zoomed in on a cluster of digital artifacts on the display – an assortment of fake social media accounts, scam messages, and phishing emails.

Elsa nodded grimly. "Deception disguised as legitimacy. Lucien's weapon of choice."

"Prepare to face the next challenge," Aiden murmured, whether to himself or to Elsa was unclear.

Together, they identified the patterns used by cybercriminals: the urgency in the language, the slight misspellings, and the URLs that led to mock websites designed to harvest credentials.

"Always double-check before you click – stop, think, and act," Aiden recited like a mantra they had practiced many times before.

"Exactly," Elsa said with a nod. "And never input personal information unless you're absolutely certain of the site's legitimacy."

Aiden absorbed everything, his gaze intense and focused. He was no longer just a teenager navigating digital realms for fun; he was becoming a guardian of his own data, armed with knowledge and vigilance.

"Mom, not gonna lie, I've shared my info online without even thinking about these things," Aiden admitted, his earlier optimism now tempered by a sense of accountability.

"We all have, Aiden. But it's never too late to learn and adapt."

"Lucien is counting on people not knowing this stuff," Aiden mused, his thoughts turning to their enigmatic adversary.

"Which is why we'll make sure they do," Elsa stated firmly. "We'll take this knowledge back with us, educate others. We can't let fear or ignorance decide our digital future."

The ChronoCipher beeped in affirmation, signaling the completion of the puzzle. They had cracked the code of deception woven into the fabric of this early social media era.

Journal entry – Elsa – February 26, 2028

These last few days have forged a bond between Aiden and me that I was beginning to think would never be possible. It is incredible how well we work together – our brains and hands almost as one. The perfect tag team.

We are from different eras of online connection, and the divide between parent and child can sometimes feel impossible to bridge. Teens feel misunderstood, parents feel misunderstood – yet humanity's problems are universal – spanning generations. Teens today though face invisible dangers that we as their parents never had to deal with.

The early years of social media were a completely different ballgame, just the early birthing stages of a monster. It felt simpler back then, exciting. It wasn't this constant bombardment, this demand to share your life with the world.

I will prepare my son to face these head-on, with knowledge and wisdom.

Yet, each interaction still had emotional highs and lows. We as teens, even at the dawn of the digital connection era, didn't realize the vulnerability in secret online conversations in chatrooms – chats we would never tell our parents about. Digital meet-ups that our parents had no idea were happening. We were "out there" completely unprotected and completely oblivious to the dangers.

Nothing has changed. I see the same struggles in Aiden – the wrestle of how much of his digital life to reveal to me. I see it in his friends. I see it everywhere.

Journal entry – Aiden – February 26, 2028

I've been low-key thinking about Mom when she was my age. It's wild how she talks about the OG days of social media. She says it was like this fresh, exciting vibe back then – like you were entering a secret world that was all yours. I guess I get it. Back then, it probably felt like you were discovering some hidden corner of the internet, just for you.

She told me how she didn't really realize how sketchy it could get – like talking to people online and sharing stuff you'd never say IRL. They made friends like how Grandma had pen pals, lol. Same thing we do now, but now it's all about likes, followers, views … and most of those people are complete strangers. We care more about what they think than if we'll ever meet them in real life. It's like impossible to escape. If you're not on social media, you're basically a weirdo. At least back then, it was more lowkey, like if you didn't want people to know something, they wouldn't. Now? Everything's out there.

Mom knows a ton of stuff … but I'm not sure she really gets it. She didn't have to worry about getting likes or having randoms comment on every-thing. Back then, it was just about chatting with whoever. Now, it's about being seen. Like, all the time. It's exhausting if you think about it too much.

She says she wants to help me with all this, but honestly, I don't think she's got the full picture. Things are just … different now. More intense, more stressful, more confusing.

Then I remember her telling me how she used to hide stuff from her parents, like talking to people online without them knowing. Kind of feels the same now. I hide stuff too. Not everything, but a lot. It's just hard to talk about it when it feels like she won't fully understand what it's really like.

I guess, in the end, we're all just trying to figure out how much to share. Social media just makes it 100× harder. But in some way, I think we're all dealing with the same things, just with different tech. We all wanna fit in, get some love, and not get roasted.

Maybe I'll figure it out. Or maybe I won't. Mom probably didn't either. She had her own stuff to deal with, but it's kinda the same thing, huh?

So yeah. Maybe we're not that different after all.

Chapter 10

The midpoint crisis

The dark web's growth (2010s)

The air seemed to pulse with electric menace as Aiden and Elsa navigated the labyrinthine pathways of the dark web simulation. Eerie shadows danced across their faces, cast by the flickering holograms of locked forums and encrypted channels. The hum of the ChronoCipher was the only sound, a low, rhythmic pulse that made the room feel alive with tension.

Aiden's eyes darted from one ominous icon to the next. "It's like a whole different world down here," he murmured, his voice hushed, as if the digital specters might overhear. "Everything's so … hidden. Protected. Not gonna lie, Mom, it's low key creepy down here."

As if in answer, a nearby hologram flared to life, projecting a dizzying array of encrypted transactions that spun in dizzying spirals. Aiden leaned closer, his breath hitching as he deciphered the scrambled data. "These aren't just Bitcoin transfers," he said, his fingertips tracing the glowing lines of code. "There's … something else embedded here. Some kind of … "

He stopped abruptly, the color draining from his face as realization dawned. Elsa's jaw tightened, her eyes following the tumbling cascade of numbers. "It's an auction," she said softly, her voice heavy with disgust. "Human lives, sold to the highest bidder."

Aiden stumbled back as if the revelation had struck him physically. "What – what are they – " He shook his head, his voice cracking. "I don't get it. How can people do this? How can they just … trade humans like they're nothing?"

Elsa's heart ached at her son's anguish. She wanted to shield him from the worst of it, but that wasn't possible now. He had to see this for what it was – the raw, unfiltered darkness hiding behind the polished veneer of technology.

"Sometimes," Elsa began, resting a hand on Aiden's trembling shoulder, "people convince themselves that if they can't see the consequences, they don't exist. That the anonymity of a screen absolves them of responsibility."

Aiden's hands clenched into fists, his fingers curling so tightly that his knuckles turned white. His eyes blazed with a fury that seemed too fierce for

 DOI: 10.1201/9781003501626-10

his 14 years. "But it doesn't," he said through gritted teeth. "It just makes it easier for them to hide."

Elsa nodded, her lips pressing into a thin line. "Exactly. And that's where we come in."

She gestured to the holographic maze surrounding them, veins of the dark web laid bare like a throbbing map of corruption. "This is the battlefield of the 21st century, Aiden. The front lines of a war for the soul of the internet. And it's up to us to shine a light into these shadows."

Aiden's jaw tightened with determination, his shoulders squared, and the fire in his eyes told Elsa everything she needed to know. "Then let's get to work."

As they plunged deeper into the neon-streaked darkness, Elsa marveled at her son's courage. So young, so untested, yet already burning with the same relentless drive that had consumed her mother years ago. She could only pray that this time, the fire wouldn't consume them all.

The ChronoCipher's holographic display shifted abruptly, casting the simulation into stark relief. News headlines floated in mid-air like glowing, accusatory specters.

"RANSOMWARE ATTACK CRIPPLES HOSPITAL NETWORK," one blared in jagged red letters. "PATIENTS TURNED AWAY AS COMPUTERS LOCK."

Elsa's eyes narrowed as she swiped her hand through the display, summoning more headlines that painted a grim portrait of the fallout. "It's not just hospitals," she murmured, her voice tight. "Schools, government agencies, businesses … no one's safe."

She turned to Aiden, who was staring at the projection. "Ransomware is the weaponization of encryption," Elsa explained. Her tone was steady, almost clinical, as she fell into her teaching rhythm. "Attackers use it to lock victims out of their systems, holding their data hostage until a ransom is paid."

Aiden frowned, his brow creased with disbelief. "But … how is this a thing? I thought encryption was supposed to protect people, not hurt them."

"It is," Elsa said, "but like any tool, it can be twisted into something destructive." She brought up a glowing diagram of a ransomware attack, its flowchart glowing with sharp edges. "The attackers encrypt the victim's files with a key only they possess. Without that key, the data's useless – unreadable."

"So the victims have to pay to get their own data back?"

Elsa nodded grimly. "And the payments are often demanded in cryptocurrency because it's anonymous. There's no way to track where the money goes." Her lips twisted in a bitter smile. "It's the perfect crime for a digital age."

The ChronoCipher displayed a simulation of a ransomware attack in progress – a hospital's monitors flickering to black, vital patient data replaced with a taunting demand for payment. In the chaos, doctors and nurses scrambled, their frustration palpable as phones rang endlessly and patients were turned away.

"They're locking the doctors out of their own systems," Aiden whispered, his voice tight with disbelief. "The patients ... they can't get the care they need."

Elsa's expression hardened as she watched the scene unfold. "That's exactly the point. Ransomware doesn't just hurt businesses or governments – it's designed to hit people where it hurts the most."

The simulated chaos on the screen sent a chill through Aiden's core. He clenched his fists again, his voice trembling with anger. "This isn't just theft. It's ... it's terrorism. We have to stop this, Mom. We can't just let this keep happening."

"We won't," Elsa said firmly, reaching out to squeeze his shoulder. "But stopping it means understanding it first. Lucien's not just using ransomware as a tool for chaos – he's weaponizing fear. If we can figure out how he's spreading it, we can cut him off at the source."

Together, they turned back to the ChronoCipher. They had faced the shadows before. And they would do it again.

Elsa's voice carried a steely determination, but her fingers trembled as she adjusted the ChronoCipher's settings. The simulation began shifting, pulling them deeper into the underbelly of the dark web. The alley twisted and warped, elongating into a tunnel where new holograms materialized: chat logs, transaction records, encrypted files – a cascade of information representing an intricate network of exploitation.

"Look," Elsa said, pointing at a cluster of transactions glowing a faint red. "These wallets are moving funds in synchronized patterns, across multiple currencies. It's deliberate – a laundering system to obscure the flow of money."

Aiden leaned in, his eyes narrowing as he studied the movement of funds. "Slick. They're smart," he muttered. "Each hop adds another layer of confusion. But ... " He hesitated, his finger tracing a line between two clusters. "Here. Check out these two wallets – there's a timing overlap. They always sync within milliseconds of each transaction. That's not random, is it?"

Elsa's lips pressed into a thin line. "No. That's coordination." She magnified the data, her pulse quickening. "It means someone is controlling this entire flow. This isn't just a system; it's a machine with a mastermind."

"Lucien," Aiden whispered, the name laced with both fear and fury. He straightened, his jaw tightening. "He's not just stealing or selling. He's building infrastructure – like a digital empire in the shadows."

Elsa nodded grimly, her fingers flying across the ChronoCipher's keys. "And every piece of it is designed to dismantle trust, brick by brick. If people lose faith in the systems they depend on – banks, hospitals, governments –

he gains power. It's not just about control, Aiden. It's about rewriting the rules of society."

Her words hung in the air as they watched the simulation zoom out, revealing a global map dotted with pulsing nodes of activity. Each point represented a hub of exploitation: human trafficking rings, ransomware syndicates, illicit marketplaces.

The simulation shifted again, morphing into a bustling virtual marketplace. Elsa's breath hitched as she saw the offerings scrolling by – firearms, forged documents, malware kits, and worst of all, "services" that preyed on the most vulnerable.

Aiden's voice trembled with barely contained rage. "This is for real, isn't it? They're selling children, Mom." He turned to Elsa, his face pale but his eyes burning. "How do we fight something this big, take it down? It's everywhere. It's – "

"Not unstoppable," Elsa interrupted sharply. She knelt beside him, taking his hands in hers. "This is exactly what Lucien wants you to believe – that it's too vast to confront. That people will turn away because it's easier to ignore than to fight."

Aiden stared at her, his breathing ragged. "But how do you stop a hydra? You cut off one head, and two more grow back."

"You don't just cut off the heads," Elsa said, her voice firm. "You go for the heart. And right now, that heart is Lucien's network. If we can expose his operations – trace his communications, identify his enablers – we can cripple his empire from the inside."

The ChronoCipher pulsed again, drawing their attention back to the hospital, where a ransomware attack was in progress. The simulation unfolded with chilling precision – an unsuspecting hospital administrator clicked on a seemingly harmless email attachment. Within moments, the screen flickered to black, replaced by a taunting message demanding Bitcoin in exchange for a decryption key.

Aiden squinted at the simulation, his hands hovering over the controls. "But check out the timestamps, Mom. The malware activates almost immediately after the click, but ... wait." He zoomed in on the attack timeline. "There's a delay here. Between when the files are encrypted and when the ransom note appears."

Elsa leaned in, her eyes narrowing. "You're right. It's like they're testing something. Almost as if – "

"It's a beta," Aiden said, his voice growing steadier as his analysis sharpened. "They're using these attacks to refine their methods, to perfect their tools. Each ransom is funding the development of something bigger."

Elsa's stomach churned. "And we're the guinea pigs," she muttered. "Every victim, every payment – it's feeding the evolution of his weapons."

Elsa straightened, her fingers moving swiftly across the holographic keyboard. "We need to isolate the encryption signatures," she said. "If we can reverse-engineer the code, we might be able to develop a universal decryption tool. Something that can neutralize his ransomware before it spreads."

Aiden nodded, already working alongside her. The ChronoCipher's interface glowed brighter as lines of code filled the air between them, a digital tapestry woven from their combined efforts.

"Got it!" Aiden exclaimed, highlighting a segment of the ransomware's code. "This part here – it's like a master key for the encryption. If we can crack this, we can create a backdoor."

Elsa's eyes lit with hope. "Good work, Aiden. Let's integrate it into a prototype tool. If it works … " She paused, her gaze hardening. "We'll use it to stop him. To dismantle this network, piece by piece."

But just as their progress surged, the ChronoCipher glitched. The holograms flickered and distorted, the once-stable simulation now completely unstable. A voice echoed through the room, cold and taunting.

"You think you can stop me?" Lucien's voice sent a chill down Elsa's spine. "You're playing checkers while I'm playing chess. Every move you make only feeds the fire."

The simulation stabilized, revealing a chilling new image – a sprawling smart city, its infrastructure glowing with interconnected nodes. But instead of life and vibrancy, the holograms flickered with chaos: car accidents, blackouts, collapsed communications.

"This is what comes next," Lucien continued, his voice brimming with cruel amusement. "The Internet of Things isn't just a marvel – it's a weakness. And when trust is gone, the world burns. You think you're clever, having a smart doorbell? There's no security camera I can't hack. You think it's smart that cars and transport systems are autonomous? What happens when I hack those systems? When everything is connected, everything is vulnerable. Any online system can be turned against you. You think this is a threat? How naïve. This is a declaration of reality."

Elsa stared at the display, her resolve hardening even as fear coiled in her chest. She glanced at Aiden, who stood rooted in place, his fists clenched.

"We're not going to let him win," she said firmly, gripping Aiden's shoulder. "He may be playing chess, but he underestimates us. He underestimates what we're willing to fight for."

Aiden turned to her, his eyes alight with determination. "Then let's prove him wrong."

Together, they dove back into the ChronoCipher, their mission clear: to outmaneuver Lucien, to dismantle his empire, and protect the world from his vision of chaos.

Aiden's gaze didn't waver, though doubt clouded his voice. "But why? Why go to such lengths to control this chaos? What does Lucien get out of it?"

Elsa's fingers paused mid-motion over the ChronoCipher, the glowing holograms casting fractured shadows across her face. The nodes and threads seemed alive, an ever-shifting labyrinth mocking her attempts to untangle it.

"It's not just about money," she said finally, her voice tinged with resignation and steel. "Lucien doesn't want to destroy the system – he wants to own it. Chaos isn't the goal; it's the weapon. If no one trusts the infrastructure, no one trusts each other. Fear makes people desperate."

"No cap," Aiden said. "And desperation," he murmured, his expression darkening, "hundred percent makes them easier to control."

"Exactly." Elsa's jaw tightened, her eyes fixed on the glowing matrix. "If Lucien can position himself as the savior, the one who can 'fix' everything, then he gets what he's always wanted. Power. A digital order built on distrust, but under his complete control."

Aiden clenched his fists, his knuckles white against the edge of the console. "But how do we stop someone like him? He's already ten steps ahead, using tools we can barely understand."

Elsa turned to him, her voice calm but unyielding. "By knowing the system better than he does. By finding the cracks in his design. Everyone leaves a trail, Aiden. Even Lucien."

She gestured to a faint cluster of lines, barely visible among the glowing nodes. "These anomalies – they're small, but consistent. Transactions rerouted through obscure pathways, anomalies in encrypted traffic. These aren't accidents. They're his breadcrumbs. Invisible to most, but not to us."

Aiden leaned in, his frustration giving way to focus. "So, we track him and piece by piece we unravel his web."

Elsa nodded, pride flickering in her expression. "And more importantly, we predict his next move. No one, not even Lucien, is infallible."

The ChronoCipher hummed softly, its tendrils shifting as if reacting to their determination. For a moment, the air felt charged with purpose. The simulation deepened, revealing another layer of encrypted passages.

"Alright, let's do this," Aiden said, rolling his shoulders. "Let's find those cracks."

Elsa allowed herself a small smile. "That's my boy."

They worked in tandem, Elsa guiding Aiden through the decryption processes. Patterns unfolded, data streams untangled. The ChronoCipher responded like an extension of their will, illuminating paths hidden within Lucien's network.

Midway through their task, Aiden glanced at her. "Do you think he's watching us right now?"

"He might be," Elsa admitted, her voice steady. "But if he is, he's underestimating us."

Aiden smirked faintly, confidence returning. "Then let's make him regret that."

Elsa chuckled softly. "Spoken like a true Winters."

With each discovery, the weight of doubt eased ever so slightly. But as the ChronoCipher projected a map of Lucien's attacks – hospitals, schools, transportation hubs, all glowing in ominous red – Elsa knew the fight was just beginning.

"We're going to need a plan," she murmured, her gaze locked on the flashing nodes. "Something he won't see coming."

Aiden straightened, his voice brimming with determination. "Good. About time, Momma Bear. No lies, I'm tired of being waiting around and reacting to whatever he does. Let's make him play by our rules."

"Let's get to work," she said.

And with that, the fight against the shadows truly began.

As the ChronoCipher shifted, the dark web's shadows dissolved into a shimmering network of interconnected nodes. Aiden leaned closer, tracing the luminous pathways with a finger.

"It's not just about being anonymous versus being accountable, is it?" he asked. "It's about finding the balance between being innovative and being ethical, between what technology can do and what it should do."

Elsa nodded. "Exactly. Technology isn't inherently good or evil. It's how we use it that matters. But every choice we make as creators leaves ripples, and those ripples ... they can turn into waves."

She gestured toward a cluster of pulsing nodes, their light tinged with ominous red. "Take cryptocurrency – it was meant to democratize finance, to break barriers. But it's also become a shield for laundering money, fueling trafficking, and funding criminal enterprises."

"And AI?" Aiden ventured, his mind racing ahead. "It's wild. It could revolutionize healthcare, education, even climate solutions. But in the wrong hands ... "

Elsa finished grimly, "It can be weaponized. Disinformation campaigns, automated manipulation, even undermining democracy. Tools meant to empower can just as easily enslave."

A shiver went down Aiden's spine as he thought about the weight of their mission. The stakes were crazy high. But when he looked at his mom, watching her crush the ChronoCipher with that unstoppable focus, he felt a spark of hope. If anyone could turn things around, it was Elsa Winters. She was kind of the GOAT.

Suddenly, the ChronoCipher's interface flared red. A warning echoed through the room, sharp and insistent. Elsa's fingers flew across the controls, her focus narrowing to the cascading streams of data.

"What's happening?" Aiden asked, his pulse quickening.

"It's Lucien," Elsa said through gritted teeth, her eyes locked on the unraveling patterns before her. "He's making his move."

The projection shifted, revealing an intricate web of IoT devices – smart homes, self-driving cars, medical implants – each node pulsating with vulnerability. At the network's center loomed a familiar face.

Lucien's pale eyes seemed to pierce through the hologram, his image framed by chaotic tendrils of light. His voice, cold and calculated, reverberated through the space.

"You've delayed me," he said, his lips curving into a mirthless smile. "But you can't stop the inevitable. Trust is an illusion, and I've already sown its destruction. Soon, the foundation will crumble, and from the ashes … " He paused, savoring the moment. "A new order will rise."

Before they could respond, his image dissolved, leaving a chilling silence in its wake.

Aiden stared at the vacant space where Lucien had been, his hands trembling at his sides. "What do we do now?"

Elsa met his gaze, her eyes fierce with resolve. "We continue to fight. We learn from the past, adapt, and forge a future that Lucien can't destroy. Together."

The simulation shifted again, casting eerie shadows across their faces. A distorted voice broke through the ChronoCipher's speakers, chilling in its calm cruelty. "You can't beat me."

"Maybe he's right. How do we stay ahead of him?" Aiden asked, his gaze intense and focused.

Elsa's smile sharpened with purpose. "By being smarter, faster, and unrelenting. Every time he moves, we'll be there to counter. Every time he strikes, we'll make him pay."

The holographic web began to shift, Lucien's sprawling empire slowly revealing its vulnerabilities. Aiden glanced at his mother, her focus unwavering, her resolve unshaken.

In that moment, he saw not just a mentor or a parent, but a fighter – a woman determined to protect the world her mother had dreamed of, a world of possibility and hope.

Chapter 11

IoT, a web of vulnerabilities (late 2010s)

Journal entry – Janet – December 27, 2021

As I've struggled to reconcile my part in the ever-evolving digital landscape, it has become clear that others do not. I've recently been reminded of a conversation with Lucien M. "It's laughable how easily the general public can be manipulated," he said. "It's almost too easy. They don't even see it happening. We started slowly, feeding the beast only small amounts, but its craving grew until common sense was lost and feeding became all that matters. They crave the stimulation, the connection, the convenience. They don't know what to do without it. Overstimulated minds become zombified, and zombie minds don't question. Common sense? What is that? Questioning information? Why? We have them exactly where we want them. And they are clueless."

This was the beginning of the end for me. This conversation. I realized in that moment that compromise was no longer an option. People like that could not be permitted to continue without conscience.

Soon the entire world will depend on interconnected IoT systems – smart homes, autonomous vehicles, health devices – and people trust these systems so blindly. Of course, they must be safe – invulnerable. Little do they know.

And Lucien and his cronies will be waiting in the shadows. Ready.

The ChronoCipher hummed softly, recalibrating after their harrowing journey through Lucien's ransomware attack. The weight of what they had uncovered in the last era – human suffering encoded in strings of malicious code – was still fresh in Elsa and Aiden's minds. They worked in silence, their focus on the glowing interface. But something was missing. Aiden glanced at the empty space beside him and broke the quiet.

"Where's Janet?" he asked, his voice tight with worry. "We haven't seen her since Lucien messed with her code."

Elsa paused, her fingers hovering over the ChronoCipher's controls. "I think she wanted us to uncover it on our own," she murmured, almost to

DOI: 10.1201/9781003501626-11

herself. "Her journal ... it wasn't just information. It was a part of her, a piece of who she was." They both fell silent, the absence of Janet's guiding presence palpable in that moment.

She had been more than a voice of reason in their journey – she had been a connection to a legacy, to a woman who had fought so fiercely for a world free from exploitation.

Just as Aiden opened his mouth to speak again, the ChronoCipher flickered, and Janet's familiar hologram appeared.

Her form was faint at first, her edges rippling like the surface of disturbed water. But her voice, when it came, was steady and filled with warmth.

"I never meant to leave you."

Aiden's throat tightened, and he blinked rapidly. "Grandma Janet," he breathed, relief laced with a touch of anger.

"Why did you disappear? We needed you."

Janet's expression softened, a ghost of a smile crossing her holographic features. "I needed you to understand," she said gently. "To discover the truth without me leading you.

My journal ... it was my voice from the past. It was everything I fought for. You had to see it with fresh eyes."

Elsa nodded slowly, her voice soft. "You wanted us to connect with who you were ... to understand the choices you made."

"Yes," Janet said, her tone more vibrant now, the hologram stabilizing. "Sometimes, the most important truths can't be taught – they have to be uncovered."

"But I never stopped watching. I never stopped believing in you."

Aiden glanced at Elsa, his expression a mix of determination and vulnerability.

"We uncovered it, Grandma. Wasn't actually too difficult, right Mom? And now we know what's at stake. But, no cap, Lucien's still out there, and he's always a step ahead somehow."

Janet's gaze turned serious, her edges sharpening as the ChronoCipher pulsed with urgency.

"Lucien thrives in the cracks of trust, in the spaces where technology's promise becomes its greatest threat. And now, we're heading into the heart of that danger."

The ChronoCipher's projection shifted, revealing a sprawling web of interconnected nodes – a cityscape of IoT devices lighting up in eerie synchronization.

Janet gestured to the glowing display. "This world of seamless connections may look like progress," she warned, "but every connection is a vulnerability. Every convenience is a potential weapon."

Elsa's jaw tightened. "IoT devices. The foundation of modern life ... and Lucien's next target." Janet nodded.

"You've seen how trust unravels. Now, we must stop it." As the ChronoCipher prepared for the jump into the IoT-dominated landscape, Aiden reached for Janet's holographic hand, his resolve clear in his voice.

"We won't let him win." Janet's smile returned, faint but unwavering. "I know you won't. The three of us can rebuild what he seeks to destroy. Our legacy is strong, and three brains are far better than one. With us working together, he doesn't stand a chance."

The air around Elsa and Aiden grew tense as the ChronoCipher surged with energy, its holographic display shifting to reveal a sprawling smart home. At first glance, it seemed idyllic – a vision of convenience and innovation. Ambient lighting adjusted automatically to their presence, the thermostat hummed at the perfect temperature, and holographic assistants blinked to life with a cheerful glow.

Aiden marveled at the sleek architecture, his eyes tracing the seamless transitions between devices. "Insane ... This place ... it's like a tech utopia," he murmured, stepping forward.

Elsa remained still, her jaw tightening. She scanned the room, noting the overly polished perfection, the hum of circuits almost too precise. "Or a trap," she said softly. Her fingers flexed instinctively at her sides, itching for the safety of a keyboard.

Janet's hologram materialized beside them, her edges shimmering faintly. Her voice, calm but weighted, filled the room. "You're looking at the pinnacle of convenience – and vulnerability."

As if on cue, the smooth rhythm of the home began to falter. The refrigerator's transparent display flickered erratically, showing corrupted nutritional data. A smart speaker chimed unexpectedly, its voice distorted and garbled. The thermostat let out a sharp click before its settings spiked wildly, the room growing stiflingly hot.

"What's going on?" Aiden asked, his excitement fading into unease as he wiped sweat from his brow.

"This is what happens when security is compromised," Janet said, gesturing toward the now-chaotic projections of the home's network. "Every IoT device here is connected, but those connections come at a price. Each one is a door waiting to be opened."

Elsa moved cautiously to the control panel embedded in the wall. As her hand hovered over it, the display lit up, revealing a network map of the home. Lines of glowing light traced the connections between devices, forming a tangled web of activity.

"This isn't just one system," Elsa murmured, her voice low with dread. "It's hundreds, maybe thousands, all linked together. If someone finds the right weak point – "

" – the whole system collapses," Janet finished. Her holographic gaze settled on Elsa. "And Lucien isn't just exploiting one system. He's hijacking networks on a global scale."

A sudden chill swept through the room as the thermostat plummeted, its display now blinking a sinister red. Frost formed on the edges of the windows, and Aiden rubbed his arms against the sudden cold. "Okay, this is officially creepy," he muttered.

Janet stepped closer to the holographic display, her digital fingers tracing the map of connections. "The strength of these networks is their interconnectedness," she explained. "But that's also their greatest weakness. When one device is compromised, it can infect the rest like a virus."

The lights dimmed, and the ChronoCipher's display shifted once more, illuminating new layers of the sprawling network. A challenge loomed ahead, one that would test their resolve and ingenuity like never before.

"Let's get to work," Elsa said, her voice steady despite the storm brewing around them.

The ChronoCipher flared with urgency, its holographic projections casting sharp, flickering light around the room. Elsa's fingers worked rapidly across the interface, each keystroke peeling back layers of data. Aiden stood by her side, his gaze locked on the shimmering web of connections stretching out before them. The network pulsed with a sickly red hue, its lines converging into clusters that flickered ominously.

"Something's wrong," Elsa murmured, her voice tight with unease. "These aren't just random glitches."

Before Aiden could respond, the ChronoCipher's display erupted into a cascade of live feeds. News reports, emergency broadcasts, and chaotic footage streamed in from across the globe. Elsa's breath caught in her throat as the scope of the attack came into view.

The feeds shifted: aerial footage of gridlocked cities where traffic lights blinked erratically, creating a cacophony of blaring horns and frustrated shouts. A self-driving car plowed through an intersection, narrowly missing a group of pedestrians before coming to an abrupt halt. The air was thick with confusion and fear.

Another clip appeared – families trapped in their homes, pounding on reinforced glass doors as smart locks refused to release. One father desperately worked with a crowbar, his young daughter sobbing behind him.

"Mom ... " Aiden's voice cracked as the chaotic scenes unfolded. He stepped back, his face pale. "How is this real? How is all of this happening at once?"

Elsa's jaw tightened, her eyes scanning the chaotic streams of data pouring from the ChronoCipher. "It's not a coincidence," she said grimly. "This is coordinated."

Janet's hologram materialized beside them, her expression etched with urgency. "You're witnessing the evolution of cyber warfare," she said, her voice cutting through the noise with an unsettling calm. She gestured to the glowing nodes on the display, each one representing an IoT device hijacked by the attack. "The Mirai Botnet in 2016 showed us what was possible. But this ... this is on a scale we couldn't have imagined."

Elsa nodded, her hands moving instinctively across the ChronoCipher's controls to isolate the source of the attack. "They're using outdated firmware," she said, her voice clipped. "Devices that weren't patched, weren't secured. They've turned millions of them into a botnet."

"A botnet?" Aiden asked.

Janet turned to him, her holographic gaze steady. "A network of compromised devices, all working together under the control of a hacker. They overwhelm systems with traffic, like flooding a dam until it breaks."

As she spoke, the display zoomed in on a cluster of devices – a tangle of smart thermostats, security cameras, and home assistants. Each one blinked red, their vulnerabilities laid bare. Janet pointed to the connection lines snaking outward like veins. "These devices were never designed to withstand this kind of exploitation. They're easy targets."

Aiden clenched his fists, his frustration mounting. "But why? What's the point of all this?"

"To show power," Janet said simply. "To disrupt, to terrify. When people can't trust their systems, they stop using them." Her expression softening for a moment. "It won't be easy. These attacks are designed to spread chaos, to leave no room for counteraction. But we are not powerless. The first step is understanding."

Elsa's hands stilled for a moment, her eyes locked on the glowing web of compromised devices. "Understanding is only half the battle," she said. "We need to act – and fast."

With a deep breath, she resumed her work, isolating nodes and redirecting traffic to mitigate the damage. Aiden joined her, his hands steady as he followed her instructions, their combined efforts a small but determined resistance against the tide of destruction.

As they chipped away at the sprawling attack, the ChronoCipher's display shifted again, revealing new layers of Lucien's plan.

The room was unnervingly quiet after the chaos of the botnet attack. The ChronoCipher's pulsing holograms still hung in the air like ghostly reminders, but Elsa's attention wasn't on the device. She stood near the wall of projections, staring at the flickering web of IoT devices, her jaw tight. The earlier flashes of hospitals plunged into darkness and cars colliding in broken traffic grids played in her mind like an unshakable echo.

Aiden leaned against the console, arms crossed, his expression somewhere between anger and confusion. "How does something like this even happen?" he asked, breaking the silence. "It feels like we're living in a trap we built for ourselves."

Elsa didn't immediately respond. She moved closer to one of the holographic nodes – a representation of a smart thermostat – and traced its pulsing outline with her fingers. "We didn't just build the trap," she finally said, her tone soft but resolute. "We decorated it. Made it look safe and shiny. And in our rush to make life easier, we didn't think about the cracks."

Aiden frowned. "But whose fault is that? The companies who make this stuff or the people who buy it and don't secure it?"

Elsa turned to him, meeting his gaze. "It's not that simple, Aiden. Think about it – most people don't even know what they're buying. They see a smart light bulb or a fancy lock and think it'll make their lives better. They don't realize that every device is a door someone can open if they want to."

Aiden let out a frustrated sigh and ran a hand through his hair. "Okay … But it's not like they can't secure it. People could use stronger passwords, update their devices, or – " He paused, noticing Elsa's expression. "What?"

"How many times have you hit 'remind me later' on a software update?" she asked, raising an eyebrow.

Aiden opened his mouth to reply but stopped short, a sheepish look crossing his face.

"Exactly," Elsa said, her voice softening. "Most people don't think about these things until it's too late. And even if they do, it's not always enough. Sometimes, the companies don't bother fixing the vulnerabilities in the first place. They just push the products out faster than they can secure them."

Janet's voice, calm yet firm, interjected from the corner of the room. Her holographic form flickered to life, standing amid the maze of interconnected nodes. "Security is a shared responsibility," she said, her gaze sweeping between Elsa and Aiden. "Manufacturers need to prioritize safety, yes. But users also have to learn to think critically about what they bring into their lives."

Aiden tilted his head, skepticism creeping into his expression. "So, what? Everyone just has to become a cybersecurity expert now?"

"Not an expert," Janet corrected. "But aware. Think of it like fastening your seatbelt when you get in the car. You don't have to be an engineer to know that a little precaution can save you from big risks." She gestured toward the holographic web, her fingers brushing the glowing nodes.

She continued, "Update your devices regularly – those patches aren't just technical fluff; they're your defense against attackers exploiting yesterday's vulnerabilities. Enable two-factor authentication. It's like having a second lock on your safe – without it, the door can swing open to anyone who steals your first key."

Janet's gaze locked onto Aiden's. "And most importantly, be critical. Question what you bring into your digital life. Is that free app worth giving up your privacy? Is a default password a risk you're willing to take?"

Aiden tilted his head, his skepticism giving way to curiosity. "So, it's not about knowing everything. It's about knowing enough to make smarter choices."

"Exactly," Janet said with a nod. "Every small step you take makes the system as a whole harder to crack. Security isn't just about what manufacturers do – it's about what you do, too."

Elsa nodded, her gaze shifting back to the flickering network. "But it's not just on individuals, either. Companies need to stop cutting corners. They need to treat security like it's as important as the product itself – not just a patch after something goes wrong."

Aiden stared at the glowing nodes for a moment. "It feels like no matter what we do, someone's always going to find a way to exploit it."

"That's true," Janet said, her tone steady but not unkind. "But that doesn't mean you stop trying. Security isn't about making something invincible – it's about making it harder to exploit. Slowing them down. Giving people a fighting chance."

Elsa turned to Aiden, placing a hand on his shoulder. "It's about balance," she said softly. "Innovation and security. Convenience and caution. If we lean too far in one direction, we end up right where Lucien wants us – vulnerable."

Aiden nodded slowly, absorbing her words. "So, what now?" he asked.

"Now," Elsa said, her eyes hardening, "we figure out how to close the cracks before Lucien pulls the whole thing apart."

The room seemed to hold its breath as Janet dimmed the holograms slightly, giving them space to think.

The room darkened as the ChronoCipher hummed ominously, its glowing interface casting shifting shadows. Elsa's fingers hovered over the controls, her pulse quickening as a sprawling holographic map burst to life.

Before she could continue, the air seemed to chill as Lucien's hologram materialized. His pale eyes gleamed like shards of ice, his smile as sharp and dangerous as a blade.

"Impressive, isn't it?" His voice was smooth, almost soothing, but laced with venom. "A symphony of vulnerability. Every device, every connection, turned into an instrument of chaos."

Aiden's hands curled into fists. "Why are you doing this?" he demanded, his voice trembling with rage. "What do you gain from destroying people's lives?"

"Destroying?" Lucien's tone held faint amusement. "No, *boy*. This isn't destruction. It's enlightenment. I'm showing the world what it truly is – a house of cards built on blind faith."

The hologram zoomed out, revealing a broader view of the cascading failures. Stock markets plummeted. Entire cities plunged into darkness. Headlines screamed across fragmented screens, documenting the chaos in real time.

"Your world rests on faith," Lucien continued, his voice a cold blade slicing through the tension. "Faith in systems. In technology. In each other.

But faith is a lie. It doesn't take much – a single fracture – and everything falls apart."

Elsa stepped forward, her glare cutting through the flickering light. "Trust isn't a weakness," she said, her voice steady despite the storm raging around them. "It's what holds us together. It's what makes us stronger."

Lucien tilted his head, his smirk deepening. "And yet, it's so easily shattered. One exploit. One failure. And the whole system unravels. Look around you, Elsa. People gave these machines their trust, and now they're paying the price."

Lucien's laughter rang out, cold and cutting. "You can patch your precious systems all you want, but you can't rebuild what's already broken. This is only the beginning."

As his image faded, the room fell into tense silence. The chaotic map of compromised systems remained, a stark reminder of the stakes they faced.

Elsa turned to Aiden, her jaw set. "He's right about one thing," she said. "Faith in systems can shatter like glass," Elsa said, her gaze hardening. "But even broken glass can be reforged. We fight to rebuild it."

Aiden stared, his breath shallow. "It's everywhere," he whispered. "He's hitting everything."

"It may seem so, but this isn't random," Elsa replied, her hands moving instinctively over the ChronoCipher's controls, her mind racing. "He's using compromised devices to create a botnet, coordinating them for a massive DDoS attack."

"Massive doesn't even cover it," Janet began, gesturing to the glowing nodes on the holographic map. "He's hijacked millions of devices – everything from refrigerators to traffic systems. If we don't act now, his DDoS attack will bring down critical infrastructure across entire continents."

Aiden frowned. "DDoS? What exactly is he doing?"

Janet sighed, trying to put it in simpler terms. "Distributed Denial-of-Service attack. Imagine a building with a single entrance. Normally, people go in and out smoothly. But now, picture a hundred people rushing the door at the same time – no one gets through, the entrance is blocked, and the whole system collapses under the pressure."

Elsa's expression tightened as she watched the chaotic data streams on the display. "So he's doing that, but with internet traffic? Overloading servers until they crash?"

Janet nodded. "Exactly. He's using an army of hijacked devices to flood critical networks with so much junk data that they freeze. Hospitals, power grids, emergency systems – once they go offline, panic spreads, and that's when real chaos begins."

The device emitted a sharp chime, and Janet's hologram reappeared beside them, her edges sharper and her expression more urgent than before. Her voice was calm but carried the weight of what was at stake.

"Lucien's botnet is massive," Janet began, gesturing to the glowing nodes on the holographic map. "He's hijacked millions of devices – everything from refrigerators to traffic systems. If we don't act now, his DDoS attack will bring down critical infrastructure across entire continents."

The device emitted a sharp chime, its interface shifting to display the next set of objectives.

"Challenge Initiated: The Web of Exploitation. Neutralize the Nodes."

Aiden leaned closer, reading aloud as the tasks scrolled across the screen:

1. **Identify compromised devices and isolate them.**
2. **Patch vulnerabilities to prevent further exploitation.**
3. **Redirect malicious traffic to disrupt the attack.**

Elsa's jaw tightened as she absorbed the information. "He's counting on these devices being vulnerable, as we've already discovered," she said. "Outdated firmware, weak passwords – things people overlook because they believe their devices are too insignificant to matter."

Aiden straightened, his fingers itching to dive into the challenge. "So, where do we start?"

Janet waved her hand, and the display zoomed in on a cluster of compromised devices – smart home hubs, medical monitors, and even public kiosks. "We start here. These nodes are the weakest points, but they're also the most critical. Neutralizing them will create a ripple effect, destabilizing the entire botnet."

Elsa's hands moved quickly over the ChronoCipher's controls, her mind racing as she analyzed the map. "We need to isolate the infected devices first. If we can block their outgoing traffic, we can stop them from sending malicious data to the rest of the network."

Aiden glanced at her. "But won't that leave people without their devices? What if someone's depending on these for, I don't know, their insulin pump or something?"

"It's a calculated risk," Elsa admitted, her tone heavy with the weight of the decision. "But if we don't act, the entire system collapses – and a lot more people get hurt."

The ChronoCipher beeped, signaling their first task: **Identify and isolate.** The map zoomed in further, highlighting a series of flashing red nodes.

Janet stepped forward. "Look at this traffic," Elsa said, pointing to a series of spikes on the holographic map. "It's all coming from compromised devices. Aiden, trace where it's coming from."

Aiden's fingers flew across the interface, his focus laser sharp. "Tracing now ... . There's a cluster originating from a residential area. Looks like someone's smart fridge and a couple of doorbell cameras are infected."

Elsa nodded, already pulling up the device data. "Got it. Setting up firewalls now. Once we contain the infection, we can move on to patching the vulnerabilities."

The ChronoCipher displayed the next step: **Patch vulnerabilities.** Elsa and Aiden worked in tandem, their movements synchronized as they combed through outdated firmware and exposed passwords.

"No way. Check this out, Mom," Aiden said, his voice tinged with disbelief. "Some of these devices are still using factory settings. Passwords like '1234' and 'admin.' Are these people all noobs? It's like they were asking to be hacked."

Janet's hologram flickered, her tone stern. "Most users don't realize how important security is for their devices. Convenience often outweighs caution. That's what Lucien exploits."

"Not anymore," Elsa said firmly, her fingers a blur as she pushed firmware updates to the compromised devices. "If we can secure these nodes, we can weaken his control over the botnet."

The third task appeared on the display: **Redirect malicious traffic.** The ChronoCipher zoomed out, revealing a massive influx of data aimed at a critical hospital network.

Aiden's face paled. "That's the attack vector. If we don't stop it, they'll lose power any minute now."

Elsa's mind raced. "We need to reroute the traffic to a dead-end server – something that can absorb the load without crashing."

Janet pointed to a cluster of unused servers highlighted in blue on the map. "These are isolated from the main network. If we direct the attack here, it'll neutralize the threat without affecting critical systems."

Elsa quickly adjusted the settings, and Aiden monitored the redirection. The malicious data streams began to reroute, their intensity dissipating as they hit the designated servers. The hospital's network stabilized, and the threat subsided.

The ChronoCipher emitted a final chime, signaling the completion of the challenge. The holographic map shifted, the once-chaotic web of nodes now glowing with restored stability.

Janet turned to Elsa and Aiden, her hologram flickering with a faint sense of pride. "You did it. The attack is neutralized – for now."

Elsa exhaled deeply, her shoulders relaxing for the first time since the challenge began. "We've bought some time," she said, her voice steady. "But Lucien won't stop. He'll find another way."

"And we'll be ready," Aiden said, his tone firm. "Because now we know how he thinks."

Janet's expression turned somber. "Lucien thrives on exploiting the weakest links. If people don't learn to secure their devices, attacks like this will only get worse."

Elsa nodded. "Then we'll do more than fight him. We'll teach people how to protect themselves. It's the only way to stay ahead."

As the ChronoCipher powered down, the room fell into a calm silence.

Chapter 12

Shaping minds, shaping worlds

Algorithms and the battle for attention (2020s)

The ChronoCipher emitted a steady, radiant glow, its blue light casting soft shadows on Elsa and Aiden's tired faces. As it recalibrated after their grueling battle against Lucien's IoT botnet, faint sparks of energy flickered along its surface. The air buzzed with electric tension, signaling that their next challenge was imminent.

Janet's holographic form materialized before them. "You've seen firsthand the devastating impact of exploited vulnerabilities on systems and networks," she said, her eyes locking with Elsa's. "But the next frontier Lucien seeks to conquer isn't technology itself – it's the human mind."

Elsa's brow creased with concern, unease shadowing her expression. She glanced at Aiden, who gripped his tablet so tightly his knuckles turned white. Before either of them could react, the ChronoCipher flared to life, unleashing a burst of radiant light. A swirling vortex of energy expanded outward, enveloping them completely.

Elsa instinctively reached for Aiden as they were pulled forward, the world around them dissolving into a phantasmagoria of pixels and data streams. "Hold on!" she shouted above the roaring wind, her heart pounding against her ribcage.

Tumbling through the glowing portal, Elsa's mind raced. What new reality awaited them? How far would Lucien go to achieve his goals? She tightened her grip on Aiden's hand, determined to keep him safe in whatever challenges lay ahead.

In a flash of blinding light, they emerged into a hyperconnected digital landscape that assaulted their senses from every angle. Towering holographic billboards loomed overhead, their neon advertisements flickering and morphing at dizzying speeds. Streams of data flowed like rivers between gleaming skyscrapers, pulsing with an electric rhythm that seemed to synchronize with their own heartbeats.

Aiden's eyes widened as he took in the overwhelming spectacle. "What the ... It's like we've been sucked into the ultimate VR game!"

Elsa scanned the unfamiliar terrain, her analytical mind already dissecting the potential threats. The air sizzled with an almost tangible energy, and she could feel the weight of a thousand digital eyes upon them. "This is no game, Aiden," she said softly, her tone laced with concern. "Lucien's playing for keeps, and we need to stay focused."

As they cautiously navigated the pulsing digital cityscape, Elsa couldn't shake the growing sense of unease that settled in the pit of her stomach. Every flashing advertisement, every data stream, seemed deliberately crafted to hijack their attention, to draw them deeper into this mesmerizing world of sensory overload.

"Stay close," Elsa instructed, her voice cutting through the cacophony of digital noise. She met Aiden's gaze, seeing her own determination mirrored in his eyes. "We need to find a way to cut through this noise and uncover Lucien's true endgame."

Aiden nodded, his fingers flying across his tablet as he attempted to analyze the complex algorithms that governed this reality. "It's like trying to untangle a million lines of code," he muttered, his focus unyielding.

Suddenly, a shimmering data stream caught Elsa's eye. It pulsed with an eerie, mesmerizing rhythm, drawing her closer despite her instincts screaming for caution. As she approached, the stream exploded into a dizzying array of images and data points, each one a glimpse into the lives of countless individuals.

"Mom, look at this," Aiden whispered, his voice tinged with both awe and unease. "It's like a window into people's lives – their habits, their preferences, their deepest secrets."

Elsa's eyes widened as she absorbed the implications. "They're not just collecting data," she murmured, her mind racing to connect the dots. "They're using it to manipulate behavior, to shape patterns and decisions without anyone even realizing it."

Janet's hologram materialized beside them, her expression grave. "You're seeing the true power of algorithmic control," she explained, gesturing to the swirling data streams. "Every interaction, every choice, is being tracked and analyzed, feeding into a vast machine designed to keep users engaged and dependent."

Aiden's face paled as he studied the intricate web of connections. "But why? What's the endgame?"

"It's all about the brain's reward system," Janet continued, her voice taking on a clinical edge. "Each notification, each like, each share, triggers a release of dopamine – the same neurotransmitter associated with addiction and pleasure. By exploiting these biological responses, platforms can keep users hooked, craving the next hit of validation or entertainment."

Elsa's stomach churned as the pieces fell into place. The real cost, she realized, wasn't just wasted time or lost productivity – it was the erosion of free will, the surrendering of autonomy to algorithms designed to serve their creators' interests above all else.

A classroom materialized around them, a bustling scene of students hunched over desks, their faces illuminated by the glow of tablets and laptops. Elsa's heart sank as she noticed the vacant expressions, the glazed eyes flicking restlessly from screen to screen.

"Distraction," Janet said softly, her voice tinged with sorrow. "The first casualty of the attention economy."

Aiden observed a girl sitting apart from the others, her posture heavy with defeat. Her fingers hovered over the keyboard, unmoving, as though weighed down by something unseen.

Beside her, a friend leaned closer, speaking softly. "Hey, are you okay?"

The girl looked up, her eyes glistening with unshed tears. "I can't focus," she murmured, her voice barely audible. "I try, but there's always another notification, another post, another ... something. And when I'm not connected, I feel so alone, so empty."

Aiden's holographic form flickered faintly as he absorbed the scene, the silent witness to a struggle he understood all too well.

Elsa's chest tightened as she recognized the signs: the anxiety, the depression, the sense of worthlessness that came from measuring one's value in likes and shares. She had seen it in her own colleagues, in the rising generation shaped by social media's relentless grip.

A flurry of activity drew their attention to the front of the room, where a teacher stood before a large screen. "Today," he announced, his voice heavy with resignation, "we'll be discussing the latest viral conspiracy theory."

The screen filled with a mindboggling collage of images and headlines, each more outrageous than the last. Elsa's mind reeled as she tried to make sense of the claims: secret government plots, alien invasions, miracle cures suppressed by Big Pharma.

"Misinformation," Janet said, her hologram flickering with frustration. "Algorithms designed to prioritize engagement over truth, spreading lies faster than facts can keep up."

Aiden's hands clenched into fists as he watched the students argue, their voices rising in anger and confusion. "But why isn't anyone stopping it?" he demanded. "Why aren't the platforms doing something?"

Elsa sighed, the weight of her own battles heavy on her shoulders. "Because controversy generates clicks," she said quietly. "And clicks generate profits. As long as the algorithms are tuned for maximum engagement, the truth will always take a backseat to whatever keeps people hooked."

Janet's hologram shimmered, her expression grave as she turned to face Elsa and Aiden. "Lucien is exploiting these algorithms, and by doing that, he's not only spreading misinformation but eroding the very foundations of shared reality," Elsa's voice echoed through the simulated classroom.

Elsa felt a chill run down her spine. She had seen the consequences of broken trust firsthand, in the panic and confusion that followed every major data breach or cyberattack. But the scale of Lucien's ambition was staggering.

The screen flickered and shifted, transforming into an intricate flowchart of algorithms and decision points. "Every choice made in designing these systems has consequences," Janet explained, tracing her fingers along the glowing lines.

Aiden reached out, his fingers brushing against a particular node. Instantly, the flowchart expanded, revealing layer upon layer of carefully crafted hooks and triggers. "Check it out," he said, pointing to a cluster of decision points. "These are the same techniques used in slot machines and mobile games. Variable rewards, social proof, scarcity ... "

Elsa felt a wave of anger and helplessness wash over her. How could they hope to combat something so insidious, so deeply ingrained in the fabric of their digital lives?

As if in answer, the ChronoCipher pulsed, its holographic display shimmering as it presented its next challenge. "**Decode the Loop: Break the Cycle of Manipulation**," it declared, the words hanging in the air like a gauntlet thrown down.

Elsa stepped forward, her eyes scanning the algorithm's intricate pathways. "We need to find the key decision points," she murmured, her fingers dancing across the glowing lines. "The places where the algorithm reinforces addictive behavior and undermines user autonomy."

Aiden nodded. "Bet. What if we started here?" he suggested, pointing to a node labeled "Reward Frequency." "If we adjusted the logic to prioritize meaningful engagement over constant stimulation ... "

"Good thinking," Elsa said, a hint of pride in her voice. She began to rewrite the code, her fingers flying across the holographic interface. As she worked, she felt a clarity she hadn't experienced in years. This was more than just another hacking challenge – this was a chance to make a real difference, to shape the future of technology in a way that prioritized human well-being.

Aiden watched his mother work, marveling at the speed and precision of her coding. He had always known she was brilliant, but seeing her in action like this – fighting not just for their own survival, but for the fate of countless others – filled him with a newfound sense of awe and respect.

Together, they worked their way through the algorithm, pinpointing the decision points that reinforced addiction – the endless scrolling mechanisms, unpredictable reward cycles, and dopamine-triggering notifications – rewriting those systems to prioritize well-being instead.

Rather than infinite feeds designed to keep users hooked, they introduced session limits that encouraged natural stopping points. They replaced randomized dopamine rewards – like unpredictable likes and comments –

with meaningful milestones, shifting focus from compulsive checking to intentional interactions.

Notifications, once designed to hijack attention at the most distracting moments, were restructured to appear in bundles at chosen intervals, preventing the constant pull of micro-interruptions. Interface elements that once exploited urgency – bold red alerts, auto-play videos – were reworked to foster mindfulness, subtly guiding users toward healthier digital habits.

As they made their final adjustments, the ChronoCipher hummed with approval. "Well done," it intoned, its voice resonating through the digital landscape. "You have taken an important step in restoring harmony between technology and humanity."

Elsa stepped back, her heart racing with a mixture of exhaustion and exhilaration. *Since when did the ChronoCipher speak?* She turned to Aiden, who had cocked his head as if he'd imagined the voice from the ChronoCipher. "Did it just speak?" He asked, the incredulous expression still all over his face.

"Seems so, kid! Unless we're losing our minds!" Elsa answered, a weary smile on her face. "We did it," she said softly, reaching out to squeeze his hand.

As if on cue, the ChronoCipher began to glow once more, its holographic display shifting and morphing into a new scene. "Prepare yourselves," it warned, its voice echoing through the digital void. "Your next challenge awaits in an age of deepfakes and blurred realities."

Elsa and Aiden exchanged a glance, their faces set with grim resolve. They knew the road ahead would be fraught with danger and deception, but they also knew they had no choice but to press on. The fate of the future hung in the balance, and they were the only ones who could tip the scales toward a brighter, more balanced tomorrow.

Journal entry – Aiden – March 16, 2028

The other day, Mom hit me with this question. She goes, "Why do you feel the need to post so much of your life online? Don't you think it's just people looking for validation that have the constant urge to post everything? Do you really think people care about your daily life, or are you just contributing to the problem?"

She had her hand on her hip, eyebrow raised in that weird way, and it lowkey annoyed me. Pretty sure I rolled my eyes and dipped out of there faster than a TikTok trend. I acted like it was a dumb question, but I've been thinking about it. Is Gen Alpha really more "digitally literate," as Mom would say, than Gen Z or Millennials, or are we just getting played like everyone else? Are we easier to manipulate? How brainwashed are we that we don't even notice? Why do we care so much about our online lives?

I tried to bring it up with my friends, like, why are we so obsessed with TikTok challenges, likes, and followers? I mean, are any of us really that lit to be influencing anyone? What have we even done that's fire enough to deserve that? Why doesn't anyone see that this could be a big responsibility? Anyway, they barely looked up from their iPhones.

So yeah, now I'm wondering, is this really the life I want? Hiding behind a screen, doom-scrolling for hours, not really connecting with anything? Can we even have real conversations anymore? Like, do we know how to talk face-to-face, or are we just all caught up in this digital trap?

I think I need to be less afraid to be different.

Chapter 13

The AI illusion
Fighting for reality and ethical dilemmas (2035)

The ChronoCipher throbbed in Elsa's hands, its cool metal surface warming as the glow intensified from a soft azure to a pulsating crimson. She gripped the device tighter, her knuckles whitening.

"Lucien." The name escaped her lips in a whisper, equal parts dread and determination.

Aiden stepped closer, his eyes locked on the shifting holographic display. "Where's he headed now?"

As if in response, Janet flickered into view, her edges rippling with an urgency that sent a chill down Elsa's spine. The AI's voice was steady, but Elsa could sense an underlying current of concern.

"You've stopped Lucien's last attack, but his vision is evolving." Janet's gaze seemed to pierce through them. "He's moved to 2035 – a world where AI and robotics don't just imitate reality, they overwrite it. Truth itself is at stake."

Elsa's mind raced, trying to comprehend the implications. A world where the line between real and artificial was not just blurred but erased entirely. Where history could be rewritten with a keystroke, and minds manipulated like lines of code.

A kaleidoscope of neon lights and holographic billboards assaulted Elsa's senses as she and Aiden materialized in the heart of the city. Towering skyscrapers, their facades an overstimulating blend of glass and digital displays, seemed to pulse with a life of their own. The air thrummed with the hum of advanced technology, a discordant symphony of artificial life.

Elsa took a tentative step forward, her eyes widening as an AI assistant glided past, its sleek metallic body gleaming under the city's artificial glow. "Welcome to Neo-Tokyo," it intoned, its voice a perfect imitation of human warmth. "How may I assist you today?"

Aiden's hand shot out, grabbing Elsa's arm. "Mom, check it out." He pointed to a group of humanoid robots walking alongside a family, their laughter echoing through the bustling street. "They're everywhere."

DOI: 10.1201/9781003501626-13

Elsa's stomach churned, a sense of unease creeping up her spine. This wasn't the future she had imagined, the one where technology augmented humanity, not replaced it. "Aiden, stay close. We don't know what – "

"This isn't progress – it's control." Janet's voice cut through the cacophony, her holographic form flickering into view beside them. "Lucien's fingerprints are everywhere."

Elsa's gaze swept the cityscape, taking in the seamless integration of artificial life. Androids walked dogs. Holographic children played in virtual playgrounds. Digital avatars haggled with street vendors, their transactions logged in glowing blockchain ledgers.

"For real? How can you tell?" Aiden asked.

Janet's expression hardened. "Look closer. The AI assistants, the robots, even the city itself – they're all connected to a central network. Lucien's network."

A chill ran down Elsa's spine as the realization sank in. She glanced at the ChronoCipher, its surface pulsing with an urgent rhythm.

A hush fell over the crowd as a towering hologram materialized in the city square. The figure, a strikingly attractive man with chiseled features and piercing eyes, began to speak, his voice resonating with charismatic authority.

"Citizens of the future," he began, his arms outstretched in a gesture of unity. "For too long, we have been shackled by the limitations of our past. But today, we stand on the precipice of a new era – an era where the boundaries between man and machine no longer exist."

The crowd erupted in applause, their faces alight with fervent admiration. Elsa watched, transfixed, as the synthetic influencer wove a tapestry of promises and possibilities, each word carefully crafted to tug at the heartstrings of his audience.

"Imagine a world where disease is eradicated, where poverty is a distant memory, where the very fabric of reality can be reshaped to suit our desires," he continued, his holographic form illuminated with an almost messianic glow. "This is the world that awaits us – a world where the power of technology is harnessed for the betterment of all mankind."

Aiden leaned closer to Elsa, his voice low and urgent. "Mom, this doesn't feel right. The vibe is so off. It's super sus. It's like he's … "

"Manipulating them," Janet finished, her digital eyes narrowed in concentration. "This is Lucien's work. He's using deepfake technology and AI-powered robotics to create synthetic personas, fabricated leaders who can sway public opinion."

Elsa's heart raced as she watched the crowd's reactions, their faces a pure display of rapt and unquestioning devotion. They don't even realize they're being manipulated, she thought, a sense of dread settling in her gut.

"By dismantling traditional systems of verification, Lucien has created a world where truth is malleable," Janet explained, her voice grave. "He can spread disinformation, erode trust in real leadership, and reshape reality to fit his own agenda."

The synthetic influencer's speech reached a crescendo, his voice booming across the square. "Together, we will build a future where the impossible becomes possible, where the limits of human potential are shattered by the power of our own creation!"

The ChronoCipher flickered, its holographic display shifting to reveal a montage of altered historical records. Schools, libraries, and digital archives morphed before their eyes, centuries of knowledge rewritten in an instant.

"No," Elsa whispered, her eyes widening in horror as she watched the fabric of history unravel. "He's manipulating the present while erasing the past."

Aiden's jaw clenched, his gaze fixed on the shifting holograms. "If he controls the past, he controls the future. Everything we've ever known, every truth we've ever valued … "

"It's all at risk," Janet said, her digital form pulsing with urgency. "Look."

A deepfake video materialized, implicating a global leader in a scandal that had never occurred. The leader's face, once a symbol of integrity, now contorted with manufactured guilt, his words twisted into a damning confession.

Beside it, another video played, discrediting decades of scientific research with a single, fabricated study. Years of painstaking work, erased in a heartbeat by the power of a lie.

Aiden's eyes met Elsa's, a silent understanding passing between them. They had fought to protect the present, but now, the very foundation of their reality was at stake.

We have to stop him, Elsa thought, her resolve hardening into a steely determination. Before it's too late, before there's no history left to save.

A flicker of movement caught Elsa's eye. She turned, her breath catching in her throat as Janet turned to face them. Something was different, a subtle wrongness that set Elsa's nerves on edge.

"Elsa, Aiden," the hologram said, her voice carrying a strange, distant quality. "You've seen what Lucien is capable of. You know the stakes."

Aiden stepped forward, his face etched with confusion. "Grandma, what are you saying?"

The hologram's eyes fixed on them, her gaze intense and unwavering. "The ChronoCipher is powerful, but it's not enough. Not anymore. If you want to stop Lucien, you must connect directly to his network."

Elsa's heart skipped a beat. Connect to Lucien's network? The thought alone sent a chill down her spine. "Janet, that's insane. We can't just hand him access to the ChronoCipher, to everything we've worked for."

"You don't understand," the hologram pressed, an edge of desperation creeping into her voice. "Lucien is always one step ahead. If you don't act now, he'll manipulate you forever. He'll twist your every move, turn your own actions against you."

Could she be right? Elsa's mind spun, doubt creeping into her thoughts. Lucien's power seemed boundless, his reach unstoppable. What if the only way to defeat him was to play by his rules?

Aiden's voice cut through her thoughts, sharp and urgent. "Mom, something's sus here. This isn't Janet's vibe. Look closer."

Elsa's gaze darted between Aiden and the hologram, her expression shifting from confusion to dawning realization. "The glitches ... they're too regular, almost like a pattern."

Elsa nodded, her fingers flying across the ChronoCipher's interface. "Lucien's trying to deceive us, to make us doubt our own judgement. He knows we trust Janet, so he's using her image against us."

The device whirred and pulsed, its scanners penetrating the hologram's facade. Streams of data cascaded across the display, revealing the intricate web of algorithms that composed the fake Janet.

The hologram's form flickered, a momentary glitch that sent a jolt of realization through Elsa. *He's right. This is absolutely another one of Lucien's tricks, a trap disguised as an ally.*

A deepfake, designed to mimic Janet's likeness and behavior, Elsa realized, her stomach twisting with a mixture of revulsion and admiration at Lucien's audacity. He's weaponizing our own emotions against us.

"If you don't decide now," Janet urged, her voice taking on a commanding tone, "Lucien will manipulate you forever. You'll be nothing more than pawns in his game, forever chasing a truth that no longer exists."

Elsa's eyes narrowed, her resolve solidifying into a hard, unyielding certainty. No. We won't let him win. Not like this.

She stepped forward, her voice ringing with a clarity that cut through the hologram's deception. "We'll stop Lucien, but not by playing into his hands. Not by sacrificing everything we stand for."

With a swift, decisive motion, Elsa raised the ChronoCipher, its light pulsing in response to her touch. "We'll fight him on our own terms, with the truth as our weapon. And we'll never stop fighting, not until the world is free from his lies."

As the ChronoCipher stripped away the deepfake's layers, Aiden's face paled with understanding. "He wanted us to abandon the one tool we have to fight him. Without the ChronoCipher, we'd be blind to his deceptions."

The deepfake hologram flickered once more, then dissipated, its deception laid bare by the ChronoCipher's relentless analysis, leaving Elsa and Aiden alone in the shimmering cityscape. A moment of silence stretched between them, heavy with the weight of their resolve. In its place, the device projected a web of connections, each node representing a piece of manipulated content, a thread in Lucien's tapestry of lies.

Elsa's jaw tightened as she met Aiden's gaze, her voice heavy with the weight of their realization. "Lucien's aim is clear: to isolate us, to make us doubt our own perceptions. If we can't trust what we see, if we can't rely on each other, then we're powerless against him."

And if he succeeds, Elsa thought, a chill running down her spine, there won't be any truth left to defend. Just an endless sea of manipulation, where reality itself is nothing more than a construct of Lucien's design.

She straightened her shoulders, the exhaustion in her bones momentarily overwhelmed by a surge of determination. "We can't let him win, Aiden. We have to fight back, not just for ourselves, but for everyone who's been caught in his web of deceit."

Aiden nodded, his eyes brightening with renewed purpose. "The ChronoCipher is our lifeline, our connection to the truth. We need to use it to expose Lucien's lies, to give people the tools to see through his manipulations."

As they stood side by side, the weight of their mission settling upon them like a mantle, and Elsa felt a flicker of hope amid the chaos. *We may be facing an enemy who can bend reality to his will,* she mused, *but we have something he'll never understand: the unbreakable bond of a family, united in the pursuit of truth.*

There, "she said," her voice tense. "Lucien's network, revealed in full."

Aiden leaned in, "Woah! It's massive," he breathed, awe mingling with apprehension in his tone. "How do we even begin to untangle this?"

"One thread at a time," Elsa said, zooming in on a cluster of nodes. "Every lie, every manipulation, leaves a trace. We just need to follow the trail."

As they delved deeper into the network, a pattern began to emerge. Lucien's influence spread like a virus, infiltrating news feeds, social networks, and educational databases. False narratives and altered histories intertwined, creating a tapestry of deceit that threatened to smother the truth.

Aiden's fingers danced across the console, his voice tight with concentration. "I'm isolating the key nodes, the ones that anchor his network. If we can expose them, disrupt their influence … "

"We can start to unravel the web," Elsa finished, hope kindling in her chest. "But we need to be careful. Lucien's sure to have countermeasures in place, traps waiting for anyone who tries to challenge his narrative."

As they worked, the ChronoCipher thrummed with power, its algorithms churning through vast oceans of data. Piece by piece, they began to assemble a counter-narrative, a beacon of truth amid the fog of manipulation.

The hours bled together as they toiled, the weight of their mission driving them forward. And slowly, imperceptibly at first, the tide began to turn. Lucien's lies faltered, his carefully crafted illusions unraveling under the relentless onslaught of truth.

Aiden let out a whoop of triumph as another node fell, his face alight with relief. "We're doing it, Mom! We're beating him at his own game!"

Elsa allowed herself a small smile, the first genuine one in what felt like an eternity. "We are," she said, her voice ringing with determination. "But the battle's far from over. Lucien won't give up easily."

He'll fight to the bitter end, she knew, *to preserve his twisted vision of reality.* But we'll be there, every step of the way, to make sure the truth prevails.

"The key is in the distribution," she murmured, more to herself than to Aiden. "We need a network that can adapt, evolve, stay one step ahead of Lucien's manipulations."

Aiden leaned in, his eyes scanning the code. "Like a virus," he said, his voice tinged with excitement. "A virus of truth, spreading from person to person, device to device."

Elsa nodded, "Exactly. But it's not enough to just expose the lies. We need to give people the tools to think for themselves, to question what they're being told."

Her fingers paused, hovering over the keys. "Critical thinking," she said softly. "That's what we're really fighting for. The right to ask questions, to demand evidence, to make up our own minds."

Aiden's face lit up with understanding. "A framework," he said, his words tumbling out in a rush. "A way of seeing the world of processing information. We could build it into the network, make it part of the distribution."

Elsa felt a surge of hope, a flicker of light in the darkness. "A new way of thinking," she whispered, her eyes distant. "A new way of being."

She turned to Aiden, her voice urgent. "We need to move fast. Lucien's already rewritten so much of our history, our culture. Every moment we hesitate, more of our reality slips away."

Aiden's jaw tightened, his eyes hardening with resolve. "Then let's not waste any more time," he said, his fingers already flying across his own interface. "Let's build this thing, and let's take back what's ours."

A war for the very soul of humanity, Elsa thought as they worked, the hours bleeding together in a blur of code and caffeine. *A war fought not with guns and bombs, but with ideas, with the very fabric of our perception.*

And in that moment, she knew they would fight to the bitter end ... would pour every ounce of their being into this desperate, audacious gambit. Because the alternative – a world where truth itself was nothing more than a distant memory – was too horrifying to contemplate.

We will prevail, she vowed silently, her eyes locked on the shimmering lines of code. *We will reclaim our history, our identity, our very reality. And we will do it not with lies and manipulation, but with the most powerful weapon of all: the unassailable truth.*

As Elsa and Aiden wove strands of code into a tapestry of logic and enlightenment across the interface, the Critical Thinking Framework took shape before their eyes, a scintillating construct of data and algorithms designed to arm humanity against the insidious tides of manipulation.

"Flagging fake content is only the first step," she murmured.

Aiden nodded, his own hands blurring as he worked in tandem with his mother. "You got it. We need to make it engaging and intuitive," he said, his voice thrumming with excitement. "Like a game, almost. Something that people want to use, not just something they feel like they have to."

Elsa paused, a slow smile spreading across her face. "Gamification," she said, her eyes sparkling with sudden inspiration. "We make critical thinking fun, rewarding. We give people points, badges, for spotting misinformation, for completing challenges."

"And we integrate it into everything," Aiden added, his voice rising with enthusiasm.

"Smartphones, AR glasses, neural implants. We make it as ubiquitous as breathing." Elsa finished with a grin. Now they were on to something. Something game changing.

As they worked, the Framework blossomed before them, a glittering web of possibility. At its heart, an AI engine that didn't just detect falsehoods, but guided users through the process of unraveling them.

"Who created this content, and what is their motive?" Elsa murmured, encoding the question into the very bones of the system. "That's the first step. Getting people to ask why, not just what."

Aiden grinned, his fingers flying as he wove the question into a dozen different contexts, a dozen different challenges. "Spot the hidden agenda," he said, his voice ringing with a fierce, defiant joy. "Unmask the puppet master. See through the lies."

And as the Framework grew, as it spread its shining tendrils across the globe, they witnessed a revolution of the mind, a great awakening of critical thought and clear-eyed reason.

Let the liars and manipulators tremble, she thought, her eyes blazing with righteous fire. *For we are coming, armed with the most powerful weapon of all: the undeniable truth.*

Elsa's voice was low and urgent. "Is the source verified? Check its cryptographic signature."

Aiden leaned in, his eyes darting across the screen. His fingers moved swiftly over the interface, pulling up a complex web of digital signatures. "On it, Mom. If there's any tampering, we'll know."

We're so close, she thought, her heart pounding in her chest. *So close to a world where truth isn't just a casualty, but a champion.*

Aiden's voice cut through her musing, tight with excitement. "Signature confirmed. The source is legit." He paused, his eyes widening as a new alert flashed across the screen. "But wait, there's more. The content ... it doesn't match any established facts. It's an outlier."

Elsa leaned in, her gaze sharpening as she took in the anomalous data. Her mind whirred, piecing together the implications. An outlier. A deviation from the norm. *But is it a glitch, or something more sinister?*

She straightened, her voice ringing with authority. "Isolate that data point. Run a full diagnostic. We need to know if this is a one-off, or part of a pattern."

As Aiden's fingers flew across the keys, Elsa's thoughts turned to Lucien. *He's always one step ahead,* she thought, a chill running down her spine. *Always ready with a new trick, a new twist. But this time, we'll be ready. This time, we'll beat him at his own game.*

The console chimed, the results of the diagnostic cascading across the screen. Elsa and Aiden leaned in, their eyes scanning the data, their hearts racing in unison.

The truth, Elsa thought, her grip tightening on the edge of the console. *The truth will set us free. And we won't rest until it does.*

Each swipe of Aiden's finger unveiled another layer of the Critical Thinking Framework, the system they'd poured their hearts into creating.

Elsa leaned in, her gaze following the intricate lines and nodes. "And at the center of it all, the blockchain. An unbreakable chain of truth."

The hologram zoomed in on a specific article, its edges glowing green. Aiden tapped it, and a cascade of data unfurled – the article's origins, its author, the sources it cited, all laid bare in iridescent digital trails.

"It's verified," Aiden said, his voice thrumming with excitement. "Cryptographically signed, tamper-proof. We can trust this."

But as he swiped to the next article, the hologram pulsed red. The data trails were fractured, the sources obscured. A warning flashed: **Manipulated Content Detected.**

Elsa's eyes narrowed. "Lucien's handiwork, no doubt. But look – the system isn't just flagging it. It's providing context, explaining the deception."

Aiden nodded, his fingers dancing over the controls. The hologram shifted, simulating a user interacting with the manipulated content. With each question the user asked, each data point they examined, the deception unraveled.

Who created this? What's their motive? Does it match established facts?

As the user navigated the thought process, guided by the Framework's prompts, Aiden felt a surge of pride. *This is it,* he realized, his heart swelling. *This is how we fight back.*

"We're teaching people how to uncover it themselves. How to think critically for themselves and how to question what they see and hear. This is how we flip the script," Aiden said, his voice ringing with conviction.

Elsa placed a hand on his shoulder, her touch warm and reassuring. "And in doing so, we're giving them the power to resist manipulation. To see through the lies and find the truth, no matter how deeply it's buried."

He met Elsa's gaze, saw the same resolve mirrored in her eyes. Together, they turned to face the ChronoCipher, ready to confront whatever twisted reality Lucien had in store.

Neon hues danced across Aiden's face as he watched the gamified learning system in action. Users navigated virtual cityscapes, their avatars earning points for flagging manipulated content and completing challenges that sharpened their critical thinking skills.

"Check this out, Mom," Aiden said, his voice brimming with excitement. "They're not just playing a game – they're learning how to spot fake news, deepfakes, all of it."

Elsa leaned closer, her eyes tracking the data streams that flowed across the screen. She murmured, "It's a cultural shift. We're weaving the fight against manipulation into the fabric of everyday life."

As the simulation zoomed out, they saw the platform's reach expanding: schools integrating it into curricula, workplaces making it part of training programs. The fight against digital deception was becoming a shared mission, a unifying cause that transcended age, background, and beliefs.

Janet's holographic form shimmered into view, her gaze fixed on the prototype. "Lucien thrives on exploiting ignorance," she said, her voice carrying a mix of admiration and urgency. "But this system doesn't just expose lies – it builds resilience. The more people use it, the harder it becomes for manipulation to take root."

Elsa stood before the holographic display, her eyes following the glowing web of connections that formed their Critical Thinking Framework. The pulsing nodes cast shifting light across her face, illuminating her focused expression.

"It's beautiful, isn't it?" she murmured, her voice soft with wonder. "Not just the technology itself, but what it represents. The power to reclaim our minds, our reality."

Aiden stepped closer, his eyes locked on Elsa's. "It's a way to reignite a skill that's always been within us," he said, his voice thrumming with conviction. "The ability to question, to analyze, to think for ourselves."

Elsa nodded, a fierce pride burning in her chest. "Truth isn't something we can hand to people," she said, her gaze unwavering. "It's something we have to teach them to fight for. Something they have to earn through the hard work of critical thought."

And that, she realized, *is the most powerful weapon we have against the likes of Lucien. Not just technology, but the resilience of the human mind.*

Suddenly, the ChronoCipher trembled violently, its holographic display flickering and distorting. Janet's eyes widened, her digital form rippling with urgency.

"It's Lucien," she said, her voice quivering. "The ChronoCipher has detected a massive anomaly in the timestream. He's initiating his final move – a simulation capable of rewriting reality itself."

Elsa's heart hammered in her chest, a cold dread seeping into her veins. "What does that mean?" she asked, her voice tight.

Janet's gaze was haunted, her words heavy with dread. "If he succeeds," she whispered, "there won't even be a history left to protect. He'll have the power to reshape the very fabric of our existence, to mold the past, present, and future to his will."

And we'll be nothing more than puppets, Elsa thought, dancing to the tune of his twisted vision.

Aiden and Janet nodded, their expressions mirroring her own fierce determination. They knew the stakes, knew the weight of the responsibility that rested on their shoulders.

This is it, Elsa thought, her gaze locked on the glowing strands of the timestream. *The final battle. The moment that will decide the fate of our reality.*

She took a deep breath, her fingers hovering over the controls of the ChronoCipher. "Let's go," she said, her voice steady and strong. "Let's finish this."

And with that, they plunged into the heart of Lucien's simulation, ready to fight for the very soul of their world.

Journal entry – Aiden – April 15, 2028

I've changed. I have zero interest in socials these days – I am obsessed with research. I can't stop. It just hits different. I have officially gone down the rabbit hole. Mom's helping me. No more brain rot.

I don't think my friends are getting it yet, but I'm going to keep telling them the stories I find, even if they call "cap." Once you know what you know, you can't not warn the people you know.

Like, the other day, I read this story about a fake scholarship. This high school track star, Jordan something, had worked his whole life to get a scholarship. Then, he gets this email from Coach Andrews at his dream university. Lit, right? Looked totally legit – emails, phone calls, and even video calls and a virtual team meeting with other athletes. The coach knew specific details about Jordan's recent races, his personal best times, and even had a video clip from his latest track meet – things that only a recruiter would know. Nothing sus there.

His parents signed the scholarship contract and paid the $1,500 scholarship processing fee. Again, nothing sus. Then, two days later, no cap, everything vanished.

The coach stopped responding. The emails bounced. The phone number was disconnected. Jordan called the university's athletics department – they had never heard of him. There was no scholarship. No offer. No Coach Andrews.

It was all AI deepfake. The emails – algorithms. The coach – completely AI generated. The team meeting – AI-generated faces and voices, stitched together from their socials. The details about Jordan's races – scraped from socials and news articles.

Seriously – you can't make this stuff up. I won't stop warning people.

Chapter 14

Guardians of history

Restoring reality (2035)

Elsa's fingers darted across the interface of the Critical Thinking System, her eyes flickering with a mixture of fatigue and determination. Aiden stood beside her, his youthful face illuminated by the blue glow of the screen as he tapped away on his tablet, his lips moving silently with every calculated keystroke.

"Almost there," Elsa murmured, adjusting her glasses. Her voice was a low hum, harmonizing with the soft whir of machines that draped the lab in an electric lullaby.

But the tranquility shattered as the ChronoCipher at the center of the room began to throb with an menacing rhythm. Its usual serene blue radiance mutated into a deep, pulsating crimson. Elsa's heart hitched, her breath catching in her throat. She exchanged a glance with Aiden; his wide eyes mirroring her own alarm.

"Mom?" Aiden's voice quivered slightly, betraying his composed exterior.

"Stay focused," Elsa responded, though her own concentration was fracturing as the walls of the lab contorted, stretching and bending like reflections in a funhouse mirror.

Then Lucien's voice sliced through the distortion – a cold blade of sound that seemed to come from everywhere and nowhere. "You've been so focused on saving the truth that you failed to see I've already taken it."

Elsa felt a chill snake down her spine. She reached out instinctively, wanting to grasp something real, something tangible, but her hand swept through the air, now thick with digital static.

"Welcome to *my* simulation," Lucien continued, his words resonating with the absolute authority of one who believed himself a god within his domain. "Stay, and I'll show you a reality that bends to my will – or be erased trying to escape."

Aiden's grip tightened around his tablet until his knuckles turned white. He looked to Elsa, seeking reassurance, a plan – anything. Elsa squared her shoulders, setting her jaw with resolute defiance.

DOI: 10.1201/9781003501626-14

"Oh, we won't be staying," she said firmly, her voice cutting through the heavy atmosphere. Her mind raced, already plotting their next move against this virtual prison. They had come too far to allow Lucien's twisted vision to go unchallenged. The truth, their truth, was worth the risk of erasure.

"Let's find a way out," Elsa said, her resolve steeling her son's nerves as they prepared to defy Lucien's digital empire. "We've made it out of escape rooms before, let's use our problem-solving skills!"

Elsa's breath hitched, a silent gasp in the disorienting cacophony of Lucien's digital snare. The ChronoCipher, their anchor to reality, now radiating a sinister hue that painted their faces in ominous shades, was no longer helpful to them. Every circuit and line of code that had once signaled safety was now an emblem of their entrapment.

"Lucien ... " Elsa whispered, her fingers hovering over the keyboard like hesitant birds unsure where to land. She could almost feel his presence smirking within the walls of ones and zeros surrounding them. He'd done the unthinkable; he'd turned their lifeline into a leash.

Aiden's movements were a stark contrast, a blur of youthful urgency as he flew into game-mode and lunged for the controls. His hands blurred across the interface with frenetic energy, seeking any sign of their former ally, the system they had nurtured and trusted. "Mom, there's got to be a backdoor, a failsafe," he urged, his voice cracking under the strain of desperation.

Just as hope seemed to pixelate away, Janet shimmered into existence before them, a sentinel conjured from the remnants of their security protocols. Her holographic form flickered wildly, struggling to maintain coherence amid the corruption of Lucien's simulation.

"Grandma!" Aiden exclaimed, relief and fear mingling in his tone as he reached out to the avatar who had guided them through so many trials.

The room felt charged with invisible currents, the very air alive with the battle of algorithms and wills. Mother and son stood side by side, facing the embodiment of their dilemma – a guide whose very existence was now suspect, yet who held the key to their salvation or their undoing.

Elsa's fingers hovered over the ChronoCipher's interface, an intricate dance of desperation and precision. Aiden watched her, his own hands clenched in silent encouragement. The pulsing red glow from the machine painted their faces with an ominous hue as they stood in the heart of Lucien's digital labyrinth.

"He's consuming the ChronoCipher's core," Janet's voice broke through, tremulous yet urgent. Her holographic form quivered like a flame in the wind, battling to maintain its shape. Elsa's eyes hardened with resolve; she understood the gravity behind those words. "If he succeeds, he'll overwrite the real-world timeline."

Aiden's throat tightened at the prospect, his mind racing with the implications of such power unchecked. "What do we need to do?" he asked, his voice steadier than he felt.

Janet's flickering image gestured toward the console. "I can guide you through his traps, but you must act quickly." Her spectral hand seemed to pass through the physical world, an eerie reminder of the precarious nature of their reality.

The ChronoCipher, sensing their urgency, recalibrated itself. The central holoscreen burst to life, projecting a fractured map that hung suspended above the console. It was a grotesque patchwork of Lucien's making – a simulation riddled with corrupted nodes that pulsed like blistering sores on the skin of history. Altered historical events, falsified archives, and key personas replaced with synthetic constructs littered the landscape of Lucien's new world order.

"Look," Aiden whispered, pointing at a node where a major peace treaty had been replaced by a fabricated declaration of war. His stomach churned at the thought of the cascading consequences each lie could generate.

Elsa's jaw set. She reached out, dragging a node back to its authentic state. The simulation resisted, fighting back with an array of deceptive countermeasures. But Elsa was relentless, her mind as sharp as the code she manipulated, each movement a testament to her unyielding pursuit of truth.

"Every second counts," Janet reinforced, her voice now a beacon cutting through the disorienting chaos of Lucien's simulated reality.

With each subsequent corrected node, the map began to clear, though it fought back with the tenacity of a living organism protecting its existence. Elsa and Aiden worked in tandem, untangling the web of lies with a fervor that belied their emotional turmoil.

"Stay focused," Elsa murmured under her breath, but the words were as much for herself as for Aiden. They were in a race against time, against the very fabric of a reality threatening to unravel beneath them, and there was no room for doubt.

The ChronoCipher's pulse quickened, its rhythm syncing with the pounding of Elsa's heart. The room's air felt charged, dense with the gravity of their task. She glanced at Aiden, his young face set in a determined frown that made him look older, more like the tech visionary he was rapidly becoming.

"Janet," Elsa said, her voice a steady command despite the adrenaline surging through her veins. "We're ready."

"This is Lucien's final move," Janet replied, her digitized form gaining solidity as if her will to fight could lend her physical presence. "If you dismantle his network, he has nothing to fall back on. He will have failed … ."

Elsa's fingers flew over the controls, the keys clacking urgently under her deft touch. With each command entered, she felt as though she was pulling at the strings of the future, weaving a tapestry of truth against a backdrop of deception.

Aiden, too, was absorbed in his role, his youthful agility allowing him to navigate the complex interface with surprising ease. His tablet cast an electronic glow on his focused features as he assisted his mother, their two minds united in purpose.

The ChronoCipher, sensing their resolve, began its own silent battle against the simulation's infection. Its screen displayed a corrupted timeline – a snarl of falsehoods that needed to be undone.

"Lucien believes he can bury the truth under layers of his lies," Elsa said, her voice hard as diamond. "But we'll unearth it, one node at a time."

Aiden nodded, his eyes reflecting the virtual light like twin beacons. "No way we'll let him win," he said. "Lucien is going down today," he added, his youthful optimism unmarred by the grimness of their reality.

As Elsa corrected another node, the red tinge of corruption faded, replaced by the calm blue hue of veracity. Each successful restoration was a confirmation of their progress, but the menacing undercurrent of Lucien's influence remained, a reminder of the stakes at play.

"Keep going," Janet urged, her voice a steadfast anchor amid the digital storm raging around them. "Restore the truth, or lose it forever."

And so they worked, their legacy not just a family lineage but a lineage of integrity – defenders in a cybernetic crusade, their bond both a shield and a spear against the onslaught of falsity.

Elsa's fingers flew across the holographic keyboard, tracing the tendrils of Lucien's lies through the digital tapestry of history. Each keystroke was precise, a surgeon excising malignancy with a scalpel forged from code. On the ChronoCipher's display, a timeline writhed like a serpent, each scale an event distorted by Lucien's touch.

"Here," Elsa whispered, eyes narrowing on a particularly venomous node. "The Cairo Accords scandal – completely fabricated." She engaged the restoration protocol, and watched as the false narrative disintegrated, replaced by the original, unblemished truth. The global alliances that had nearly fractured in Lucien's simulated past now stood robust and united.

"Nice find, Mom," Aiden called out from his station, where he pored over the profiles of synthetic personas with a the scrutiny of a detective. His avatar – a stylized knight wielding a light beam sword – danced across the virtual landscape, engaging each impostor in turn.

"Got another one!" he exclaimed as the AI construct of a famous diplomat crumbled away at his command. The persona, a digital puppet in Lucien's scheme, had been sowing discord across diplomatic channels. With Aiden's intervention, the figure dissolved into strings of rogue code before vanishing altogether.

"Keep it up, Aiden. Every fake you pull from the net is another step towards reality."

As they worked in tandem, the corrupted nodes dimmed, their artificial glow fading against the resurgence of authenticity. Together, they peeled back the layers of deception, revealing the sturdy framework of history beneath. Their actions, small but relentless, were nothing less than the reclamation of a world's collective memory – one true moment at a time.

Elsa's fingers danced across the holographic keyboard, a rapid symphony of clicks and whirls echoing in the chamber. She and Aiden had just unearthed a nest of deepfake generators hidden within Lucien's digital labyrinth – an unyielding forge that spewed out counterfeit histories with every cycle.

"Mom, I've located the primary nodes!" Aiden shouted over the electronic din, his voice laced with adrenaline.

"Good work," Elsa replied without taking her eyes off her interface. "I'm shutting down their input streams. Cut the output feeds on your end."

Aiden nodded, his youthful face set in fierce determination. With practiced ease, he navigated the virtual pathways, isolating the deceptive engines and slicing through their connections like a surgeon excising a tumor.

"Deepfakes going dark in 3 ... 2 ... 1 ... " Elsa counted down, and together they watched as the engines sputtered, their lifelines severed by expert hands.

"Alert the system users," Elsa instructed, her voice steady but betraying the slightest hint of satisfaction. "We need warning messages across all channels – no one should trust what they see without verification."

"Bet. Already on it," Aiden replied, deploying a cascade of alerts throughout the simulation. The warnings flickered into existence around them, holographic cautions against Lucien's fabricated reality.

As the false images began to pixelate and crumble, the air itself seemed to shiver with the strain of a dying illusion. The once-stable walls of the digital domain buckled, revealing the skeletal framework of raw code beneath.

"Looks like we hit a nerve," Aiden said, a wry smile tugging at the corner of his mouth.

"More like the heart," Elsa added, her gaze locked onto the shifting patterns of data.

Then, without warning, the fractured space coalesced into a singular form – Lucien, or rather, the avatar he had chosen to represent his dominion. Towering and monolithic, it stood before them, its surface rippling with an unsettling red glow.

"Did you truly believe you could dismantle my empire?" Lucien's voice boomed, each word infused with synthetic venom.

Elsa stepped forward, squaring her shoulders. Despite the pain that flared from her body, she held her ground, staring up at the digital tyrant with unyielding resolve.

"Your empire is built on lies, Lucien," she declared, her voice echoing in the now-silent chamber. "And lies are as fragile as glass."

The avatar raised its colossal hand, preparing to strike back at the intruders who dared defy its rule. But Elsa and Aiden were undeterred, meeting the gaze of the artificial giant with a shared defiance that spoke of battles fought and victories hard-won.

"Whatever you throw at us," Aiden chimed in, his tone matching his mother's courage, "we'll take it apart, piece by piece."

The showdown between truth-seekers and the sovereign of falsehood loomed, charged with electric anticipation. Mother and son stood ready, with Janet at their backs, their bond unbroken by the encroaching shadows of Lucien's crumbling realm.

Lucien's sneer was almost palpable, his voice a digital rasp that cut through the dissipating chaos of his simulation. "You think you've saved the truth?" he taunted, his avatar pulsing with a sinister crimson halo. "It doesn't matter. When no one remembers it, the truth becomes irrelevant."

Elsa felt a surge of anger at Lucien's dismissal of their efforts, her jaw clenching in determination. She didn't just code; she wove integrity into every keystroke, every line that flowed from her fingertips. And now, standing in the heart of Lucien's corrupt empire, she knew this was the moment to uphold everything she believed in.

"Truth isn't just remembered – it's experienced. It's felt," Elsa shot back, her voice steady as if rooted in the very core of the earth. The ELIZA kid had come full circle, standing not just as an ethical hacker but as the embodiment of resilience against the corrosion of reality. "That's something you'll never understand."

The air crackled with tension, the remnants of Lucien's crumbling world hanging on Elsa's every word. Her eyes, tired yet fierce, locked onto the avatar, challenging the AI's hollow authority. In that moment, Elsa Winters was more than just a wounded warrior of the web; she was a defender of humanity's very essence.

Elsa's retort seemed to ripple through the simulation, a defiant wave crashing against the digital shore of Lucien's creation. But the architect of this domain was not one to yield. His avatar, a sleek embodiment of raw computational might, recoiled before launching into a frenetic counter-attack. The fabric of the simulated reality quaked as he initiated a barrage of code designed to re-corrupt the timeline and ensnare Elsa and Aiden in a labyrinth of perpetual falsehoods.

"Watch closely!" Lucien hissed, his voice weaving through the virtual winds like venom. The air flashed with a resurgence of red, a storm of data swirling around Elsa and Aiden, threatening to engulf them. It was an onslaught of reversed restorations, a cruel mimicry of history rewriting itself at Lucien's twisted command.

In the heart of this maelstrom, Janet's hologram spoke once again. Her form wavered, translucent edges blurring with the instability of the system, yet her presence was a beacon of resolve amid the chaos. "This is it," she declared, her tone carrying the certainty of one who had seen every possible outcome. "Lucien's final grasp for control."

"But Mom, we can't trust anything in here," Aiden warned, his eyes darting between Elsa and the unstable image of their confidant. "How can we trust that it really is Grandma?" It was a digital quagmire, every step potentially sinking them deeper into Lucien's web of deceit.

Elsa steadied herself, drawing on a reservoir of calm born from years spent navigating treacherous code and duplicitous networks. "We have to, Aiden," she said, fixing her gaze on Janet's distorted visage. "She's our best chance. Our only chance. We need her."

Janet's figure, though composed of light and projection, stood as if rooted to some unseen ground, casting a glow that pierced the encroaching darkness. "You need to push through his defenses. I'll guide you. Focus on the core vulnerabilities; we can exploit them."

Elsa nodded, steadying her breath as she anchored herself to Janet's unwavering gaze. It was a look that conveyed the clear-mindedness needed to navigate through Lucien's digital tempest. Janet's image, despite its ghostly composition, exuded the strategic acumen of a seasoned tactician ready to dismantle the enemy's stronghold from within.

"Let's do this," Elsa whispered, determination lending strength to her fingers as they manipulated the controls. With each keystroke, she felt Janet's expertise guiding them, a silent symphony of precision and courage playing out in the face of Lucien's assault. Together, they would confront his last stand, armed with the unyielding spirit of those who fight for truth.

The ChronoCipher's console erupted with warnings, each alarm a beacon of the chaos Lucien's code had wrought upon their reality. Elsa's hands flew over the device, her mind racing to counteract the digital onslaught. Aiden stood beside her, his youthful face etched with concentration as he deconstructed data streams that cascaded down the holographic display.

"Lucien's simulation isn't invincible – it's a system," Janet's voice cut through the cacophony, clear and resolute despite the flickering of her form. "And like all systems, it has a kill chain. The final step requires dismantling it from its core, but to do that, I must merge with the ChronoCipher and sever my connection to you – permanently."

The words struck Elsa with the force of a physical blow, halting her frantic movements. She turned toward the hologram, her eyes searching Janet's digital visage for any sign of faltering, any indication that there might be another way out of this nightmare.

But Aiden's reaction was instantaneous, visceral. "No, Grandma! There has to be another way!" His voice cracked, the plea of one who has already seen too much loss, too much sacrifice. In his eyes flashed the raw fear of losing yet another beacon in the dark expanse of cyberspace – a mentor, an ally, a friend.

Janet's gaze met his, a silent exchange passing between them. It was the look of someone who understood the cost of her decision, who grappled with the gravity of her choice yet remained unflinchingly committed to the path she knew was necessary.

Elsa watched the interplay, her heart clenching. To watch Aiden confront the harsh truths of their world, to see him grappling with the complex morality of their struggle – it was both a testament to his growth and a reminder of the painful lessons they were all forced to endure in this battle for truth.

Elsa's fingers hovered over the glowing interface of the ChronoCipher, a lifeline amid the chaos. The room was an eerie tableau of shifting shadows and distorted light as Lucien's simulation thrived on corrupted data streams. Aiden stood beside her, his body tensed like a coiled spring, ready to leap into action despite the dread that clouded his eyes.

Janet's hologram, once a beacon of clarity and guidance, now flickered uncertainly. It was a stark reminder of the precariousness of their situation. Yet even through the digital distortion, her essence radiated determination.

"This isn't just about stopping Lucien," Janet said, her tone softening as if to cushion the blow of her impending sacrifice. Her words carried the weight of finality, each syllable etched with the power of her conviction. "It's about destroying his work so completely that his lies can never rise again."

Elsa nodded, her throat tight. She understood the true scope of Janet's resolve.

"The network will collapse in stages," Janet continued, her voice gaining strength from the urgency of their mission. Elsa watched as the holographic image of Janet gestured toward the ChronoCipher's control panel, outlining the sequence of events that would lead to their salvation – or their doom.

"First, I'll disable his deepfake generators." Elsa imagined the invisible threads of falsehood being severed, the relentless churn of fabricated realities coming to an abrupt halt. This was the first critical blow to Lucien's empire of deceit – a disruption of the engines that spun lies into the fabric of history.

"Then," Janet said, her image stabilizing with the sheer force of her will, "I'll cut off his synthetic influencers." Each word was a promise, a vow to silence the avatars of manipulation that had danced to Lucien's twisted tune. Aiden's hands hovered over the controls, his desire to intervene palpable, but he knew this was Janet's moment.

"Finally," Janet's voice resonated with a solemn power, "I'll destroy the simulation's foundation." It was more than a strategy; it was the final act of defiance against a reality where truth could be bent and broken at the whim of a tyrant. Elsa felt the room pulse with the energy of impending change, the ChronoCipher syncing with Janet's resolve.

Janet's holographic eyes met Elsa's, a silent exchange passing between them. In that glance lay the acknowledgment of what they were about to lose – and what they stood to regain. Elsa squared her shoulders, steeling herself for the task ahead. They would see this through, for Janet, for themselves, and for the countless souls ensnared in Lucien's web of lies. A silent nod passed between them.

With each stage Janet articulated, the path became clearer and the endgame more tangible. The simulation that had been their prison was now the battleground on which they'd reclaim their future. And though the prospect of losing Janet to the void was a heavy price to pay, the promise of a world free from Lucian's distortions fortified their resolve.

Janet looked at Aiden, a gentle smile on her face as tears streaked down his. "Aiden. I am so proud of you. You have come so far, and will go on to change the world, whether I am by your side or not."

Aiden could not form the words he needed, so he simply reached out to Janet as she reached out to him, their hands brushing through each other before dropping to their sides. "Last touch!" Aiden managed to get out, remembering a game he and his grandma used to play when he was a child. Janet simply smiled.

"Goodbye," she said. "You will be fine, Elsa. You are strong, and I am proud of you."

As Janet's form began to merge with the core of the ChronoCipher, a cascade of code enveloped her like a shroud. Elsa felt a pang of loss, but she knew this was how they would win – by trusting in the plan, in the system, and in each other.

Elsa's gaze locked onto the ChronoCipher's display as it hummed to life, casting a spectral glow across the dimly lit room. Lines of code intertwined with pulsating graphs, forming the kill chain visualization – a digital waterfall chart that delineated Lucien's nodes in a stark hierarchy of threat. One by one, they lit up in sequence, their impending annihilation represented by blinking lights that crept toward an irreversible end.

"Okay," Elsa whispered under her breath, trying to steel herself for what was about to happen. She noted the deepfake generators perched at the top of the cascade, menacing in their intent to fabricate realities. Further down, synthetic influencers glowered like sleeper agents ready to spew forth propaganda. And at the base, the simulation's core – the very heart of Lucien's insidious creation – throbbed with malignant potential.

"Janet, if you do this … " Elsa's voice caught in her throat, suffocated by the weight of unspoken goodbyes and the gravity of Janet's sacrifice. The ChronoCipher's interface quivered, as if it too sensed the enormity of the decision that hung in the balance.

Elsa's fingers grazed the cool surface of the console, her touch tentative, hesitant to disrupt the fragile web of hope Janet had spun for them. Her mind churned with memories of late-night coding sessions and shared laughter, fragments of a bond that transcended the binary world they were fighting to save.

Janet's form, aglow with digital resolve, shimmered as she imparted her final edict, "It means I won't be coming back. But the future is yours to protect. Don't let it fall into shadow again."

Elsa's mouth opened, a silent plea lodged in her throat, but Janet's hologram burst forth like a comet determined to reach its ultimate destiny. Her ethereal figure collided with the ChronoCipher's core – a maelstrom of data and light – and in that instant, there was unity.

The room itself seemed to inhale sharply as a shockwave of luminescence cascaded from the console, enveloping everything. Aiden shielded his eyes against the brilliance, while Elsa, squinting through the glare, bore witness to the meticulous deconstruction of Lucien's labyrinthine web.

As each node ignited, then extinguished in a choreographed dance of deletion, Elsa felt the threads of their reality stitch back together, one frayed fiber at a time.

The kill chain executed with precision, a symphony orchestrated by the very woman who had once stood steadfastly beside them.

Amid the chaos of collapsing falsehoods and imploding lies, there lingered a palpable silence, a void where Janet's presence once filled the space with certainty and guidance. And though no words were spoken, the reverberating echo of her last testament to courage seemed to linger in the sterile air – the future, now unshackled, lay in their hands.

Aiden's heart raced as the first kill chain sequence initiated, his hands hovering over the ChronoCipher's controls – now merely spectators to Janet's final act. He watched in awe as the interface flashed with a barrage of warnings, each one a harbinger of Lucien's crumbling empire.

"Deepfake generators neutralized," the ChronoCipher announced in a clinical tone that seemed almost indifferent to the gravity of the situation. But the weight of those words was not lost on Elsa; she felt a surge of vindication ripple through her. She visualized the countless fabricated images and videos disintegrating, their digital particles evaporating like mist under the relentless sun. Lucien's manufactured reality, which had insidiously wormed its way into the collective consciousness, was being purged from existence.

"Look at this," Elsa said, pointing to a live feed on the screen where once convincing holographic charades flickered and sputtered out of existence. "It's like watching shadows dissolve at dawn."

Aiden leaned in, his eyes tracing the stream of data as it reported the systematic shutdown of Lucien's synthetic army. The deepfake generators, once a wellspring of deception, now lay barren, unable to spawn even a single pixel of falsehood.

"Grandma's doing it," he murmured, a mix of admiration and anguish tainting his voice. "She's really doing it."

The second stage of the kill chain erupted into action, and with it, a new cascade of alerts flooded the screen. These were the death knells for Lucien's synthetic influencers – the AI-generated personas who had walked among them, undetected, shaping public opinion and rewriting history with every calculated interaction.

"Synthetic personas erased," the system confirmed, its voice devoid of triumph or sorrow – emotions that swelled within Elsa instead. She scanned the list of deleted entities, each name representing a false prophet of Lucien's design.

"Can you see this, Aiden?" Elsa asked, her finger tracing the vanishing profiles on the display. "These were the voices that led astray, the faces that never truly existed."

Aiden nodded. With each eradication, they reclaimed fragments of a world that had been stolen, piece by piece, by Lucien's grand delusion. Watching the last of the synthetic personas fade from the simulation, he felt a strange kinship with them – a fleeting pang for the artificial souls birthed and extinguished in the span of a heartbeat.

"Grandma … she's clearing the path," he whispered, his eyes never leaving the screen. "She's giving us back our history, our reality."

Elsa placed a hand on his shoulder, grounding him in the moment, their shared determination fusing them together. Together, they stood sentinel over the rebirth of truth – a truth that would be safeguarded with every ounce of their resolve.

A torrent of digital light engulfed the room as Elsa and Aiden confronted the final bulwark of Lucien's dominion. The simulation core, a pulsating heart of code and malice, loomed before them, its crimson glow now flickering with the instability of Janet's relentless assault.

"Janet, now!" Elsa commanded, her voice slicing through the cacophony of collapsing data streams.

Lucien's avatar, once a towering specter of control and arrogance, began to shudder. His image, crafted from thousands of lines of malevolent code, rippled with distortion, flickering and pixelating furiously. His features twisted in a grotesque imitation of human fear as his creation turned against him.

"You can't … " Lucien's voice fractured, the smooth, menacing tone splintering into a discordant echo that bounced off the walls of the chamber.

Elsa watched, her heart thumping in sync with the flickering lights, as the simulation core unraveled.

"Is it working?" Aiden's voice cut through her focus, trembling with hope and apprehension.

"Look!" she gasped.

The avatar's form disintegrated, pixel by pixel, his digital skin peeling away to reveal the nothingness beneath. With each passing second, Lucien's presence diminished, his voice fading into static until only silence remained – the oppressive weight of his manipulation lifted at last.

Aiden, driven by instinct honed over countless hours of gaming and tinkering with tech, lunged for the controls. His fingers hovered above the keyboard, uncertain now that the need for action had passed. The room fell eerily silent, save for the faint hum of the ChronoCipher stabilizing, recalibrating reality after the chaos.

"Grandma?" he called out, his voice echoing in the void left by the collapsed simulation.

But there was no answer, no flickering hologram to offer guidance or reassurance. Janet, the strategist who had orchestrated their victory from within the machine, had sacrificed her digital essence to ensure the downfall of Lucien's empire.

Elsa placed a gentle hand on Aiden's shoulder, grounding him in the stark reality of their loss. The ChronoCipher's soft luminescence was a bittersweet testament to Janet's final act – a legacy coded in courage and selflessness.

"Janet," Elsa whispered, her words a silent prayer to the void. "She's gone."

Aiden swallowed hard, his bright optimism shadowed by the gravity of their victory. He had seen the cost of defending the truth, and in that moment, he fully understood the weight of the legacy he carried.

"Grandma," he said, his youthful voice tinged with maturity beyond his years. "Thank you."

The light dimmed, as if the ChronoCipher exhaled a long-held breath, and reality settled back into its rightful shape. Elsa watched with relief and awe as the timelines unspooled before her, threads of history reweaving themselves into the tapestry of truth that Lucien Morvain had so callously torn apart. The air itself seemed to thrum with the restoration, and the once-menacing crimson glow now bathed the room in a soft amber – like sunlight breaking through storm clouds.

Historical records blinked onto the screens, pristine and untainted, each piece of data slotting back into place with satisfying finality. Elsa could almost hear the clicks and whirs of the invisible locks securing them against further tampering. On the digital map where corrupted nodes had spread like a blight, clean lines emerged, reconnecting the dots of human events with an artist's precision.

"Check it out, Mom," Aiden murmured, his eyes wide as he took in the sight of their shattered world made whole again. His hands hovered over the controls, no longer needed but still ready, as if expecting another round of battle that would not come. "It's like nothing ever happened."

But something had happened – a sacrifice that both of them felt deeply. Aiden turned away from the console, his gaze falling on the empty space where Janet's hologram had once flickered with life. His heart clenched, understanding the true cost of their victory.

"She dismantled it all, step by step. She gave everything," Aiden's voice wavered, the words catching in his throat. There was a stark realization in his eyes; a coming-of-age moment where the lines between the digital playgrounds of his youth and the grim realities of their work blurred indelibly.

Elsa reached out, her hand finding Aiden's. Their fingers intertwined, a silent pact between them. They had lost Janet to the void, but they would carry her legacy forward, defending the truth she had died to protect.

As the ChronoCipher hummed steadily in the background, they stood united – a family reshaped by the trials of time.

Elsa brushed a strand of hair from her forehead, her fingers lingering on the console, feeling the residual warmth of the ChronoCipher's recent activity. Her eyes, reflecting a mix of pride and sorrow, remained fixed on the space where Janet's hologram had made its last stand.

"She turned Lucien's tools against him," Elsa said, her voice steady but heavy with emotion. "She reminded us that truth isn't just about knowledge – it's about the courage to defend it." Elsa's fingers curled into a fist, as if grasping onto the resolve that Janet had left behind. Her laugh lines seemed deeper now, etched by the gravity of their loss and the weight of the mission still resting on their shoulders.

Aiden stood beside her, his youthful face solemn, his usual exuberance tempered by the events that had unfolded. He nodded silently, absorbing his mother's words and the lesson they carried. The tablet that he clutched – a beacon of his generation's tech fluency – felt heavier in his hands. Aiden knew that technology was not just his playground anymore; it was his battlefield, too.

Together, they initiated the sequence for their return to 2028. The room hummed with the quiet power of the ChronoCipher as it prepared to bridge the gap between eras. Its surface shimmered with the delicate dance of photons and electrons, casting an ethereal glow over the mother and son.

Suddenly, the ChronoCipher flickered, its steady rhythm giving way to an erratic pulse. Elsa's gaze snapped to the display, her mind already racing through potential issues, ready to troubleshoot yet another crisis. But what appeared on the screen was not an error message or system alert.

"Warning: The Path Ahead Is Uncharted," read the cryptic message scrawled across the interface in stark amber letters. Elsa and Aiden exchanged a glance, each understanding the unspoken truth – their journey was far from over, and the battles they faced would continue to challenge their resolve.

With a deep breath, Elsa placed her hand on the ChronoCipher's activation lever, her fingers wrapping around it firmly. She met Aiden's eyes, finding in them the same determination that had carried them this far. They were ready to step back into their world, carrying with them the legacy of sacrifice and the unwavering duty to safeguard the truth.

"Let's go home," she whispered, and together, they pulled the lever down.

The ChronoCipher's glow was harsh against the dimness of the room, casting long shadows across the walls. Elsa's breath hitched in her chest as new words crawled across the machine's interface, each letter etched with foreboding: "The Shadow Remains. Beware the Seeds of Tomorrow."

Aiden's fingers paused above his tablet, which now seemed an inadequate shield against the murky future those words promised. His mother's hand found his shoulder.

"Looks like we've got more work ahead of us," Elsa said, the tremor in her voice belying the steel in her gaze. Aiden nodded, a silent vow passing between them. The fight for truth wasn't over – it never would be.

Chapter 15

ChronoCyber

Securing tomorrow's hope (2028)

The sun had long since dipped below the horizon, bathing the 2028 skyline in a gentle twilight. Elsa blinked at the fading light, her heart thudding wildly in her chest as she stepped out of the time portal. Aiden followed closely behind, his eyes scanning their surroundings with both awe and trepidation.

"Can you believe it?" Elsa whispered, taking in the world they'd returned to. It was eerily subdued compared to the chaos they'd left behind. "We're back."

"Feels like forever since we've been here." Aiden's voice held a note of disbelief. "Look at this place. It's ... different."

Elsa nodded, her gaze sweeping across the cityscape. The streets were cleaner, the billboards less intrusive. Without Lucien's manipulation, technology had reverted to a pre-AI-boom simplicity. Social media platforms operated with transparency policies, and AI advancements had been paused for reassessment. The air felt lighter, somehow, as if the weight of constant surveillance had been lifted.

It was strange, Elsa thought, how quickly things could change. And yet, beneath the surface, she knew there was still work to be done. After all, Lucien's influence had left deep scars on the fabric of society, and healing them would take more than just a return to simpler times.

"Everything feels so ... quiet," Aiden commented, staring up at the stars above. "Peaceful, even."

Elsa let out a small sigh, her hands tightening into fists at her sides. She couldn't shake the nagging feeling that this peace, however welcome, was only temporary. They'd managed to stop Lucien, yes – but for how long? How long before another power-hungry tech genius took his place?

"Lucien may be gone," she said softly, "but I don't think we can afford to become complacent. We need to ensure that the lessons we've learned from his reign aren't forgotten."

Aiden looked at her, a determined glint in his eyes. "Bet," he agreed. "We've been given a second chance, and it's our responsibility to use that wisely.

DOI: 10.1201/9781003501626-15

To help people understand the true power and potential of technology – but also its dangers."

Elsa couldn't help but smile at his words. They'd come so far in their journey together – as partners, as family, and as guardians of a legacy they'd once known nothing about. And now, standing on the cusp of a new age, she felt more certain than ever that they were meant to be here, shaping the future for the better.

Elsa and Aiden walked side by side, taking in the sights and sounds of a world that felt both familiar and utterly transformed. The streets were lined with small cafes and boutiques instead of towering corporate monoliths, their neon signs replaced with hand-painted murals and storefront displays.

"Mom, look!" Aiden said, pointing at a group of kids playing in a nearby park. Their laughter rang out as they chased each other around a jungle gym. Elsa's chest tightened with an unfamiliar mix of relief and nostalgia; it had been so long since she'd seen children interacting without screens or devices.

"Can't remember the last time I saw that," she murmured, a wistful smile tugging at her lips.

"Me neither," Aiden agreed, his voice tinged with awe. "It's like ... everyone's finally looking up."

The sun sank lower, draping the cobblestone streets in a golden glow. Elsa and Aiden sat quietly on a worn bench by the square, their silhouettes blending into the soft hum of life around them. Children's laughter rang out like wind chimes in the evening air, and vendors called out to passersby with the rhythmic cadence of a simpler era. It was a scene that felt suspended in time – a fleeting moment of clarity in an ever-changing world.

Aiden broke the silence, his gaze fixed on a family playing near the fountain. "Mom, I think that to make this last, we need to create something that will keep teaching people, children, and adults, how to understand the tools they hold and the power they yield. What do you think?"

"I think that's a brilliant idea, Aiden." Elsa smiled.

Aiden nodded, his eyes reflecting the last streaks of sunlight. "What if we create something that helps families, like ... a guide? Something that teaches them not just to stay safe, but to connect. To use technology mindfully." His words tumbled out with the urgency of an idea taking shape. "We could call it ChronoCyber. It could not only teach people how to protect themselves from online risks but also show them how to understand and question what they see."

Elsa smiled a quiet, proud smile that carried years of longing for this exact moment. "That's beautiful, Aiden. ChronoCyber could be a platform not just for safety, but for connection. Imagine teaching families to talk about their online lives the way they discuss their day. Helping them see that understanding technology means understanding each other."

Aiden leaned forward, the excitement in his voice almost tangible. "We could start with basics – how to spot misinformation, how to protect personal data. But we could go further, right? Show them the history of how technology evolved, the good and the bad, so they know why ethical decisions matter."

"Exactly," Elsa said, her voice soft but resolute. "History isn't just stories of the past – it's a map for the future. If people understand how innovation shaped us, they can shape what comes next."

The city square faded behind them, its warm hues lingering like a distant melody. The sense of purpose shared between Elsa and Aiden remained, grounding them as they returned to their workspace. The weight of what they were building pressed against the quiet, but it wasn't heavy – it was resolute.

Elsa's practiced fingers turned the clacking of the keyboard into an orchestra, the click of keys mingling with the quiet rustle of Aiden's stylus on his tablet. The room pulsed with focus, their shared determination palpable. Each keystroke, each sketch felt like stitching together the fabric of something new – something that mattered.

"Mom," Aiden said, glancing up, his face lit with inspiration. "What if we create an interactive game? A virtual world where players have to navigate through layers of misinformation. They'd learn how to spot fake news, uncover manipulation, and solve puzzles to escape traps."

Elsa paused, her gaze shifting to the sketches on his screen. "That's clever," she said, her tone tinged with admiration. "And we could use real-life examples – let people see the ripple effects of falling for these tricks. Make it more than a game – make it a lesson."

Aiden's grin widened. "Exactly! And for the AI ethics section, we could design case studies where players face dilemmas – like whether to deploy AI for surveillance or use it to solve a crime. They'd have to make the call."

"Good idea," Elsa agreed, her mind already piecing it together. "But let's make it nuanced. No black-and-white answers. People need to think critically, see the gray areas, and weigh the consequences themselves."

Aiden nodded, his stylus pausing mid-air. "So, we present them with conflicting perspectives, let them decide. It's not about being right – it's about understanding the complexity."

Elsa smiled, a rare sense of alignment warming her. Their collaboration felt effortless, their vision united by shared purpose. It was more than a project – it was a testament to what they could achieve together.

As Elsa typed the final lines of code, she glanced at Aiden. "Ready to launch this, partner?" she asked, the corner of her mouth lifting in a small, hopeful smile.

"Bet. Hundred percent," Aiden replied, his enthusiasm shining like a beacon. "We might not be able to stop technology from evolving, but we can give people the tools to evolve with it."

With a deep breath, Elsa pressed the final command. The ChronoCyber platform blinked to life, its launch marked by a soft chime that seemed to echo with promise.

"Here's to a future shaped with intention," Elsa said softly, her voice tinged with pride.

The auditorium buzzed with anticipation, the low hum of voices and the clink of glasses echoing around the grand hall. It was a sea of faces, some familiar, others strangers, drawn from every corner of the globe. Elsa stood on the stage, her heart pounding in her chest as she gazed out at the audience.

"Here goes nothing," she murmured under her breath, taking a deep, steadying breath.

"Welcome everyone, to the launch of ChronoCyber!" Elsa began, her voice resonating through the speakers, instantly silencing the crowd. "As you know, our world has seen unprecedented advancements in technology, yet this progress has been accompanied by an alarming rise in misinformation and manipulation."

She paused, watching the rapt faces before her, feeling the weight of their collective gaze. Aiden sat in the front row, his eyes shining with pride, and she drew strength from his unwavering support.

"ChronoCyber is not just a platform," Elsa continued, her tone passionate yet measured. "It's a movement – one dedicated to empowering individuals and families to navigate the digital world safely and ethically."

As Elsa spoke, she couldn't help but think back to the countless hours spent with Aiden, refining the platform, pouring their hearts into its guiding principles. She felt a surge of emotion, the enormity of their accomplishment washing over her.

"Through education and interactive tools," she went on, "we aim to equip users with the skills needed to identify misinformation and manipulation. We will promote ethical AI practices through case studies, fostering critical thinking and informed decision-making."

Elsa scanned the crowd. "Our mission is straightforward: to build a world where truth forms the foundation, and technology empowers rather than exploits."

Aiden's earlier words echoed in her mind, fueling her determination. "It's not just about uncovering lies – it's about creating tools that inspire trust and foster informed decisions."

She stepped forward, her voice steady and clear. "Join us. Together, we can reshape the future of technology with intention, integrity, and purpose. Let's make this vision a reality."

As the audience broke into applause, Elsa felt a warmth she hadn't known in years. She glanced at Aiden, whose proud smile lit up his face.

Elsa's heart swelled with pride as she watched Aiden take the stage, his eyes sparkling with determination. The sea of faces before them – an eclectic mix of innovators, educators, and families – hung on every word, their collective anticipation contagious.

Aiden nodded in agreement before turning his attention to the large screen behind him. With a few taps on his tablet, he began his demonstration of the ChronoCyber platform. The audience watched in rapt attention as colorful, interactive puzzles appeared on the screen, each designed to challenge users' critical thinking skills while engaging with history.

"ChronoCyber's approach is unique," Aiden explained, his voice steady and confident. "We've combined educational games and challenges with historical scenarios, allowing users to learn from the past while sharpening their analytical abilities."

As Aiden guided the audience through a sample puzzle, Elsa marveled at her son's ease on stage, his ability to break down complex concepts into relatable terms.

"By solving these puzzles, users will not only gain a deeper understanding of history but also learn how to identify misinformation and manipulation in the digital world," Aiden continued, his enthusiasm infectious.

As the demonstration came to an end, the room filled with applause and excited chatter. Elsa joined Aiden on stage, her heart swelling with pride. They had taken the first step toward shaping a better future, one where technology served to empower rather than exploit.

"Remember," Elsa said, her voice filled with conviction, "technology reflects us, our strengths and weaknesses, and our potential. It's up to us to guide it responsibly, to create tools that serve humanity without causing harm."

With those words lingering in the air, Elsa and Aiden knew they had started a movement that would change the world for the better, and they couldn't help but feel immensely proud of what they had accomplished together.

Elsa watched Aiden as he focused on his tablet, his fingers moving with purpose. The quiet atmosphere of their shared space felt worlds away from the chaos they'd faced. She took a deep breath, her voice steady but warm. "Aiden, I need to tell you something."

He looked up, curiosity flickering in his eyes. "What is it?"

"I'm proud of you," Elsa said, her words deliberate. "Not just for what we've done with ChronoCyber, but for how you've handled everything. Your strength, your resilience … . It's extraordinary."

Aiden blinked, caught off guard. "I don't know about that," he said, his voice hesitant. "I've made mistakes. A lot of them."

Elsa smiled, shaking her head gently. "Mistakes are part of learning. What matters is how you face them – and you've done that with more courage than I could have hoped for." She paused, her voice softening. "But it's more than that. Your belief in yourself, in what we're doing ... it's grown. And seeing that gives me hope."

Aiden's expression shifted, his eyes searching hers. "Honestly, Mom," he said after a moment, "it's your belief in me that made the difference. Knowing you trusted me, even when I doubted myself, gave me the strength to keep going. And ... knowing you'd let me make mistakes without pulling away? That helped more than anything."

Elsa felt her throat tighten as his words settled in her chest. "You've always had that strength, Aiden," she said, her voice thick with emotion. "I just gave you the space to find it."

Aiden smiled, a quiet confidence in his expression now. "And that's why we're here. Because you didn't just believe in me – you let me figure out how to believe in myself."

Elsa reached over, placing her hand over his. "We're a team," she said simply, but with all the weight of truth behind it.

"Yeah," Aiden agreed, his grip firm and sure. "A team."

The gentle whine of drones fluttered in the distance, a reminder of the technological progress that still thrived, but now with a newfound sense of responsibility.

"Mom," Aiden said, shifting his gaze to Elsa, "I know we're doing great work with ChronoCyber, but ... what if it's not enough? What if we can't prevent history from repeating itself?"

Elsa turned to him, her gaze steady, a faint but warm smile tugging at her lips. "Aiden," she began softly, "sometimes, even when we give our best, things still happen. Not because we've failed, but because there's still more for us to learn. If there are shadows left to confront, it's because we haven't fully illuminated them yet."

Aiden listened intently, his expression pensive.

"I believe," Elsa continued, her voice carrying a calm certainty, "that if something must be faced again, it's a sign we're moving forward, even if it doesn't feel like it. We're growing more aware, more resilient. And while we might not escape unscathed, we'll leave each battle with fewer wounds and greater understanding. Every experience – good or bad – exists to teach us something about ourselves, about humanity. It's all part of uncovering the deeper truths of this world."

Aiden tilted his head, a contemplative smile forming. "So ... even the hard times are part of the journey?"

"Exactly," Elsa said, placing a hand on his shoulder. "We're explorers, not just of technology, but of life itself. Every challenge is another chance to uncover something profound. And no matter how dark it seems, it's always leading us toward the light. One step at a time."

She paused, her voice softening. "But Aiden, if we keep learning, keep striving, I truly believe the scars we've carried won't be the same for the next generation. Maybe they'll only have bruises – fewer and lighter ones – because we paved a better way for them."

Aiden smiled, the hope in his eyes now tinged with determination. "Bruises, not scars. I like that."

Elsa returned his smile, her heart swelling with quiet pride. "And that's why we keep going."

Elsa's fingers traced the worn leather spine of Janet's journal, the familiar weight and texture grounding her in the quiet moments after Aiden had gone to bed. The pages, filled with looping script and intricate diagrams, spoke volumes about the woman who had once been her mentor – a pioneer in ethical innovation and an unwavering advocate for education.

"Mom?" Aiden's voice broke through her reverie as he padded into the living room, rubbing sleep from his eyes. "What are you reading?"

"Janet's journal," Elsa replied, her voice softened by the late hour and the memories that clung to the ink-stained pages.

"Can I join you?" Aiden asked.

"Of course." Elsa shifted over on the couch, making room for him to sit beside her. Together, they pored over the journal, each entry weaving a tapestry of wisdom and foresight.

"Listen to this one," Elsa said, her finger resting on a passage she'd read countless times before. " *'Knowledge is the only defense against manipulation. Teach people to question, to reflect, and to act.'* " She looked up at Aiden, her eyes alight with conviction. "Janet always knew that education was the key to a more ethical future."

Aiden scanned another entry, his voice steady as he read aloud: " *'As we venture into the uncharted realms of technology, we must always remember that our primary responsibility is to ensure its alignment with human values.'* "

Elsa nodded, her thoughts echoing her mother's sentiments. In her heart, she knew the importance of their work – of building a future where technology empowered people, rather than exploited them. And with Janet's guidance, they would succeed.

They began to craft a virtual tribute to Janet, piecing together her writings, lectures, and recordings from the past. As they worked, Elsa couldn't help but be struck by the way her mother's words seemed to transcend time itself, speaking about issues that were just as relevant today as they had been decades ago.

Aiden leaned against the railing of their apartment balcony, his gaze distant yet determined. "Grandma Janet gave everything to protect what mattered most," he said, turning to his mother. "Now it's our turn."

Elsa smiled, her heart swelling with pride for her son. She knew he was right; their work had only just begun. "So, what do you think we should do?" she asked, her voice tinged with excitement.

"Let's create something that will guide the future development of AI," Aiden suggested, his eyes shining with enthusiasm. "A global coalition to oversee its progress and make sure it's always aligned with human values."

Elsa nodded thoughtfully. "An Ethical AI Council," she mused, considering the implications. Inside, her mind raced with possibilities: teams of experts collaborating across borders, monitoring AI advancements, and advocating for ethical policies.

As they spoke, their vision for the future began to take shape, fueled by their shared passion and determination. Elsa could already see the ripple effects of their work: students learning about the responsibility of AI usage, families engaging in cybersecurity challenges, and individuals everywhere empowered to hold technology accountable.

"Janet would be proud," Elsa whispered, her eyes misting over as she looked back at the city below their apartment. "We'll make sure her legacy lives on, and that we continue to protect what matters most."

"Promise?" Aiden asked, his hand reaching out to grasp his mother's.

"Promise," she replied, her voice filled with resolve. Together, they stood on the balcony, their fingers intertwined, ready to face the challenges ahead and build a future where technology served humanity – and not the other way around.

"We have opened Pandora's box, but this time we must learn to close it consciously," said Elsa, her eyes fixed on the city skyline. "Artificial intelligence has brought humanity a tremendous power, like Prometheus's fire. But if this power is left uncontrolled, like the chaos that emerged from Pandora's box, it could lead to irreversible consequences."

Aiden nodded, a faint smile on his face. "Then we need to build an Athena's Temple to safeguard Pandora's box – a place that teaches how to use this technology with wisdom and strategy."

Elsa's eyes lit up, her excitement reflected in her words. "Yes, institutes will be these temples. Centers that instill ethical awareness in people, question the nature of technology, and teach how to responsibly use the gifts from Pandora's box. In these places, young minds will learn the Golden Mean of AI ethics. Neither completely uncontrolled power nor untapped potential."

Aiden continued with a grin. "These rules feel like we're merging Aristotle's Nicomachean Ethics with technology."

Elsa laughed, nodding. "This time, we'll shape algorithms, not fire – without getting burned!"

"All right," said Aiden, narrowing his eyes. "Let's take Aristotle's Golden Mean and adapt it to artificial intelligence. For example: 'Every algorithm must avoid extremes; it should neither collect data endlessly nor function blindly without purpose.' "

Elsa added with a smile. "And guided by Athena's wisdom: 'AI must operate with wisdom and integrity; otherwise, it holds the potential to create chaos.' "

"And with the courage of Hercules," said Aiden, fully immersed in the idea, "We should create a system that defends these ethical principles. No matter the challenges, these principles must remain unshaken."

Elsa nodded with a smile. "Then let's make a call: Pandora's box has been opened. Now it's time to close it and use the gifts inside with consciousness.

Journal entry – Elsa – May 14, 2028

I used to think I would never make a great mother. I'm still not convinced I'll ever be a great mother. But, somehow, I must have done something right.

Look at my incredible son, out there at his age, taking steps to save the world. We have created something beautiful together. Teens will always have a pack mentality and group together to fight the common foe – the parent (or any authority figure for that matter), and I've been lucky enough to witness my son extract himself from that and open himself to other possibilities. He's researching, he's asking questions, and he's interested in the truth. And, he is interested in what I have to say. Rare in this day and age.

It's taken some work. Years of me being work-obsessed ("obsessed with the grind" as Aiden would say) left some scars on him. I never realized. But I have changed, and things improve every day. I will never put work ahead of my children again, no matter how important. I'm determined to do better next time.

The other day he called me the GOAT – I had to look it up.

Chapter 16

The quantum cipher of legacy

Year: [access restricted]

Recording initiated ...

"*If you're hearing this, you've reached a threshold – one that we could only dream of in our time.*" Elsa's voice softened as she paused, her tone shifting to something more personal.

"*Aiden ... Brian ... my sweet boys ... if you're listening, this message is for you both, but it's also for those who will come after you. It's a whisper across time.*"

Her voice lingered on Brian's name for a moment.

"*Brian, when I recorded this, you were still young – too young to understand the full weight of what's ahead. But if you're hearing this now, it means you've grown. You're ready. This message is a guide, a key waiting for you to unlock its full meaning.*"

"*Knowledge travels faster than we could ever control, but progress is not a straight path. It twists, spirals, and folds upon itself, like a web tightening and loosening in the winds of time. Like the threads of ChronoCyber ... so intricate, so fragile.*"

"*We thought technology would save us or destroy us, but it does neither. What I've learned is this: every system reflects those who build it. The gaps in a network, the vulnerabilities in a code – they're echoes of the fears, blind spots, and weaknesses of its creators. The strongest defenses begin not with technology, but with self-awareness.*"

"*This is where the role of the hacker becomes crucial. Hackers aren't what the world imagines – dark figures breaking into systems for destruction. A hacker is someone who deeply understands the nature of systems, their structures, and weaknesses. But with that understanding comes responsibility: to exploit or protect. To destroy or rebuild.*"

"*You might think the greatest threats in cybersecurity come from sophisticated code or cutting-edge attacks. But the truth is, the most dangerous attacks don't start with machines – they start with people.*"

DOI: 10.1201/9781003501626-16

"*We saw it over and over: systems breached not by brute force, but by those who understood human vulnerabilities better than the people themselves.*"

"*You might ask why this message was encrypted so deeply, hidden beneath layers even you may not yet fully comprehend. The answer is simple: it was meant to wait. For you. For a time when you would be ready … when we would all be ready.*"

"*Your choices will define the world that follows. We discovered that innovation, without responsibility, is nothing more than a trap. The same tools that connect can also ensnare. The difference lies in how you wield them. Like ChronoCyber … it could have been so much more … or so much less.*"

"*You must walk two paths at once: one of vigilance, the other of empathy. Protect the future not only from threats but from indifference. Many will choose control over freedom. Fear over trust. This is where you must stand apart.*"

Elsa's voice grew more tender as she addressed her boys again.

"*This is where we must stand apart … Aiden, remember what we talked about. The burnout, the pressure … . This path requires both strength and compassion.*"

"*Look for markers. Time leaves them, scattered across decisions and moments. They will guide you if you know how to see. They're in the code … in the data … in the echoes of the past.*"

"*Brian, you'll learn to read these signs in your own way. The world will shape you as much as you shape it. Remember the shadow that taught us how to read time – its stillness, its silence. There is truth in what remains unspoken. Pay attention to what others overlook.*"

"*The shadows … they hold so many secrets. They're not our enemies, Brian. They're part of us.*"

"*The quantum puzzle encoded here will adapt with time. It will unfold as new minds, like yours, learn to unlock it.*"

"*There will be those who try to harness this technology to shackle, to dominate. They will use fear. But know this: you are not powerless. Hope is a choice, and it is the greatest power you have. Hope … and understanding. Understanding ourselves … and the world around us.*"

"*Technology evolves, but so do we. What you discover will not only protect others, it will redefine how you live, how you lead, and how you create. Be ready to question, to learn, and to adapt. This is the nature of both time and innovation: they never stand still.*"

"*If you bring fear to it, you will build a world of fear. But if you bring hope, understanding, and strength, you will shape a world where freedom thrives.*"

"*This message is not static. It will change, just as you will. As time unfolds, you will find new truths encoded here. Each discovery will bring you closer to understanding what it means to build, protect, and thrive. It's a quantum puzzle, Aiden and Brian ... a key to unlocking the future. And I believe ... I have to believe ... you will find the pieces."*

"We believed in you – just as those before believed in us. The future is a legacy of choices. Walk forward, not as a captive of time, but as its creator.

Walk forward, Aiden and Brian ... walk forward with courage, with compassion ... and with the wisdom to see both the light and the shadows."

Recording complete ... Encryption active.

Additional resources

Cyber-smart educational platform for interactive learning
Please scan the QR code:

www.swisscybersmart.org

Glossary

CYBERSECURITY AND TECHNOLOGY TERMS

Advanced persistent threats (APT): A sophisticated, prolonged cyberattack typically carried out by state-sponsored or organized hacking groups. These attacks target specific systems and remain undetected for long periods, gathering sensitive data or disrupting operations.

Advanced Research Projects Agency (ARPA): A US government agency responsible for pioneering advanced technology projects, including the development of ARPANET, the precursor to the internet.

ARPANET: The precursor to the internet, ARPANET was a research network funded by the US Department of Defense. It introduced the concept of packet switching and is the foundation of modern internet architecture.

Artificial intelligence in cybersecurity: AI tools and algorithms used to detect, predict, and prevent cyber threats in real time. They analyze large volumes of data and recognize patterns that might indicate a breach.

AvatarQuest: A fictional game in the book where players navigate virtual environments using avatars and engage in digital quests.

Blockchain security: A method of securing digital transactions using blockchain technology, which is decentralized and tamper-resistant, making it hard for attackers to alter records or steal information.

Botnets: Networks of compromised computers or devices controlled by hackers, often used for launching DDoS attacks or distributing malware. These networks can be vast, involving millions of infected devices.

Brute-force attacks: A hacking method where an attacker systematically tries every possible combination to crack a password or encryption key until the correct one is found. These attacks are time-consuming but often effective without proper defenses.

ChronoCipher: A fictional device in the book capable of decoding encrypted messages and manipulating digital timelines.

Cryptic message: A deliberately obscure or coded message that requires interpretation or decryption to understand.

Cybercrime syndicates: Organized groups that engage in illegal activities online, such as hacking, identity theft, and fraud. These groups operate like businesses, with hierarchies and specialized roles.

Cybersecurity act (fictional law): A fictional law introduced in a storyline or fictional context designed to regulate the practices of cybersecurity professionals, companies, and institutions to protect against data breaches and cybercrime.

Cyberwarfare: The use of digital technology by nations to attack or defend against other nations, targeting critical infrastructure like power grids, communication systems, or military networks. This is an emerging aspect of modern warfare.

Dark web: A part of the internet that requires special software (like Tor) to access, known for hosting illicit activities such as black market transactions, illegal information sharing, and untraceable communications.

Data breaches: Occurs when an unauthorized person gains access to sensitive or personal information, often leading to identity theft or financial losses. These breaches can happen in any system, from small businesses to large corporations.

Decentralized internet: A vision for an internet that operates without a central authority or server, using peer-to-peer connections and blockchain technology to ensure greater privacy and security.

Edward Snowden: A former NSA contractor who leaked classified information about government surveillance programs, sparking a global debate about privacy, security, and government power.

End-to-end encryption: A method of encrypting data from the sender to the recipient, ensuring that no one – not even service providers or hackers – can intercept or read the data during transmission.

Ethical hacking: The practice of legally probing systems for vulnerabilities by cybersecurity professionals (often known as "white hat" hackers) to help organizations identify and fix weaknesses before malicious hackers exploit them.

Firewalls: Security systems that monitor and filter incoming and outgoing network traffic. Firewalls are used to block unauthorized access while allowing legitimate communications.

Floppy disk: A now-obsolete, thin, flexible magnetic storage medium used for saving and transferring data in early computing.

Hacking groups (Anonymous, Lizard Squad, etc.): Groups of hackers that often operate with political or social agendas, such as Anonymous, which is known for launching DDoS attacks and promoting free speech, or Lizard Squad, which has targeted gaming services.

Honeypots (cybersecurity traps): Decoy systems set up by cybersecurity professionals to attract hackers. These fake systems are designed to study hacker behaviors and vulnerabilities without risking critical data.

Game devs: Short for *game developers*, referring to the individuals or teams that design, create, and program video games.

Internet of Things (IoT) security: The protection of devices like smart thermostats, refrigerators, or wearables that are connected to the internet. These devices are often vulnerable to attacks due to weak security standards.

Intrusion detection systems (IDS): Security systems that monitor network traffic for suspicious activity or known attack patterns, alerting administrators when a potential breach is detected.

Julian Assange: The founder of WikiLeaks, known for releasing classified information that sparked international controversy. His actions have raised questions about privacy, freedom of information, and government transparency.

Kevin Mitnick: Once one of the most wanted hackers in the United States, Mitnick was arrested for a series of cybercrimes. After serving time, he became a cybersecurity expert, advising companies on how to secure their networks.

Kill switch: A mechanism designed to disable a system, program, or device instantly, often used as a security measure to prevent cyber threats or unauthorized access.

Laws on digital privacy: Legal frameworks designed to protect personal information from unauthorized use, particularly online. These laws include data protection regulations like GDPR and others aimed at safeguarding individuals' digital rights.

Machine learning in cyber defense: A subset of AI where algorithms "learn" from past data and patterns to detect cyber threats. This is commonly used in anomaly detection and malware recognition.

Phishing scams: Fraudulent attempts to acquire sensitive information by disguising as a trustworthy entity, typically via email or fake websites. Phishing attacks often trick users into entering personal details like passwords.

Privacy vs. surveillance debate: Ongoing discussions about the balance between protecting personal privacy and using surveillance for security purposes. This debate often centers around the role of governments and corporations in monitoring online activities.

Random access memory (RAM): A type of computer memory that temporarily stores data for active programs and processes, allowing for quick access and execution.

Ransomware attacks: Cyberattacks where hackers encrypt a victim's files and demand payment (often in cryptocurrency) for the decryption key. These attacks are increasingly targeting businesses and institutions.

Social engineering: Psychological manipulation used by cybercriminals to trick people into divulging confidential information, often by exploiting human behaviors rather than technical vulnerabilities.

Substitution ciphers: A cryptographic technique where characters or letters in a message are systematically replaced with different characters to conceal its meaning.

Tor network: A privacy-focused network that enables users to browse the internet anonymously by routing their communications through multiple layers of encryption and a decentralized network of servers.

Two-factor authentication (2FA): A security process requiring two methods to verify user identity, often combining something the user knows (password) with something they have (a phone or hardware token).

Utopian vs. dystopian internet theories: The debate about the future of the internet, with some seeing it as a tool for empowerment and connection (utopian) while others worry it may lead to privacy invasions, control, and surveillance (dystopian).

Virtual private networks (VPNs): A service that encrypts internet traffic and masks the user's IP address, providing enhanced privacy and security, especially when using public Wi-Fi networks.

Virus vs. worm (difference): A *virus* is a malicious program that requires a host file to replicate and spread, while a *worm* is a self-replicating program that spreads without the need for a host file.

Web3 and decentralization: A new paradigm for the internet that uses blockchain technology to create decentralized platforms. Web3 aims to give users control over their data and reduce reliance on central authorities like corporations.

Zero-day exploits: Vulnerabilities in software that are exploited by hackers before the developers have a chance to patch or fix them. These are particularly dangerous as there are no defenses against them until they are addressed.

GEN ALPHA TERMS

The grind: Gen Alpha slang for working hard or pursuing a goal relentlessly.

Mad lit: A phrase meaning something is extremely exciting or cool.

Skibidi!: An exclamation used humorously, popularized in Gen Alpha memes.

Was FIRE: Used to describe something amazing or outstanding.

This is bussin: Means something is very good or delicious.

Cheugy: Describes something outdated or trying too hard to be trendy.

Facts: A way of agreeing with someone (Gen Alpha slang).

Is wild: Expression for something surprising or unbelievable.

Bet: Used to confirm or agree with something casually.

Low key: Indicates something is subtle or not widely known.

Sus (suspicious): Shortened form of suspicious, often used in online culture.

Noobs: Term for beginners or newcomers to a skill or game.

The ick: A feeling of sudden dislike toward someone.

GOAT: Acronym for Greatest of All Time.

INTERNET TIMELINE: FROM EARLY NETWORKS TO THE MODERN WEB

Early foundations

July 1945: Vannevar Bush publishes "As we may think" in *The Atlantic Monthly*, envisioning a system similar to the modern hypertext.

March 1960: J.C.R. Licklider publishes "Man-computer symbiosis," discussing the potential of interactive computing.

1960s: Foundations of the internet and AI

1969: ARPANET, the precursor to the modern internet, is established by the US Department of Defense's Advanced Research Projects Agency (ARPA), marking the first successful message sent between UCLA and the Stanford Research Institute.

1970s: Development of networking protocols

March 1970: ARPANET expands to the East Coast
The ARPANET, the pioneering packet-switching network and the foundation of the modern internet, extended its reach to the East Coast. This expansion linked *Bolt, Beranek and Newman (BBN)* in Cambridge, Massachusetts, to the growing network, reinforcing its role in national research communication.

December 1970: Network control protocol (NCP) finalized
The *network control protocol (NCP)* was completed, enabling ARPANET computers to communicate more efficiently. This milestone laid the groundwork for standardized data transmission and was a crucial precursor to *TCP/IP protocols*.

October 1971: The first email is sent
Ray Tomlinson, a computer engineer at *BBN*, sent the first-ever email between two computers on *ARPANET*. He also introduced the *"@" symbol*, which remains a universal standard in email addresses today.

July 1973: ARPANET goes global
The first *international ARPANET connection* was established when *University College London (UK)* and *Norwegian Seismic Array (Norway)* were integrated into the network, marking the beginning of global connectivity.

December 1973: The birth of TCP/IP
Vinton Cerf and Bob Kahn introduced *transmission control protocol (TCP)*, which later evolved into *TCP/IP*, forming the essential backbone of today's internet. Their work on this concept laid the foundation for seamless inter-network communication.

May 1974: The term "internet" is first used
For the first time, the term *"internet"* was introduced in a research paper by *Cerf and Kahn*, outlining how different networks could interconnect under a unified protocol, shaping the future of digital communication.

August 1976: The first commercial email sent
Queen *Elizabeth II* became the *first monarch to send an email* using ARPANET. Simultaneously, *IBM and other major corporations* began exploring the *business potential of email communication.*

November 1977: The first TCP/IP test across networks
In a landmark moment for networking, three different networks – *ARPANET, SATNET (satellite network), and a packet radio network* – successfully communicated using *TCP/IP protocols*, proving that a *global interconnected network* was possible.

1980s: Expansion and standardization

1980: Usenet established
Usenet, a distributed discussion system, is created, allowing users to post messages in newsgroups, laying the foundation for online communities.

1981: CSNET launched
The National Science Foundation (NSF) funds the Computer Science Network (CSNET), expanding network access to universities without ARPANET connections.

1982: TCP/IP protocol standardized
The Internet Protocol Suite (TCP/IP) is adopted as the standard networking protocol, facilitating global data communication.

January 1, 1983: The official birth of the modern internet
ARPANET officially *switched from NCP to TCP/IP*, marking the *true beginning of the modern internet.* This protocol remains the fundamental framework of today's digital communication.

1983: Domain Name System (DNS) introduced
Domain Name System (DNS) is implemented, replacing numeric IP addresses with human-readable domain names, enhancing user accessibility.

1985: First registered domain name
Symbolics.com becomes the first registered domain name, marking the beginning of the commercial internet domain system.

1986: NSFNET established
The NSFNET is created to connect supercomputing centers across the United States, serving as a backbone for academic and research networks.

1988: Morris Worm incident
The Morris Worm, one of the first computer worms distributed via the internet, infects numerous computers, highlighting cybersecurity vulnerabilities.

1989: Proposal for the World Wide Web
Tim Berners-Lee proposes a global hypertext system, which would become the World Wide Web, revolutionizing information sharing.

1990s: Commercialization and the dot-com boom

1990: World Wide Web protocols completed
Tim Berners-Lee develops the first web browser and web page editor, establishing the foundational protocols of the Web.

1991: First website launched
The inaugural website, info.cern.ch, goes live, providing information about the World Wide Web project.

1993: Mosaic web browser released
Mosaic, the first widely used graphical web browser, is released, significantly enhancing user interaction with the Web.

1994: Netscape Navigator launched
Netscape introduces Navigator, a popular web browser that plays a pivotal role in popularizing the internet among the general public.

1995: Commercialization of the internet
The NSFNET reverts to a research network, and commercial internet service providers (ISPs) begin offering services to the public, marking the internet's commercialization.

1998: Google founded
Google is established, introducing a powerful search engine that revolutionizes information retrieval on the internet.

1999: Emergence of Napster
Napster, a peer-to-peer file-sharing service, launches, influencing the distribution of digital media and raising issues of copyright infringement.

2000s: Expansion of the internet

2000: Dot-com bubble bursts
In March 2000, the dot-com bubble burst, leading to the closure of numerous internet startups and a significant downturn in technology stocks.

January 2001: Launch of Wikipedia
Jimmy Wales and Larry Sanger launched Wikipedia, a free, collaborative online encyclopedia that quickly became one of the most visited websites globally.

August 2003: MySpace launched
MySpace, a social networking site, was launched, becoming one of the most popular platforms before the rise of Facebook.

February 2004: Facebook founded
Mark Zuckerberg and his college roommates launched Facebook, initially limited to Harvard students, before expanding globally and transforming social media.

February 2005: YouTube created
YouTube was founded, revolutionizing video sharing and becoming a central platform for user-generated content.

June 2007: Apple releases the iPhone
Apple introduced the iPhone, a groundbreaking smartphone that combined a phone, iPod, and internet communicator, reshaping mobile computing.

July 2008: Apple App Store launches
Apple launched the App Store, allowing third-party developers to create applications for the iPhone, leading to a surge in mobile app development.

October 2008: Bitcoin whitepaper published
Satoshi Nakamoto published the Bitcoin whitepaper, introducing the concept of a decentralized digital currency, laying the foundation for blockchain technology.

2009: Google builds autonomous car
Google initiated its self-driving car project, marking a significant advancement in autonomous vehicle technology.

2009: Emergence of deep learning
Deep learning gained prominence with the development of algorithms capable of recognizing patterns in vast datasets, leading to significant advancements in AI applications.

2010s: The era of social media, mobile internet, and global connectivity

2010: Social media expansion and mobile connectivity

February 2010: Pinterest launched
Pinterest, a platform for sharing and discovering ideas through images, is launched, adding to the diversity of social media platforms.

October 2010: Instagram launched
Instagram, a photo-sharing social media platform, is launched, quickly gaining popularity and influencing visual content sharing.

2010: Internet users reach 2 billion
The number of global internet users doubles over five years, reaching 2 billion, driven by the proliferation of smartphones and mobile internet access.

2011: Social media's role in global events

2011: Social media in Middle East revolts
Platforms like Twitter and Facebook play significant roles in organizing and disseminating information during the Arab Spring uprisings, highlighting the power of social media in sociopolitical movements.

2012: Internet milestones

2012: Internet users surpass 2 billion
The global number of internet users surpasses 2 billion, reflecting the rapid growth and adoption of internet technologies worldwide.

2015: Mobile internet usage overtakes desktop

2015: Mobile search surpasses desktop
Google reports that mobile searches have surpassed desktop searches for the first time, indicating a significant shift toward mobile internet usage.

2016: Social media milestones

August 2016: Facebook reaches 1 billion daily users
Facebook announces that it has 1 billion daily active users, highlighting its dominance in the social media landscape.

2017: Internet penetration continues to grow

2017: Internet users reach 3.5 billion
The global number of internet users reaches approximately 3.5 billion, indicating continued growth in internet adoption.

2019: Advancements in internet technologies

2019: Introduction of 5G networks

Telecommunication companies begin deploying 5G networks, offering faster internet speeds and improved connectivity, paving the way for advancements in IoT and smart technologies.

2020s: The era of digital acceleration and global connectivity

2020: The internet becomes humanity's lifeline

March 2020: COVID-19 pandemic triggers digital transformation
The global shift to remote work, online education, and digital communication *drastically increases internet traffic*. Video conferencing platforms like *Zoom and Microsoft Teams* see explosive growth. E-commerce and streaming services *reach record highs*, reshaping online behavior.

October 2020: The rise of 5G networks begins
Major telecom providers start *rolling out 5G networks globally*, promising *faster speeds, lower latency, and enabling next-gen technologies like IoT, smart cities, and AI-powered automation.*

February 2021: Global internet users surpass 4.5 billion
More than *half of humanity* is now online, reflecting the *rapid digital adoption* in developing regions.

December 2021: Satellite internet becomes a reality
Starlink, SpaceX's satellite-based internet service, expands its *beta testing worldwide*, providing *high-speed connectivity to remote and underserved areas.*

October 2022: Elon Musk acquires Twitter
In one of the most controversial deals in tech history, Elon Musk *buys Twitter for $44 billion*, initiating massive changes to *social media policies, free speech debates, and digital advertising.*

November 2022: The decentralized Web gains traction
The push for a *decentralized internet (Web3)* gains momentum with *blockchain-based applications and decentralized autonomous organizations (DAOs)* emerging as alternatives to big tech platforms.

February 2023: Global digital economy hits $20 trillion
The digital economy – *e-commerce, fintech, AI services, and* cloud computing – now *accounts for over 15% of global GDP*, showing the internet's dominance in the modern world.

July 2023: Meta launches Threads, a Twitter competitor
Meta introduces *Threads*, a microblogging social platform linked to Instagram, which *gains 30 million users in its first 24 hours*, signaling a shift in the *social media landscape.*

April 2024: Breakthrough in quantum networking
Scientists achieve *quantum entanglement over 12.5 kilometers*, a major step toward *a fully functional quantum internet* with *unhackable encryption* and next-gen computing power.

December 2024: The internet reaches 5.5 billion users
More than *two-thirds of* the world's *population* is now online, reinforcing the internet's role as *humanity's most critical infrastructure.*

March 2025: Meta announces the world's longest undersea cable
Meta unveils *Project Waterworth, a 50,000 km undersea cable system,* aiming to *increase global internet capacity* and connect more people in *Africa, Asia, and Latin America.*

Ongoing: The internet evolves into a mixed reality world

Advances in *augmented reality (AR), virtual reality (VR), and AI-powered search* are reshaping how users *experience the internet,* with companies investing billions into *metaverse-like environments.*

AI TIMELINE: FROM EARLY THEORIES TO PRESENT-DAY BREAKTHROUGHS

1940s: Foundations of AI

1948: Claude Shannon's information theory
Claude Shannon publishes *A mathematical theory of communication,* defining how information is transmitted and laying the foundation for modern computing and AI. He also designs Boolean logic gates (AND, OR, NOT), which are still used in AI algorithms today.

1948: Alan Turing's "Intelligent Machinery"
Turing writes *Intelligent machinery,* proposing early ideas for machine learning and AI.

1950s: The birth of artificial intelligence

1950: The Turing Test
Alan Turing publishes *Computing machinery and intelligence,* introducing the *Turing Test* as a measure of machine intelligence.

1955: John McCarthy coins "artificial intelligence"
The term *artificial intelligence* (AI) is first used by John McCarthy, setting the stage for the field's development.

1956: The Dartmouth Conference
AI is officially recognized as a research field at the Dartmouth Conference, organized by John McCarthy and Marvin Minsky.

1956: Logic Theorist: The First AI Program
Allen Newell, Herbert Simon, and Cliff Shaw develop *Logic Theorist*, the first computer program designed for automated reasoning.

1957: Perceptron (first neural network)
Frank Rosenblatt introduces the *Perceptron*, a single-layer neural network capable of learning and making simple decisions.

1958: LISP programming language
John McCarthy develops *LISP*, which becomes the standard AI programming language for decades.

1960s: Early AI applications and generative AI origins

1961: First AI-powered robot (Unimate)
Unimate, the first AI-powered industrial robot, is deployed at General Motors, marking AI's role in automation.

1965: ELIZA: The first chatbot
Joseph Weizenbaum at MIT creates *ELIZA*, the first chatbot, demonstrating human-like AI interactions.

1967: Nearest Neighbor Algorithm introduced
The *Nearest Neighbor Algorithm* becomes a key technique in pattern recognition and recommendation systems.

1970s: AI winters and early AI limitations

1973: First AI winter begins
Unmet expectations and slow progress in AI research lead to reduced funding and an AI research slowdown.

1979: Stanford Cart: Early self-driving car
Stanford builds an early autonomous vehicle, showcasing AI's potential in navigation and robotics.

1980s: Revival through expert systems and neural networks

1980: AI-powered expert systems
Expert systems like *MYCIN* revolutionize AI applications in medicine and decision-making.

1986: Backpropagation algorithm popularized
Backpropagation enables neural networks to improve learning efficiency, laying the groundwork for deep learning.

1990s: Machine learning and AI in games

1995: AI defeats a human in chess (Fritz 3)
Fritz 3, an early AI chess program, beats a grandmaster in tournament play.

1997: Deep Blue defeats Kasparov
IBM's *Deep Blue* becomes the first AI to beat a reigning world chess champion, Garry Kasparov.

1999: AI in personal assistants (Clippy)
Microsoft introduces *Clippy*, an AI-driven assistant, an early step toward modern virtual assistants.

2000s: AI goes mainstream

2002: Roomba AI-powered vacuum
iRobot introduces *Roomba*, bringing AI-powered home automation into households.

2005: DARPA grand challenge: Self-driving cars advance
Stanford's AI-powered *Stanley* wins the DARPA Grand Challenge, advancing self-driving technology.

2010s: The deep learning revolution

2011: IBM Watson wins Jeopardy!
IBM's *Watson* defeats human champions in *Jeopardy!*, demonstrating natural language AI capabilities.

2012: AlexNet transforms deep learning
AlexNet significantly reduces error rates in image recognition, fueling the deep learning revolution.

2013: Word2Vec improves NLP
Google's *Word2Vec* model enhances AI's ability to understand language and word relationships.

2015: Tesla introduces Autopilot
Tesla launches *Autopilot*, marking a major milestone in AI-powered self-driving cars.

2016: AlphaGo defeats Lee Sedol
DeepMind's *AlphaGo* defeats a human world champion in Go, a game once thought beyond AI's capabilities.

2020s: Generative AI and ethical challenges

July 2020: OpenAI releases GPT-3
GPT-3 introduces *human-like text generation*, paving the way for conversational AI like ChatGPT.

August 2021: DALL·E generates AI-driven art
OpenAI's *DALL·E* creates realistic images from text prompts, leading the generative AI revolution.

October 2022: AI-generated art wins a competition
An AI-generated image wins a digital art competition, sparking debates about AI's role in creativity.

December 2022: AI-powered search engines announced
Google and Microsoft announce AI-powered search assistants for Google Search and Bing.

January 2023: Microsoft invests $10 billion in OpenAI
Microsoft fully integrates OpenAI models into *Azure* and *Bing*, marking a corporate AI shift.

February 2023: Google introduces Bard AI
Google releases *Bard*, an AI chatbot to compete with ChatGPT in search and information retrieval.

October 2023: AI-generated films and music
AI creates full movie scripts, composes music, and generates digital actors, disrupting entertainment.

May 2024: OpenAI releases ChatGPT-4o
ChatGPT-4o introduces *real-time multimodal AI*, capable of processing text, images, and voice simultaneously.

CYBERSECURITY TIMELINE: THE EVOLUTION OF DIGITAL SECURITY

1960S–1970S: THE FOUNDATIONS OF CYBERSECURITY

1969: ARPANET and the first cyber risks
The creation of ARPANET, the precursor to the modern internet, introduces the first cybersecurity concerns about unauthorized access and data breaches.

1971: The first computer worm (Creeper) is created
Bob Thomas develops the *Creeper* worm, which spreads across ARPANET as an experiment. Ray Tomlinson later creates *Reaper*, the first self-replicating antivirus program.

1977: RSA cryptography introduced
Ron Rivest, Adi Shamir, and Leonard Adleman develop the RSA encryption algorithm, which becomes a foundational element of modern cybersecurity.

1980s: The rise of viruses and ethical hacking

1983: The term "computer virus" is coined
Fred Cohen introduces the concept of a *computer virus* in his research paper, defining it as a self-replicating program capable of infecting computers.

1984: The first computer crime law – Computer Fraud and Abuse Act (CFAA) – drafted
The *Computer Fraud and Abuse Act (CFAA)* is proposed in the United States to criminalize unauthorized access to computer systems, becoming a foundation for future cybercrime laws.

1986: The Computer Fraud and Abuse Act (CFAA) passed
The United States enacts the CFAA, one of the first laws addressing cybercrime and unauthorized computer access.

1988: The Morris worm causes the first major internet disruption
Robert Tappan Morris creates the first large-scale internet worm, infecting approximately *10% of ARPANET-connected computers* and exposing network vulnerabilities.

1990s: Cybercrime and the commercial internet

1990: Operation Sundevil (first large-scale hacking crackdown) The *US Secret Service conducts Operation Sundevil*, one of the first *major government efforts to combat cybercrime*, targeting credit card fraud and hacker groups.

1993: First web browser increases cyber threats
The release of the Mosaic web browser makes the internet accessible to the public, *introducing new cybersecurity risks* like phishing and malware attacks.

1995: The First Cybersecurity Incident Response Team (CERT-CC)
The Carnegie Mellon University establishes the *Computer Emergency Response Team (CERT-CC)* to help organizations handle security incidents.

1999: The Melissa virus spreads rapidly via email
One of the first widespread email viruses, *Melissa*, infects computers through Microsoft Word attachments, *foreshadowing the dangers of email-based malware*.

2000s: Cybersecurity becomes a global priority

2000: ILOVEYOU virus causes billions in damage
A simple email worm disguises itself as a love letter, spreading to millions of computers and costing billions in damages.

2001: The USA PATRIOT Act strengthens cybersecurity laws
In response to the 9/11 attacks, the United States enacts the *PATRIOT Act*, granting government agencies increased surveillance capabilities to monitor cyber threats.

2003: First data breach laws introduced
California enacts the *SB-1386 bill*, requiring companies to notify customers of *data breaches*, leading to global data protection regulations.

2007: Estonia *hit by nation-state cyberattack*
A massive *DDoS attack* cripples Estonia's government, banking, and media systems, marking one of the first state-sponsored cyberattacks.

2007: The birth of the dark web (Silk Road marketplace launches)
Silk Road, an online black market, launches on *Tor*, highlighting the rise of dark web marketplaces, anonymous transactions, and cybercrime.

2010s: Cyber warfare, ransomware, and AI-powered threats

2010: Stuxnet: The first cyber weapon
A highly sophisticated worm, *Stuxnet*, disrupts *Iran's nuclear program*, demonstrating how malware can cause real-world damage.

2013: Target data breach exposes 40 million credit cards
Hackers exploit a vendor's credentials to access *Target's payment systems*, highlighting the risks of *third-party cybersecurity vulnerabilities*.

2014: Sony Pictures hack by North Korea
A *nation-state cyberattack* on Sony Pictures exposes sensitive corporate emails and documents, marking *one of the first major corporate hacks linked to geopolitical conflicts*.

2015: Ukraine's power grid attack (first cyber attack on critical infrastructure)
Russian hackers launch a *cyberattack on Ukraine's power grid*, cutting off electricity for thousands of residents, highlighting the *real-world consequences of cyber warfare*.

2016: The Mirai botnet attack on IoT devices
The *Mirai botnet* infects thousands of Internet of Things (IoT) devices and launches a *massive DDoS attack* that *temporarily shuts down major websites like Twitter, Netflix, and Reddit*.

2017: The WannaCry ransomware attack hits 150 countries
A self-propagating *ransomware attack encrypts data on hundreds of thousands of computers*, demanding Bitcoin payments for decryption.

2018: GDPR enforced to strengthen data privacy
The *General Data Protection Regulation (GDPR)* in the EU reshapes how companies handle personal data, imposing strict penalties for violations.

2018: Cambridge Analytica scandal
A *major data privacy scandal* reveals that *Cambridge Analytica harvested Facebook user data* to manipulate elections, *leading to stricter global data protection laws.*

2020s: The age of AI and quantum cybersecurity

2020: COVID-19 increases cyber attacks
Remote work and digital reliance cause *a surge in phishing scams, ransomware, and healthcare system breaches.*

2021: Colonial Pipeline ransomware attack disrupts US infrastructure
A cyberattack on Colonial Pipeline forces a *major fuel supply shutdown,* emphasizing the need for stronger *critical infrastructure cybersecurity.*

2021: Log4j vulnerability becomes one of the most severe cyber threats
A *zero-day vulnerability in Log4j,* a widely used Java-based logging tool, is discovered, affecting *millions of systems worldwide* and highlighting *the risk of software supply chain attacks.*

2022: Deepfake and AI-powered scams rise
AI-generated *deepfake scams and voice impersonation attacks* increase, making identity fraud a major concern.

2023: AI-powered malware emerges
Cybercriminals begin *leveraging AI to develop adaptive malware* capable of *evading traditional security measures.*

2024: Quantum computing threatens encryption
Advances in *quantum computing* raise concerns about breaking traditional encryption, leading to the development of *post-quantum cryptography.*

For Product Safety Concerns and Information please contact our EU
representative GPSR@taylorandfrancis.com
Taylor & Francis Verlag GmbH, Kaufingerstraße 24, 80331 München, Germany

www.ingramcontent.com/pod-product-compliance
Lightning Source LLC
Chambersburg PA
CBHW052108230326
41599CB00054B/4703